THE CHURCH AND THE SACRAMENTS

THE CHURCH AND THE SACRAMENTS

BY

P. T. FORSYTH, M.A., D.D.

SOMETIME PRINCIPAL OF HACKNEY COLLEGE, HAMPSTEAD, AND DEAN OF THE FACULTY OF THEOLOGY IN THE UNIVERSITY OF LONDON

Wipf and Stock Publishers

150 West Broadway • Eugene OR 97401

The Church and The Sacraments
By Peter Taylor Forsyth

ISBN: 1-57910-011-2

Printed by *Wipf and Stock Publishers*
150 West Broadway • Eugene OR 97401 1996

TO

MY WIFE,

WHO CONTRIBUTES MORE THAN SHE KNOWS,
OR I CAN TELL HER, TO ALL I TRY TO DO.

AUTHOR'S PREFACE

My position is neither current Anglican nor popular Protestant. I write from the Free Church camp, but not from any recognised Free Church position—having regard, so far as I can, to the merits of the case, to early history, and the experience of religion. The ruling tendency is an effort to moralise this and other parts of theology by interpreting instead of abolishing.

The view here taken is neither memorial and Zwinglian nor is it High Catholic. It is sacramental but not sacramentarian, effective but not sacrificial. The Sacraments are not emblems but symbols, and symbols not as mere channels, but in the active sense that something is done as well as conveyed. Account is taken of the early influence of the pagan mysteries. The audience is Free Church, but the treatment means to be Great Church.

It may be expressly noted in advance that the Word does not mean the Bible, but the whole medium of communication between God's soul and man's. As this was gathered to a head in Christ, Christ is the unique Word of God. And since Christ is gathered to a head in the atoning and redeeming Cross as the incarnation not of love only but of grace, the Word is there in the most pointed way. It is the Word as an act and not simply as an exposition of God, Who acts not as a genial Father but as a redeeming Father. But as this crucified Christ comes home to a man it makes him active, and it makes him vocal. So he preaches God's gospel Christ. The Word that was preached from God to him he preaches to the world. The Word works faith, and faith works the word. We repeat with interest what God says to us. The Word is, therefore, God's new creating act on us, and then it is the act of our word through which God new creates. Since it comes from God it is pre-eminently a deed, as all the Creator's words are; as it goes out from man it is pre-eminently a word, through which God's deed works in a sacramental way. As it comes from God the Word is the

Son; as it comes from Christ through His Church it is the Spirit, the Gospel.

The Lectures were in substance delivered to students and not to scholars. This it is hoped may help to explain, where it may not excuse, two things: first, some amount of repetition; and second, a thetic rather than a dialectic note. The occasion was one for instruction rather than discussion.

There is something which Roman Catholicism and Protestantism in their extreme forms underprize, and that is the Gospel as the power of a Holy God for our moral redemption in a kingdom. The Free Churches have tended to idolise *liberty* at the cost of the truth and power which makes liberty—at the cost therefore of reverence, penitence, and humility. They have made a good servant a bad master. The Catholic Churches have tended, on the other side, to idolise *unity*, to sacrifice the Church's holiness to her catholicity, and to lose the moral power of the Gospel in a type of piety or in canonical correctness of procedure. They have sought unity in polity. That principle is here held to be fundamentally as wrong as the other, which seeks unity objectively in a mere moralism, or subjectively in a frame of mind. As to the sacraments, it may be surmised that the writer holds a mere memorialism to be a more fatal error than the Mass, and a far less lovely.

CONTENTS

PART I.—THE CHURCH

CHAPTER I

CHAPTER II

2

CONTENTS

CONTENTS

CHAPTER X

CHAPTER XI

CHAPTER XII

PART I

THE CHURCH

THE CHURCH AND THE SACRAMENTS

CHAPTER I

INTRODUCTORY

HOLY CHURCH, FREE CHURCH, AND SOUND DEMOCRACY

Church must have a positive and featured faith—it has to do not with mere spirituality but with Holy Spirituality, centring in the Atoning Cross of the Eternal Son of God. Every soul is born for the Church, which has the secret of society. Real offsets to the apparent weakness of the Church.

The special need for the Free Churches to court the idea of the Church's greatness to save them from atomism, and from the negation of an ultra-protesting spirit. The need for more positive knowledge and use of the Bible to keep the Church from being but a caterer to the public, a tribune of the people, an asset of democracy, and a client of its favour. The limits to the democracy of a Church with Christ as King and holiness for the standard of love. Spurious laicity. The escape from orthodoxy is by deeper doctrine, not poorer. The Church is made by the type of its belief and not the mere amount.

The alleged loss of influence by the Free Churches would matter little if it rose from more Christian belief. The service of women for the Church. Spirituality the fruit of regeneration—love the blossom on faith. The first liberty of a Church is evangelical, and not rational nor political.

How is it that, among the great and classic notes of the Church of a liberating Gospel as One, Holy, Catholic, and Apostolic, there is not the great modern note of Free?

In the opinion of many the Church has had its day, but it lingers on partly mischievous, as in the case of Rome, partly negligible, as with the evangelical Churches. We hear impatient questions whether religion cannot go on without a Church. To which the answer is that religion might, but Christianity could not. Not only does Christianity need a Church negatively, for protection against the world, but the

Gospel necessitates it positively, for the exercise of faith and growth of service. Christianity put into men a new power that compelled a Church by its racial nature. If Christ had not founded a Church, the thing He *did* found would have done so. He created the new life, the new Covenant which, by its nature, was bound to create the Church. So, if it is asked, "What is the security for investing our souls' sympathies and energies in this concern, the Church?" we answer, first, that the question is one that no Christian could ask and no worldling would; and, second, that no amount of subjective religion secures the Church, but the creating Word of *a positive Gospel.*

A Church building is the outward and visible sign of a local society. The spiritual has there a local habitation and a name. It has a *positive and cognisable centre.* And *that is what religion must have spiritually also*—a positive centre of fact and reality, local in time, as it were. What these buildings are on the ground, that the great events and doctrines of salvation, its great historic facts and intelligible fabrics, are for the soul. They are creative points and lines of power. We gather to them by their own compulsion, and we go out from them with power to endow and command the World. Christ, the Incarnation, the Cross, the Atonement, the Resurrection, the Spirit, the Church—what a vague, rambling, feckless religion we have without such things! A brotherhood dies out which never meets: it has no father, no focus, no force. And can it live without thinking? You cannot have Christian communion without the Christian community, nor the Christian community without its centres, its laws, and its truths. We cannot be organs of the religion of God's will without its organisation in a Church and a doctrine.

A warm spirituality without the apostolic and evangelical substance may seem attractive to many—what is called undogmatic, or even unconscious, Christianity. It will specially appeal to the lay mind, in the pulpit and out. But it is death to a Church. With mere spirituality the Church has little to do. What it has to do with is far more positive. The Christian revelation is not "God is a Spirit"; and so the Christian religion is not spirituality. Nor is the Christian revelation simply "God is Love"; and so the Christian religion is not simply charity. There are many cases when charity submerges righteousness and betrays truth. The Christian revelation is that the spiritual, personal, and loving God is holy, and only therefore eternal; so that its answering religion is the religion of the Holy Spirit; it is *Holy Spirituality*. And the site and source of that revelation, that gift, is the Cross of Christ, as the crisis of God's righteous judgment, holy grace, and new creating conquest of the world. The supreme revelation of God is the holy; and the central meaning of the Cross is less God's love than the holiness of it. We have no guarantee for the supreme thing, *the* divine thing, the eternal thing in God, namely, His holiness, except the Cross, which alone enables us not only to love His love but to *trust it absolutely and for ever*.

Every year of life it may be seen more clearly—and especially does it grow clear as age begins to discern the outline of the hills beyond the great sea, and we are moved as we used not to be moved by the thought of the celestial harpers harping on their harps,—we see more clearly, I say, that the great issue within Christianity is not between systems or doxies, but it is a battle for the body, as the one all inclusive gift of Christ, and for those intimate powers and public features in Christianity which are indispensable to such a revelation. To grasp that would be to lose the spiritual feebleness which eats the heart out of the Church's progress in so many directions. And we find it at one source only—the creative source of the atoning Cross. The Cross was required not simply by God's love, but by His holy love. It was required by His holiness and given by His love.

The Church lives on what founded it—on this positive New Testament Gospel, on the Cross of holy, judging, saving love. Its spirituality is founded on that Gospel's content of standing fact and saving truth. Of these powers the Church is the one trustee. How false it is, therefore, to say, 'Be spiritual, and you may believe anything.' 'Do good, and you can believe as you please.' An effective Church and a positive theology of the holy stand and fall together. Where a Church ceases to be a reality, and becomes a mere religious company or an audience, there positive belief tends to be despised, and forsaken for various magnetisms and sympathies. And, where theology or the knowledge of the holy is so despised, there the Church sinks to a genial and passing association, with nothing royal to suggest God's Kingdom, and nothing solemn to suggest His throne.

The Church will be just what it is made by the Gospel Word which created it. But that Word is universal and final. Therefore *every soul is born for the Church.* For every soul is born for *society*; and it is also born for *redemption*; and therefore it is born for the *society of redemption.* The Church has a right to every life. Not every Christian should be out saving souls, but every Christian should be a living member of the Church whose first great business that salvation of souls is. We are interested, of course, in the *amelioration* of society; and much is gained for its amelioration that we are so. But what society radically needs is *salvation*; and it is salvation that the Church offers to all. The Church alone has this secret—the Church, the greatest product of man's past, and the only trustee of his future.

It is singular to many that the society with the secret of society should be in such a minority and such neglect as it still is. But, when we have written off the Church's mistakes and wickednesses, past and present, which we are not likely to be allowed to forget, let these things also be remembered.

1. Let us remember its historic work after all; in spite of its defalcations its survival to-day in such power and blessing; the lie given by its immortal remnants in every age to the principle of the big battalions; its minority victory through the ages; its principle of an elect, its consecration for the many's sake of the choice few. Politics must work by majorities, but religion works most powerfully by a minority, an elect. State and Church are found as radically different here as elsewhere.

2. Yet is the true Church not in a huge and standing majority among the powers that settle things at last? For before God the Church in heaven and on earth is one. There is not an organic severance. The Church in the Unseen comes in aid. The dead we call the majority; and surely the number of those who now live to God, seen and

unseen, exceeds those around us on earth who are God's enemies.

3. But let us also add always to its numbers Christ Himself. If the presence of Napoleon on the field was worth 50,000 men, what is the value to the Church of His presence Who is more than worth the whole human race?

4. Consequently, the Church is the only society on earth whose battle is already won. The Church chiefly exists to certify that that battle was won in what was done by Christ, and that we have but to follow the victory up. Here again we see the radical difference between Church and State. The State only works forward through history to a life and a freedom always *to be* won; the Church works out a freedom already won once for all. The State can do with the legacy of the past what it will; the Church has, in its final Gospel from the past, a trust which it may not tamper with, which fashions and colours all it wills to do.

5. That is to say, the Church is the only society with a fulcrum outside the world; and therefore the only one that can move the world as a whole. Every true Church has the whole true Church at the back of it, and the one full salvation. It has all the Catholicity of the Gospel with it. It has behind it, in its Gospel, what is the true power of the very Catholicism that would not call it a Church at all, or even give it a right to live.

§

The Free Churches need to cultivate a sense of the great Church, if their freedom is not to lose all its greatness, and they are not to go down in corporate egoisms or social programmes. This is a historic sense (to lose which is to turn fantastic gnostics or fancy sectaries); but it is still more an evangelical sense (which to lose is to become fractious individualists). It is the sense and faith of the common Word of grace. And here there is much to learn, and much to do.

One recognises heartily the unspeakable service of the Free Churches to local and personal religion. But, in the first place, they have been much too *atomist*. The independence of each congregation or each member has been overdone. This is a fertile source both of their practical overlapping and their theological confusion. Their multiplication paralyses them in many a place. What might be a power is a scandal. And their theology, their truth, becomes a byword as they lose the sense of the great Church whose ordered self-consciousness any worthy theology is. It is the vast personality of the Church that wins its battle. What victory can await a religion whose regiments have on them the curse of the clans and go each its own way with some pride, following a chief and losing a Head? Each single Church is entitled by the Gospel to no more independence in the great Church than each individual man has in the small, where they are all members one of another. And each Church has the right to live only in virtue of the contribution it makes to the great Church.

In the second place, they are apt to be too *negative* in their note. Protestantism finds it hard to get over the first oppositional tone forced on the Reformers by the situation of their day. It is too much engrossed with the note of challenge and of suspicious vigilance. It suspects even the early creeds and their atmosphere. It is tempted to make more use of its liberty to attack clericalism or ecclesiasticism than to develop either the Ministry or the Church within itself. It is in danger of overdoing its protest against a false Church, of spending more on that protest than on realising a true Church, of denouncing a priestly Church till it lose its own sense of the essential priestliness of the Church. The ministers of the Churches it opposes are, on the whole at least, as earnestly spiritual as they. They are as sure they have the truth, and as loyal to Christ as the truth. Which Church in this land practises most self-sacrifice for Christ, His Word, and his Kingdom? Mere spirituality, mere devotion, is not the test of truth. We protest *against* much—what do we protest *for*? Is it for liberty, or for the truth which makes liberty? Liberty for what? Some are actually afraid for liberty if we state the belief which makes liberty. Does that not mean that their liberty is not created *by* truth, and is not spiritual, but is natural liberty applied to truth? To this point I will return.

§

To maintain such a Church and message as we cherish we must use our Bible much more than we do. And by using it I mean much more than being interested in the wonderful new knowledge and exposition of it. *If we are not going to use our Bible, it is of no use building our Churches.* We shall come to think more of our Church than of our Bible, and more of both than of Christ. And is that not Romanist? Most people make so little personal use of the Bible that they do not know if an interesting preacher is preaching the Gospel or not. The real strength of a Church is not the amount of its work but the quality of its faith. One man who truly knows his Bible is worth more to a Church's real strength than a crowd of workers who do not. If we ask the preacher, he will tell us among whom he finds his real strength. Our poverty is not in the amount of our work, but in the quality of our religion. Our religion does not make us do what patriotism does—sacrifice and die for it; else the work would be more productive. And that is not denying the passion and sacrifice that many of us do make for our Church. But is it for *the* Church?

If we are preoccupied as we should be with the One, Holy, Catholic, and Apostolic Church of the saving Word, there is a very present danger which we shall escape. We shall not be the slaves or the caterers of the public. We shall serve it, but not follow it. We shall not treat the word as the vassal nor as the colleague of the word.

We shall not look upon a Free Church merely as the religious side of the democracy. That is the most recent form of Erastianism, and the particular form of it from which the Free Churches are liable to suffer most subtly. The old Erastian position regarded the Church as the nation on its religious side. Now the Free Churches are in no danger from that view. They have existed to protest against it. And it is a view which has no longer real vitality, though it is the hollow root of an Established Church, and makes the anachronism of it. But there are other ways of establishing a Church than by law. A Church may be established in practice, when it is not in law. It may be the victim of the establishment principle even when it has not an establishment by privilege. The Free Churches can succumb to establishment in another form than that secured by Parliament. A parliamentary Church is not their nearest danger, but a parliamentary religion may be. They may come to think mainly in terms of public or social life—to say nothing of party. They may come to care more for social work than for public worship. A Church may be on quite happy terms with the world; and its Christ may be made welcome chiefly because He is "so human," or so democratic, or His worship is the correct thing. Thus a Church becomes established by the world even when it is not by the State. It does become so if it has no distinctive message over against the world; if it treat itself but as the consecrated part of the world; if its chief object is to effect and serve the world rather than to worship and glorify and commune with God; if it cease to regard its fundamental relation to the world as miraculous; if it regard its Gospel merely as the consummation of the best spiritual instincts of Humanity and not as a new creation; if its Word is simply the gathering up of the best in other faiths; if it make its final appeal to the courts of comparative religion; if it cherish the principle that its most precious thing is what unites it with other faiths and other movements, instead of what makes it different and commanding; if it is supremely concerned to have the *cachet* of the general heart, reason, and applause. What makes Christianity Christian is that grace of God which marks it off from other creeds, makes it descend on the instincts of man instead of rising from them, and seeks from them absolute obedience as truly as sympathetic recognition.

What I have just described may be called the rationalist establishment of the Church. But the Church succumbs to the democracy especially when it is tempted to forget its Holy Word, and trim it down to the happy world and the ideals of an age and culture. It is exposed to the peril of that phase of Socialism, in which the Church would be not the nation on its religious side, but democracy suffused by religion. In so far as it then survives, it does so as a branch of the public service, valuable chiefly for its social contribution. In such a state of things the minister would become, not an officer of the State, indeed, but still, a public servant, not indeed a civil servant but a social servant, the pastor of the people instead of the minister of the Gospel, the organ of the human fraternity rather than the oracle of the divine Word. He would be not so much the organ of God's grace and God's demand to the people as the tribune of the people's cause, the advocate of their rights, leading a divine sanction to their ideals, their grievances, their programme. He would be the champion of a social movement, rather than the representative of a supernatural economy, or the apostle of a holy salvation. His effect, and therefore his value, would be gone when he went out of favour with his public. He would not be free to rebuke them in God's name, nor to call for their repentance as a first condition of the Kingdom. (It is the Church's call for repentance that is the deep source of its disfavour with the democracy.) He would be hesitant about making demands which do any violence to human nature, or that cast any cloud upon burning interests. He would be constantly tempted to appeal to men's sympathies rather than their conscience. His influence would depend on their favour, which he must have for his leverage to do good. Some beneficent scheme might be endangered if he were perfectly clear and explicit about his Gospel and its requirements. Schemes must be financed, and he must not alienate supplies. He would not have a position independent of public favour. He would popularise his Gospel till he secularised it.

I am not, of course, describing a situation which exists, but one which would certainly come to exist if the Church with its Gospel were not the minister's first concern, and the democracy only came after that. He is the minister *of* the Word, *to* the Church, *for* the people. It is his Church and his Message, and not his views nor his programme, that must save the people. The democracy, after all, is but a social phase, section, or movement. It has the present hour, and it controls the future. All that is in God's good providence, on the march to the Kingdom. But the more the democracy acquires control, the more urgent is the question what is to control it.

§

And that is the great question now—not how the democracy can be served, but how it can be led, controlled, subdued to God's Kingdom. The more Humanity prevails as an ideal, the more we must ask what is to prevail with Humanity. The war[1] compels us to ask what is to cope with the cynical negation of Humanity to which the cult of Humanity has come. Democracy, after all, is but another of the ocracies which have come to the top in the history of mankind; and it is not the last. Despotism, monarchy, aristocracy, plutocracy, and so forth—they have all had their hour. And the Church has had to resist every one of them, though it has also, more or less, succumbed to every one. Is it democracy alone that the Church is never to resist in the name of its King? Must it be fatal to the Church to lose its favour, or the favour of any social movement? Does the society of Christ depend for its life and its right on the goodwill of any society of men in the world? Sooner or later a great struggle will come between the Church and the natural democracy; and then those Churches which, being supernatural in principle, have yet in practice become dependent on that democracy, will find themselves stripped of that support, torn asunder, and distressed beyond measure.

The great antithesis of Christianity in the world is "civilisation." The World, the mere mastery of nature and of man, is the chief obstacle to Christianity in the world. Well, democracy is but a phase of civilisation on its way to the Kingdom of God. It is nearer the Kingdom than the rest, perhaps not far from the Kingdom, but yet of itself not in it. To say that the Christian Church is but the religious side of democracy is to say that it is human nature turned pious—which is certainly no description of New Testament Christianity. And now that civilisation has gone to pieces in the great war, is it that part of it called democracy that is to regenerate Society?

Besides, no society which gives Christ the regal place the

[1]The First World War.

Church does can be a democracy. It is an absolute monarchy. Less might be said by us about freedom, and more about obedience in the spirit of freedom. The Church is much more bound up with the obedience of the democracy than with the triumph—its obedience, not indeed to the Church, but to Christ, His Kingdom, and His Gospel. No triumph of democracy weighs with the Church in comparison with its obedience to Christ, and to the whole, full Christ, the holy Christ crucified, and risen, and reigning, and *saving*. For this purpose of submission the *character* of Christ is quite inadequate; and even the *Person* of Christ is not enough. We must be broken to a grateful submission to the *Cross*, in which the Person of Christ comes to a head and has far more than an ideal, æsthetic, or hallowing power; it has its judging and saving, its humbling, miraculous, and new-creative power. That is the element which gives Catholicism its strength. But the religion as well as the politics of a democracy always tends to wreck on its determination to own no authority which does not proceed from itself, and to hold nothing true but what it can promptly understand and prove on the individual scale to an untaught logic. It tends to resent excellence, to be at home with mediocrity, to idolise comfort as the rich do luxury, and to be suspicious of the king, the competent, and the prophet. It is journalist. But the first condition of religion is authority. It is an authority before it is a liberty. The fundamental difference between a Church and a democracy lies thus in the principle that no numbers can create a real authority such as the Church confesses, whereas democracy as such will listen to no authority but what its numbers and majorities do create.

So, if we ask why the Church does not at once attract the democracy, we must answer that its faith is not democratic. It demands a ready and willing and absolute submission to authority, it demands obedience, which a democracy gives but partially, grudgingly, critically, or temporarily. The Church does not win the democracy because it is not a democracy. It is not based on natural right, or natural fraternity, or natural ideals. It is based on total surrender to an absolute monarch and owner in Christ, which is not natural and not egoist, and not easy. If it be further asked whether the Church can trust the democracy, trust the people, before we answer we must know for what it should trust them. Is it for political and social reform, the progress of civilisation, or for the Kingdom of God? If it is for the last, then the answer must be both "Yes" and "No." "Yes," if we are to trust it for the movements which would get rid of the abuses, oppressions, and grievances a democracy feels; "Doubtful," if we think of those grievances it inflicts and does not feel; and "No," if we mean the constructive moral relations and purposes which create the Kingdom of God. So far as it has gone, we cannot trust it to abolish the huge antichrist of war. It transfers it at best to industrial and civil war.

When we have to choose among social systems, truly it is the democracy that lies nearest to our heart and hope. It is not the Kingdom (indeed it must be taken in hand by the Kingdom), but it offers most possibility for the Kingdom if taken in hand. But, if Church or Gospel should identify itself with the democracy in the sense of giving itself up to its natural ideals, it would commit the same error in principle as when it staked itself upon a dynasty or an aristocracy. It would be risking itself upon the phase of society which happens to possess the hour. It would be canonising a passing stage of civilisation. It would be leaving the Word and choosing the world. It would be courting men at the expense of command over them.

And it would be producing a race of religious leaders with a genial way and breezy charity, who would lead only as they spared and indulged their followers, and told them what fine fellows they were; whose speech was of rights far more than of duty; who would sacrifice society to their class or sect, and who were so full of the wrongs these endure that they had no word against the sins they cherish, or the wrongs they inflict. If it is the case that none can lead the democracy but those who lay themselves out for its applause and vote, who are of an infinite good nature, and see but one side of every question; if it is the case that no one can lead it who tells it as plainly and kindly of its great faults as of its great destiny in God's name; then the ministers of the Church cannot lead the democracy except at the Church's cost and the Gospel's. If a rebuking and demanding Church must be an unpopular Church, then the Church must accept its unpopularity. It must be prepared to go into the wilderness with Christ; it must suffer outside the camp; it must show itself independent of the world it would chiefly save and bless, and perhaps be crucified by it. The Free Churches are not in so much danger from men who, in the name of religion, openly exploit the public; but they are from its caterers, from the men who follow and humour it, who minister to its ideals and sympathies at the cost of any holy discipline to its conscience.

The form of Christianity which founded modern democracy and its liberties laid more stress on the holy demand of God than did all the tyrannies which deduced the king's right from God's. Democracy was made by a Calvinism which did not humour human nature, and did not believe in it till God had done with it. It was the Arminians, the human-naturists, who stood by the Stuarts and the divine right of such kings.

§

It all comes back to be a question of the type of religion that rules the Church for the hour. And a religion of love and sympathy alone will never guide this fierce democracy, never win its respect, never control it. It is a credit to the democracy to have little sympathy with a Gospel so soft as they too often hear. If the democracy hates hard Church, it despises soft Church. But such has been the tendency of much recent religion in its reaction from hard Church. What has dropped out of our creed is the element that compels respect, the element of noble demand and solemn judgment. And that loss comes to a head in our view of the Cross. As our Cross is, so will our Church be, such will our Gospel be, and such will be our control. And if we drop from the Cross any satisfaction of God's holy demand, any reference to His holy judgment, we lose the royal thing from our moral centre. We lose what makes faith a controlling power. We are left with no more than an exhibition of love, or an apotheosis of sacrifice, which only cheers man by showing him himself at his best, instead of humbling and quickening him by the salvation of his worst.

The Church will be for the world just what it is made by its theology of the Cross. And a theology which leaves us at the mercy of our religious subjectivity, a theology which canonises a mere spiritual experience regardless of its supernatural content, a theology which just makes sacrifice divine, will leave us in the end with a Church which would simply be a sycophant of the public heart, and a waiter upon the providence of the crowd. It will be a courtier of the popular vote, and a client of political parties. And spiritual realities and distinctions will be to it but subtleties of the religious pedant. We are bidden beware of medical men who read books, and neglect experience of disease. We should beware also of the mind which, because it is interested in democracy, or civilisation, or culture, reads more about religion than it experiences, is more attracted by it than saved, is more concerned in social eugenics than in salvation by faith, knows pedagogics but cannot teach, and dissects the psychology of the child but has none of its soul. The laicising of the ministry is one of our chief perils. Let us especially beware of that laicity of mind which never experiences soul-disease and its healing, but lives only in a religiosity of interest or of feeling, whose faith is a sympathy and not a salvation, whose piety is mindless temperament and not intelligent conviction. There is much mischief done when a young and budding personal experience is submerged by the books of thinkers who have none. They do not think beyond a visible point. Their sentiments are Christian, but their foundation is only rational or humane; and they are impatient of anything which breaks up human nature for God to rebuild. The once-born are the chief spiritual peril in the Church, the religious-minded without the religious experience, with a taste for religion but no taste of it, who treat Christianity as an interpretation of life rather than a recasting of the soul, and view the Church as the company of the idealists rather than the habitation of the Spirit.

The danger of such an hour is to mistake the æsthetic for the spiritual, and the spiritual for the holy. A choral service may be so enjoyed that we think we have been engaged in an act of worship. A fraternity of gentle and creedless pietists might seem to themselves the elect remnant of the true Church. And worship which is but fine in its feeling and mystic in its note may lead people to think it is even more pleasing to God than positive faith could be. A beautiful prayer from one of George Macdonald's novels often seems to the inexperienced soul a more divine and Christian thing than a prayer of Augustine or Luther, or more moving than all the Litany. We may take a rapt religion for an exalted faith, the grace of piety for the power of the Spirit, mere calmness of nerve, mere aplomb, for confidence before God, subjective affections for objective trust. And we may think that to be *like Christ* is really to be *in Christ*. But the best of the spirits must be tried whether they be of God's historic Christ.

§

Many who have a wide knowledge of the Churches are impressed with their spiritual powerlessness, their decay in virility, moral and mental, their loss of influence with the world because of their attempt to conciliate the world by a colourless and inexigent creed. They are depressed by the world's poor opinion of the *personnel* of the Church's ministry, and its poor respect for the influence of its membership.

It is true we have gained much in realism, in service, in social sympathy, in good taste. But have we gained in reality? There are the defects I have just named (without, I hope, turning from a loyal critic to a common scold), and there are worse. And to deal with them seriously is to go far beyond spiritual precepts, suggestions, devices, and experiments. These will be tried, will galvanise up certain efforts, and will then, in due course, wear out. We must go beyond that to something more radical, more searching, more permanent, more creative. We need what the Cross of a holy Christ alone gives—a more clear sense of the Lord's controversy, of the sharp issue between God and man, Christ and the world, the Church and civilisation, the Gospel and the ideal, the true and the false in belief. We should take sanctity more seriously. There should be less vague talk about cultivating charity and the spirit of Christ, and more certainty cultivated about His Holy Spirit of our regeneration. Christian charity is, indeed, the rose-bloom of Christian faith. What is so commonly overlooked is that it *is* Christian faith that flowers there; that the flower will only come if we tend the root; first righteousness, then peace; and that a very definite Christian faith must be cultivated to produce such a bloom out of human nature in such a world. Charity which does not grow out of positive faith is but a sentimental tolerance, fashionable for the hour, and sometimes part of its cant.

The process should be arrested by which the frontiers of belief are being erased, and the Church is opened to every æsthetic adventurer of the soul, or to free trade in every opinion. Everything, it is now said, is more or less true; and so everyone is more or less good, and we know not under what king they are. We have no right, indeed, to exact from the world all that our fathers did, or to denounce as they did other religions. But are we losing that power which was the real nerve of their Gospel? Surely there was that in them which we must now reach by going deeper than even they did, and not by going round them. And the practical confession of that dynamic core we must ask from the world. We must urge submission to that Gospel —and *submission* to it we must ask, and not only sympathy. A Gospel which is not exclusive will never include the world, for it will never master it. No religion will include devotees which does not exclude rivals. Half-Gospels have no dignity, and no future. Like the famous mule, they have neither pride of ancestry nor hope of posterity. We must make it clear that Christianity faces the world with terms, and does not simply suffuse it with a glow; that it crucifies the world, and does not merely consecrate it; that it recreates and does not just soothe or cheer it; that it is life from the dead, and not simply bracing for the weak or comfort for the sad.

The Churches must be more concerned about conversion and less occupied with diversion; more interested in faith than in either sentiment, philanthropy, or theology. The

Bible should be something more than a volume of "Everyman's Library." The pulpit should draw more from its Bible than from its circulating libraries, so that the pew can trust their preachers more than their press. It is not the preachers' business, indeed, to shock and scold, and the true martyrs do not provoke martyrdom, they accept it. But more men are needed with a Gospel that will judge their people, and make them uneasy in a way the preacher himself dare not. The Church must realise that the hour has come when the question, "What do we believe?" is more great and urgent than "What should we do?" For the best we do is in the service of the things in which we most believe. If it is manhood the Churches are lacking, that means that we lack in the matter of choice, of will, of making up our minds on the greatest things, and taking our side. For the purposes of manhood, the few central issues need to be sharpened and not softened, so that we can take a man's stand.

Few things are needful or one. What is it? What is the one thing that makes the soul God's and the Church Christian? What is the one message?

The age is by when liberty had to be claimed. It is there now. What have we in it? What is the guarantee of its permanence? What is the root from which it grows, and must grow? What is the foundation it stands on? What feeds it? What is the justification of its existence? What does it serve? If everything is to serve our liberty, that means that nothing serves, or that in the end we serve ourselves. It means indulging self and brandishing liberty (or rather our natural recalcitrance) instead of plying a regenerate vocation to freedom.

The remedy for the existing state of things is not one which affects primarily either individuals or congregation, but the whole type and staple of belief. Something we do need, something which shall not be a rival nostrum, shouted against the other booths, but a new baptism in that region which lifts the Churches out of rivalry with each other and with every other agency, as Christianity is above rivalry with all other creeds. A new baptism we need; meaning by that, however, not a new piety, a new subjectivity, a mere revival. We need a new Spirit, but in the sense of a *recovered Word.*

For our present belief hardly supplies us with a Word. What Word we inherit we cannot translate into the mental and moral speech of our time. Yet the new Word does not mean a new revelation except of itself. If we could only reach a truer interpretation and deeper grasp of the old, make a revised version of the old Word, and put a new accent into the old truth!

It is not a new theology we need so much as a renovated theology, in which orthodoxy is deepened against itself, and not pared away. It is a new touch with our mind and conscience on the moral nerve of the old faith. We have had many new theologies in the last hundred years. Theological enterprise has been turning them out freely. But the vein of liberalism, which thus followed on the old Orthodoxy, has been worked out for the preacher's purpose. It is now exhausted of religious ore. The spring has given out (to change the image), and the stream runs thin, and whispers softly among little pebbles, though once it roared among great boulders now left behind in the hills. It is not sermons we need, but a Gospel, which sermons are killing. We need to go behind and beneath all our common thought and talk. Liberal theology is a standing necessity and a rich growth; but theological liberalism, abroad and at home, thins down into Unitarianism infallibly. What we require is not a race of more powerful preachers, but that which makes their capital—a new Gospel which is yet the old, the old moralised, and replaced in the conscience, and in the public conscience, from which it has been removed. We need that the Gospel we offer be moralised at the centre from the Cross, and not rationalised at the surface by thin science. We need that more people should be asking "What must I do to be saved?" rather than "What should I rationally believe?" We need power more than truth. We need a new sense of the living God as the God whose eternal Redemption is as relevant and needful to this age's conscience as to the first. It is not a ministry we need but a Gospel which makes both ministry and Church. The Church will not furnish the ministers the age requires unless it provide them with a Gospel which they will never get from the age, but only from the Bible for the age. But it is from a Bible searched by regenerate men for a Gospel, and not exploited for sermons by preachers anxious to succeed with the public. It may be best to preach to the sinners and to the saints and never mind at present the public, who feel neither. If we do that well the public will respect us. If we think of the world, let us think chiefly of the world as the arena of an eternal Redemption, and not of a professional success, or of a social revolution.

§

I have spoken of our sympathy with democracy, and I have spoken of our concomitant loss of public influence in spite of our gain of voting power—our loss as members of the Church, our gain as members of the State. This is a conjunction—loss of influence with gain of power—which is familiar to people of moral insight; and it is forced on our notice in connection with the effects of the feminist movement. But it is so strange to some that I venture to return to the situation it creates, and to do so in the interest of the Church. The Free Churches have lost influence with the leaders of public affairs, and they have not gained it with the working classes. As mediators in the great industrial war they are sometimes more anxious to be busy than qualified to be weighty. Some are mere gadflies. It is true many of the leaders of the working classes are connected with these Churches; but they would lead as much if they were not. It is not as members of the Christian Church that they have their influence. It is not the influence of their Church working through them, except indirectly. They lead in spite of their Church more than by it. And at the other end of society there is a vast difference since mid-Victorian days. Then the weighty names and moving spirits of public affairs, especially in the provinces, were also the leading members of the Free Churches. These Churches were the backbone of municipal institutions and local life. They represented the leading families of the city, and they had often the chief share in the social life of the locality. We had powerful men both in our pulpits and our Church affairs. How much it is otherwise now may be indicated by one eminent witness who went about among these Churches a great deal, and who said that their life was at present being saved by the goodness of Christian women.

If that is so, it is something like a revolution. In so far as it means that the religion of the man is feminised, it is a positive misfortune. While, in so far as it means that the best work and sympathy of the Church are left with the women, it is not to be looked on as so much fresh gain, but as showing up, by denudation, what women have all along been doing. I mean that the life of the Churches has always been very dependent indeed on their Christian women, and the retirement of the men only brings the fact to light. In the virile days of which I speak the women were well mated with their men. The one was worthy of the other in the homes as in the convictions and activities of Church life. The wives and daughters of these stout Nonconformists were of a like conviction and gravity to their men. It is not so much that we have now more female Christianity, but that we have less male. The Christianity of the men has ebbed, and left the godliness of the women more conspicuous. It is realised how much has always been due to them. The men have retired, the women have not (though too many of them have). They seem to hold the position not so much because they have been reinforced, but because they are left to it even in reduced numbers. That is what I mean when I say their conspicuous service does not so much represent a gain as became revealed by our loss.

Nobody can question the statement, I think, who compares the state of these Churches in the virile regions of Lancashire and Yorkshire with what they were fifty years ago. And some quarters are more prolific of small irritants and prickly consciences than of effective leaders and large wills.

Speaking broadly, within the Christian pale the men have tended to turn women in their religious type; while outside the Church the women have tended to turn men. The women of the Churches have in some ways been steadier than either. And many observers agree that there is growing up a far more intelligent interest in their faith among women than among men, especially among young women than among young men.

If the remark I quote is true, it suggests two things: (1) We should drop for the time a favourite but unpleasant platform phrase that our Free Church Christianity is a religion that pre-eminently breeds men. Virility is not for the hour its current type or tendency. It certainly is not its monopoly. Perhaps there is more real Puritanism of type elsewhere. Nonconformity may be the sounder principle, but has it any monopoly, or even preponderance, of Christian manhood and the social power that goes with manhood? Does its pulpit or its press show any manhood more vigorous and Christian than is found freely in the forms of Christianity that face it?

(2) If we ask what the cause is for the change we shall find it at last in the type of religion. A Church is made by what it believes. And the cause is in the type of Christianity which has been at work lowering the pitch for more than a generation. Of which, however, I have already said much.

If it is asked what we are to do, precepts, as I have said, are of no use. New devices avail not. We must go back to the first deep, distinctive, and exclusive principles of our faith, which horses and carts will not drag people to face. Men will just be what their living faith and deep belief make them. But, when we press these principles, these powers, these realities, we are charged with being academic and with offering professional theology when what is needed is practical direction. But has the Church really come to treat the moral soul's whole reliance upon Christ's judging and saving death as a piece of professional theology? There is no practical direction in *these* matters, so fundamental to the Church, but the guidance of the Holy Ghost back to the Cross and its moral regeneration. And that means something definite, a fresh and powerful grasp of the positive Gospel which alone makes Christians, and without which we may have discipleship of Christ but not membership. And Churches are not made of disciples (who turned traitors), but of these who had gone through what made them apostles, confessors, and martyrs.

What we need most is not direction but footing, not sign-posts but foundations. It is no quietive we need for a conscience uneasy over the social question, but a new moral motive, a new positive creation of the life of conscience. We are not taking a positive enough attitude to the world. We have not evangelical conviction for the purpose. The largest and deepest reference of the Gospel is not to the world or its social problems, but to Eternity and its social obligations. A positive, eternal, creative Gospel for the spiritual conscience is what we need—not a set of true beliefs to contend with false, but the holy, living God of historic grace to keep us from the idols of the religious mind and the passing age. We are the victims of the religion of the Spirit instead of subjects of regeneration by the Holy Ghost. It is a religion too exclusively pathetic and sympathetic, of personality rather than redemption—the religion of unsectarian, undenominational belief; the religion of undogmatic, unconscious Christianity, which means a Christianity without conviction and therefore without power, only too self-conscious and too little Christian. It is a Christianity more concerned to be broad than deep, more able to please than to convert, to interest than to control, to charm than to search; where love is of a futile kind because it avoids judgment, banishes fear, and blurs truth.

We turn some of the best people away from us because our one concern seems to be to get as many as possible in. We do not present clear issues, and therefore we do not evoke sure decisions, and therefore we do not appeal to manhood. We do not appeal to the strong men who have insight and decision, and who demand a faith for the mind, the conscience, and the will as truly as for the heart and for the temperament. Religion has a far more positive word to the world than politics has, a word more than critical, more than sympathetic, more than helpful. It is the word of a new heart and not a mended earth. It has a Spirit, clear, sure, incisive and decisive. Some minds, who are not at all extreme, who would be more strong if they were more extreme, never realise Christian truth except as the transfiguration of the best instincts of the natural man. And, when they handle that truth, it is like a man whose fingers are all thumbs trying to lift a sphere of moist ice. Interesting preaching may sometimes be more like the provision of a dainty meal than the word of a tingling call. We have no bugle.

It is not a question of orthodoxy but of the Holy Spirit, of a moral regeneration, and of power to keep a Church a Church, and not a sect round a doctrine, or a group round an orator. We lose what sense of a Church we had because we come to think little, or to think wrong, about the distinctive thing that makes a Church. A Church is not made by Christian sympathies or affinities. Rather are these made by a Church. A Church is made by the Christian Gospel, its creative Word of the Cross, its Holy Spirit. The religion that makes a Church is not temperamental but evangelical. It asks whether we have received the spirit of the new man, before it asks what spirit we are of in the old. It is the evangelical element in Christianity that is the Church-building element. I do not say we need less evangelical pathos (though there are forms of it we might well lose), but we do need more evangelical power, more moral grasp of our Evangel, as a basis for our freedom, and as a norm for our sympathies.

The greatest product of the Church is not brotherly love but divine worship. And we shall never worship right nor serve right till we are more engrossed with our God than even with our worship, with His reality than our piety, with His Cross than our service. It is well to dream and to talk much of brotherly love. But the brethren who love best and the love that loves longest are made by the Gospel. It is this they confess in loving, as they confess it in other ways also. Christian charity is not the sweet reasonableness of culture, nor is it natural kindliness of temper. To the lover of righteousness it does not come easy. It grows only on the stem of Christian faith, which is the tree of the Cross and its righteousness. The good live by faith and work by love. Never did Paul dream that his song of Christian love would be turned to belittle or to belabour the Christian faith on which alone it grows. The Church is the greatest product of history, and the greatest product of the Church is a holiness answering the holiness that made it, which is Holy Love. The first commandment of the Cross is "Be ye holy, for I am holy." Its call is for the confession, worship, and service of that divine Holiness of love which is the spring of our Redemption. The service of God is the root, the service of man is but the fruit. True, by their fruits shall we *know* them; but not *produce* them. The fruits are the evidence, not the principles. Love does more to show faith than to produce it. Grace produces it. We live by that faith in holy Love whose fruit is to be a love not only kind, but, still more, holy.

What then is the Church there for? The great product of a Church, I say, is that which makes God God; it is holy Love. The first business of a Church is to worship that; then, through this confession in worship, public and private, to acquire and to confess it in character and work, to reproduce it in person and conduct. It is to create holiness, then to serve and bless man in that power. A very rich man, who travelled first class through life, was asked what was the best time he ever had. His answer was: "When I was in hospital two months with typhus." Asked "What do you mean?" he answered: "I had a nurse, an angel for sweetness and patience. I can never forget her. I was a stranger. She had many on her hands besides me, and too few to help her. It was strain day and night. But in eight weeks I never saw on her face anything but the same shining kindness, never agitated, never morose. It was like heaven."

Yes, heaven lies that way, and in nothing money can get. You can hire a nurse, you cannot buy that. But the heaven was not in the work she did, but in the way she did it. It was not the service, but the soul in the service. And where is that soul made, the sanctity in the kindness? By the Gospel which makes the Church. There is nothing that can continue to make Holy Love, to make love holy, steady, and of everlasting kindness, but the Gospel of our regeneration from human nature in Jesus Christ, and Him crucified.

There are but two alternatives, an evangelical Church and a sacramental, *i.e.* a Church with the Word uppermost or a Church with the rite. There is no doubt about the earnestness and thoroughness with which the sacramental Church take their line. There is great doubt about the earnestness with which we either grasp or take ours. Yet there is no hope for us till we are as deep, thorough, and convinced as they. The attempt of the hour, however, is to avoid these alternatives by a reference to some form of the inner light.

§

Montesquieu says that each form of polity has its own principle, and that it declines and falls if this principle is either in excess or defect. The principle of despotism is fear, and the tyrant falls either when there is no fear of him, or when there is too much—when fear has made men desperate. The principle of monarchy is honour; but honour is a sentiment, and sentiment cannot keep itself noble, and the monarchy falls when the love of honour becomes either quixotry on the one hand or the passion for honours on the other. The principle of a democracy is virtue, and especially the public virtue of patriotism in peace, of public spirit; and a democracy falls either in the absence of that spirit, or in the Chauvinism, ending in the Napoleonism, of its excess. The civic liberty of the Revolution ended in the Empire. The absence of public spirit has put Germany at the mercy of her army. The lack of chivalry (which is the vice of democracy) has made the chief democracy of the world a conforming if not a consenting party.

The same thing is true, *mutatis mutandis*, of ecclesiastical polity also. Rome is weakest where she seems outwardly strong—by the fear she commands, by her claim to control the eternal destiny of souls, by her power of excommunication, and her asset of hell. Anglicanism has also had its weak side in its identification with the monarchical system and its honours, both historically, in the case of Laud and the Stuarts, and theoretically, in the episcopal system, the grades of office, the hope for promotion, and its whole aristocratic note. Independency has for its principle liberty, and, while it was weak enough in the eighteenth century through the abeyance of that principle, its peril to-day is in its excess and abuse.

But it will protect us from much misunderstanding if we are clear at the outset about what the principle really is. However democracy may mean the principle of the nation and its liberty, that is not what Independency means. It does not mean religious liberty in the sense of freedom to be *franc-tireurs*, free-lances, entitled to hold any opinion about God or none. That is liberty with which in its civic form Independency has had much to do, but it is not its own principle. It is but civil liberty on one side of it. It is liberty in the State, and not in the Church. In the Church mere latitudinarian liberty is not the principle. No Church can survive on the liberty to hold any views we think fit about religious matters so long as they are held in a religious spirit, or subject to the "great general truths of religion." They may make any groups they please on such a basis, but these would not be Churches, nor have any moral right to the property or the position of Churches. A Church has a historic and positive base. And in so far as Independency claims to be a branch of the true Church, its principle is not rational liberty, nor spiritual liberty, but evangelical liberty, which is the true Catholic tradition. It is a liberty not intrinsic to us but to which we must be redeemed and reborn. It is liberty for all thought or action which is compatible with the genius and finality of the Gospel Word, however traditional custom or theology may be affected. It is liberty for all that is created by that Gospel with its central, social, and entire Redemption. It is not merely a liberty which the Gospel does not impugn, which it finds and consecrates; it is liberty which the Gospel creates, in speech, act, or thought. The liberty of Christ is the fulness of the new man in Christ. It is not civil liberty on its religious side. It is not spiritual liberty *sans phrase*. It is not liberty, either civic or mystic, *for* Christ. But it is liberty *in* Christ, and Christ's work for the race. It is an experienced liberty which grows out of an authority, and, as its authority is, so will its liberty be. The first interest of liberty is authority.

CHAPTER II

THE CHURCH AND ITS UNITY

A Church—how different from a club. Causes leading to the present erasure of frontiers between the Church and the world; the influence of comparative politics and comparative religion. The creative centre of the Church is not simply Christ but Christ crucified. The creator and charter of the Church is the moral Gospel of grace redeeming by atonement and answered by faith. We belong to a Church because we belong to Christ, not *vice versa*. The needed recovery of the evangelical note—especially in the laity. Is the Church of the average layman equal to the tremendous moral situation? Is variety a sign of spiritual life? The loss of the idea of the great Church from the neglect of history—from the Protestant ignoring of Catholicism and the Catholic ignoring of Protestantism. Church and Sect. A Church is not a *bouquet* of individuals. There is more in a body than the sum of its parts. The first step to unity is Federation, to subdue denominational egoism. Uniformity of polity not the unity of the Church. Episcopacy optional. The analogy of a University.

WHAT is the Church? is a very old question, and it will be very much older before it is settled to general satisfaction. Many have no difficulty in defining the Church as the company of Christ. But, owing to the variety of loose ways in which Christ is understood—sometimes as no higher than a historical character, or a winsome saint—His company may mean no more than an association gathered about a religious figure, as Lutheranism rallies round Luther, or Wesleyanism about Wesley, as Islam is gathered about Mahomet, monasticism about Francis, or as a philosophical society might be called the Aristotelian. But even when His person is held to be supernatural it is yet no more than a static person in whom the soul rests; and then we have a Church devout but inert; pious but dull. So that it is a great concern to many and a grief to some to think that what were once Churches among us are ceasing to be such, and are becoming but religious groups loosely organised for family comfort, spiritual culture, or humane action. This is a danger that threatens in particular a body like Congregationalism, which, if severed from a positive doctrine of Christ and His regenerative work, would readily subside into a group of mere Christian clubs, creedless but press-led, without the feature that marks a Church off from all societies besides, religious or other. The voluntary nature of the membership tends to reduce such Churches to contractual association, in the sense which the law puts on such a phrase, without a subduing Presence or an informing Spirit, without a reality, power, and right both supernatural and supernational. But it may be asked by some *ingénu* what else a Church is than a religious club. To that it might be admitted that for some members on the roll it is little else. In a club the membership is egoistic. It is co-operative egoism. The individual joins in order to utilise for his convenience and comfort the like desire in a number of other people. They pool their social self-interest. And a Church may be joined and used for a like reason—for the religious good to be had from religious association rather than out of the love of a common Lord or the sacrificial service of His Kingdom. It may be composed of a number of people who have been persuaded that it would be for the good of their souls. But that is not a community, but only a combination. It is not a Church. The member does not come in to magnify Christ and serve upon His trust. He does not undertake responsibility, and does not with all his heart seek the others' good, a world's rescue, or a Saviour's glory. Such a group does not exist for a cause, but for a comfort. Nor is it created by any Gospel in which self is lost. Nor is it tenanted by one indwelling, overruling, and organising Presence.

This is a descent that constantly troubles the more thorough and earnest minds among us. Some of our critics put it down to the lack of an episcopate or an apostolic succession. And many of our friends try to remedy it by urging such things as a more serious use of the Church meeting—forgetting that, so to meet, the society must really be a Church already; it must know itself to be, and know what is meant by being, a Church. Our critics are right in so far as they mean that the chief necessity is a more clear, arresting, guiding and commanding theory of the Church and its ministry. A club has no theory, nor has a fraternity a principle. But there is nothing we need so much

—so long as it is not a mere academic theory but a reflection of the social nature of the Gospel. The absence of such a practical conviction about the society which has a first claim on Christians cannot be made good by any amount of social theory, nor any interest in civil society and its politics. And our Nonconformist members of Parliament might bear the suggestion that spiritual and intelligent conviction on this subject is of the greatest moment in many practical junctures round us or waiting for us.

These and the following words, then, are spoken in the conviction that for some of the Free Churches, and not in one communion alone, the sense is being lost of what makes a Church a Church. And the loss is especially serious in the pew. The note is the note of levelling down. As thus:

In other than ecclesiastical regions (in regions like comparative religion) we have been busy erasing difference, tracing continuity, and reducing collision; till the positive features of Christianity have come to be merged in a general religiosity, which is described as the action of one Spirit in a variety of forms, all much in a parity. And this is by some praised as the catholic temper in religious belief—though it is really not more than cosmopolitan. The favourite word is "broad," and the general result is thin. The true catholicity searches deep. It has a lamp given into its hand in the Gospel of Grace that nothing can put out or pale; and with that torch it explores other creeds, deeply interprets them, and gladly brings their truths or aspiration to light. But a mere cosmopolitanism has no torch, no standard, no absolute sense of relative value; it just basks in the religious weather of each climate that it finds as it roams from land to land or age to age.

Now, the like temper and method have invaded our ecclesiastical interests also. We are everywhere alive to the value of combination. We start all kinds of societies and associations of a voluntary kind, movements gathering about an idea, or clubs with a project of benefit for culture or for society. Or, taking another line, we see a large field of history covered by nationalities with similar institutions, and polities with an equal right. We study comparative politics for the fundamental social type. Or we found journals in such interests. Or at conferences we compare notes about forms of social co-operation or general eugenics. We are specially interested in the various philanthropic agencies which take the shape of societies. And chief among such associations we place the Churches, as societies for the promotion of worship, goodness, fraternity, or humanity. The Church, in its various forms, we take to be but another of the many associations that men make and unmake. And we lose the sense of the vital and eternal *differentia* which marks off the Church from every other society, from a club upwards to a nation. In the law's eye we of the Free Churches are but associations; and I cannot say that in this the law is not taking us at our own vague valuation in a growing number of cases. Either we do not really believe in the Church as supernatural, as the society whose life is the Eternal and Holy Spirit, with an atmosphere quite different from public meetings or business assemblies; or, if we so believe, we do not grasp the significance of our belief and its bearings. For the Church is not differentiated from all other societies as these are distinct from each other—by its tradition or its purpose, but by its creative Gospel and indwelling Holy Spirit. It is a body with a personality that they have not; first because it was created by an act of Redemption into which the whole perfect and final personality of its Creator was put; and, second, because it not only wears His stamp but it is inhabited by His personal Holy Spirit, which, and no mere genius, is its life principle. A mere club or association has no personality; it does not reflect a personality; it has but a more or less arbitrary cohesion. And that is all that some Churches are coming to have.

§

It is impossible to sketch here a theory of the Church. I hope to do that elsewhere. And indeed, as I have said, it is more than a theory we need, more than a theory of social religion. It is a theology, both as a source and as an expression of the corporate consciousness of the Church. It is an intelligent corporate faith which is a power for the common life. Both Church and Sacraments draw their meaning from our actual relation to a Christ Who can only be stated in more or less theological terms. If He is but a historic figure, both the Church and its rites come to the ground. The Church especially is then but another of many human and voluntary associations, only with a religious colour and interest stamped on it by a founder. Apart from a supernatural and atoning Christ, the Church is only a natural body, and therefore a body fickle and perishable. Apart from a supernatural Christ, it is non-spiritual; apart from an atoning, it is non-ethical. No cross no Christ, only a saint.

Where does the supernatural and Church-building element in Christ lie? It lies not in His character and teaching but in His office and work—in His atoning Cross and Resurrection, in His Redemption from moral death to eternal life. There He is the Son of God with power. His spirituality is evangelical. It is moral power so radical and revolutionary that it is regenerative and nothing less. He is the Christ of the Holy Father not as the Ideal of the pure, but as the Saviour of the lost. What makes Christ Christ is what He did as His life's crowning work; not how He was born or grew up, not even what He said and did from day to day —except as such words and deeds take their consummation, and have their last meaning, in His condensed word and summary work of the Cross.

It is not a question simply of living in the Person of Christ, like much clean and earnest piety, as if He were God's Temple with a niche for every soul. The Person of Christ is not a standing Temple but an Almighty Power. As in every moral personality of the first rank, it has its meaning and power in the work into which it was all put. As the Holy One He went wholly into His work of the Cross for the sin of the world. The whole value of Christ's Person for the world entered it by that strait gate. He is our God because He is our Redeemer. Our approach to Christology is through the office of Christ as Saviour. We only grasp the real divinity of His person by the value for us of His Cross. I hope the great war[1], which is doing so much to shatter our

[1] The First World War.

easy optimism and our dreamy "charity," to reveal the man of sin and the kingdom of evil, and to carry home the damnable wickedness of evil and of man, may accordingly deepen much dainty, and comely, and natural religion, and give us a new moral sense of what a World-Redeemer is and must do. And, in so far as it does this, its judgment will be a blessing to every Church that has enough conscience left to profit by it. For the first concern of every Church should be Christ's. And that was not the hearty but the holy. The first charge that He served was not the love of men, but the righteousness, the holiness of God, to Whose Kingdom all things, including love, are added. First righteousness, then peace.

The Church's one foundation, and the trust of its ministry, is not simply Christ, but Christ crucified. It is not His Person as our spiritual superlative, or even as our spiritual home and clime, but His Person as our Eternal Redeemer in His blood. It is evangelical. It is mystical, but with the mystic action working at the heart and height of moral things in a world morally wrong. The Church rests on the Grace of God, the judging, atoning, regenerating Grace of God, which is His holy Love in the form it must take with human sin. Wherever that is heartily confessed, and goes on to rule, we have the true Church. The Church is not made by men. It is no creature either of humane sympathy or of voluntary association, even though these give it a local and practical form. It is not put together by consents, contract, or affinities. It is a new creation of God in the Holy Spirit, a spiritual organism, in which we find our soul. Men unite themselves with the Church because already united with Christ, and because they are, in that very act of union with Him, already in spirit and principle organised into the great Church He created, and whose life He is.

In so far as the Church is a creature, it is the creature of the preached Gospel of God's Grace forgiving, redeeming, and creating us anew by Christ's Cross. The Church was created by the preaching of that solidary Gospel, and fortified by the Sacraments of it, which are, indeed, but other ways of receiving, confessing, and preaching it. The Church is the social and practical response to that Grace. Wherever that

Gospel is taken seriously, and duly, and statedly, there is the Church. It is the living organism (I avoid the word organisation) of the worshippers of Christ, created by His redeeming Gospel in Word and Sacrament. There is therefore but one way of recovering the idea of the Church. It is by regaining, on a scale worthy of it, the evangelical faith which made and makes the Church always. To lose that is often too easy. But it is a very hard thing to regain.

Everything appears to me to turn upon a real recovery of the evangelical note; but its recovery in a far more ample and searching sense than the phrase has sunk to denote in gatherings of Evangelicals so called—though I do not find the pitch raised in what is called the "lay Christianity" which most resents such Evangelicalism. For the Church's unity, confidence, and effect on the world, it seems to me quite necessary that the objective and moral value of the Cross of Christ which made the Church should be replaced (with whatever reforms) at the vital centre of religion. From thence it should work in such a creative way that the Thing there done by love in judgment should prescribe the whole deep tone and form of the Church's word and action with the world. Our religion needs a reality at once moral and imaginative. The source of Christian ethic must be the same as the source of Christian worship. And that is not the Sermon on the Mount, but the moral inwardness and creativeness of the Cross, which the Sermon but illustrates. It is moral weight that we have lost, because that is what has been lost from our conception of the Cross. We consent to call the Cross the centre of our faith, and yet we rather recognise it as the classic sacrifice than realise it as *the* creative moral crisis of history; the point where God and Man, Time and Eternity, Past and Future, Nature and Conscience, Judgment and Grace meet for a new Creation. This is a difference which alters the whole type of religion, and most vitally affects our relation to Church, Ministry, Sacraments, and the State. It is a difference that involves theology; and the layman will not have theology.

To some whose working capital is but religious impressionism the mention of the word evangelical suggests nothing but what they have learned to distrust, or even despise, as theological bias of an arid sort. Now, Evangelicalism, as a movement, has weaknesses, which at such a time as this are all but fatal. The chief of these have been a facile familiarity with spiritual things, falling to irreverence; its archaic treatment of the Bible in defiance of the Holy Spirit's gift of critical scholarship; and its religious individualism when the same Spirit was moving the Church to social concern. On that individualist basis, however, its philanthropy has been a glory to it when its theology had become a reproach. Yet there had once been a real strength in that theology; and it was this, that it did try to face the moral crisis and tragedy of the world's conscience—whether its constructions of the conflict always did moral justice to it or not. Often they did not—to the extent even of creating a double morality. But its attempt represents the only line of thought that does do justice to the Lord's controversy with history, that does duly gauge the sinfulness of human sin, and does appreciate the cruciality of its conquest as the radical moral problem for society and history. This must always be the note of a faith which is really, and not merely piously, evangelical, and which is truly, not formally, orthodox. It makes half the strength of the High Churchmen. The total lack of an evangelical theology, is, for a Church at least, a defect not simply theological, but moral. It is the moral defect which reduces religion in a community to moral levity and to public impotence. It takes the power out of our optimism; and it reduces the fabric of the Church to religious booths covered by gentle fern.

What we need as Churches is not more spirituality braced by more intellectual taste. It is moral virility in the deep passion and formative conscience of the religion. We need more of what turns mere religion into saving faith. We need a religion that provides its public ethic from the same authority in Christ as creates its public worship. The only theology worth much to the Church is one which gives it moral weight and action upon the world because of its moral power with God. We need more religion of the kind that gathers about a *holy* Cross; the kind of religion that goes to the roots of the moral soul, both in God and man, and does not soften the issue; the kind of religion whose intrinsic nature and property it is, by its very origin, to cope finally with the last evil of the world, to turn all that tragedy to victory in our hands, and to make such power, by a real Church, unmistakable to the public. We need a mystic religion with moral penetration. The lack of such religion is what is at the root of the social anæmia and loss of weight in some Churches that once had a different effect, even on Parliament. Nothing from official sources can cure this ill. And it is a loss that has even gone so far that adequate discussion of it may be dismissed by some as unintelligible. Of course, I speak of it as a note of the Church's faith rather than the individual's. But that dismissal is death to the Church, or, at least, to the laity in it. *It means that a layman's Church is unequal to the moral situation if such be lay religion.*

Now the demand for this deeper type of faith will be greater in the near future than the living generation has known. For, however the war goes, one thing we shall have had burned in on us which for many generations we have not had, and whose absence has lowered the whole temperature and authority of religion. We shall have had an unprecedented revelation of the evil power, the man of sin, the prince of this world. This discovery means the real end of the Victorian age, of the comfortable, kindly, bourgeois, casual Victorian age, so credulous in its humanism. We have, in a long peace and a humanitarian culture, ceased to believe in the devilry in human nature, and we have called the credulity charity. We are having our eyes opened. We have of late made several very great discoveries. We have come upon an unsuspected moral quality in our youth. We have revealed a marvellous power of improvisation in this country. We have found out Germany. And we have rediscovered Satan.

We are in the kind of world-crisis in which creeds are reborn for history. Saint Augustine wrote *The City of God* amid the sack of Rome. We shall therefore need, as none living have ever before felt the need, a religion which shows that it possesses the innate power of the Holy to deal with the wild beast which a high and Christless civilisation shows itself to be. If Orthodoxy cannot do that (and it has failed, so far as the public are concerned), let us at least be sure that we are replacing Orthodoxy by something that goes as deep as its founders did in gauging human wickedness, something with the tragic penetration and moral compass of the great Calvinism, with its power over its public and over history. For a long time we have all been acquiring a more ethical view of life, while the Church, through the abeyance of interest in the Atonement, has not made a corresponding gain in moral grasp of her new life's creative centre and controlling resource. A new baptism of moral passion and sagacity in the Church is our need now, when God takes His text and preaches judgment. We need a spirit of moral divination at evangelical depth. No amount of sympathetic treatment of a returned army will meet the case. No amount of busy interest in their new frame of mind, no amount of mere desire to face the individual problems they may present to us will meet the situation, unless it is all carried on a real, reasoned, and triumphant faith by the Churches that in Christ we have an eternal command of the worst that man can do or bear, and that His judgments are less a calamity than a salvation to the Europe that now is. Do we so grasp the Cross as to believe that "for the Christian nothing absolutely vital is at stake in any secular conflict"?

Our ailment, I said, is a world deeper than can be cured by any reforms in Church organisation or device. Nor can it be treated by a new adjustment to the social problem. However we adjust the old faith to the new intelligence or ethic, let us not lose its deeper moral connection with the Grace and Holiness of God. Let us grasp that supremacy of the moral issue for history, and that finality of its settlement by Christ's death, which makes Christianity Christian. We are failing to mission the world because of a failure in the only faith that overcomes the world, the failure of a real living faith that the world *has been* overcome. There is no man great enough to force the missionary societies to realise that such failure in the Church is the source of all their difficulties, which are but symptomatic, and beyond Boards. We have much religion in the Churches, which the pulpit rather reflects than leads. Our one lack at present is a *moral* weight, amid all our impressionism, all our humane and ethical interest. The deification of sacrifice *per se* will not give it; for sacrifice (as mere sacrifice) is morally neuter. And no devotionalism can restore it. We must, indeed, wait on God by prayer and in the Spirit. But we need, still more, vital contact with something in Christ which is the source of the Spirit, and which creates prayer as the sun touches the mountains and they steam. And that something issues from the moral depths of the Cross alone, and shakes us into peace with power. We have lost *élan* because we have become uncoupled from that in Christ which is at once source and settlement. We need prayer which is not lifting ourselves by our own waistband (as so much depressing devotion is), but prayer which is part of our answer, in moral kind, to the historic visitation and victory of holy God in the Cross of His judgment-grace.

§

Is there one Church or are there many? The New Testament says both. That is the worst of the New Testament. It does not give a plain answer to a plain question. It lives in a region beyond black and white, yes and no. Its Lord did the same. Christ was disappointing to the dilemmatists. He is all in all. "If Thou art the Messiah, tell us plainly." "I have told you. Use your soul." (John x. 24 ff.)

The divisions of Protestantism form an old and brilliant theme for the Catholic apologists. In Catholicism (divided hopelessly into Roman and Anglican) the Church's unity is a great matter—as indeed it ought to be, since its disunion is so paralysing for effect. And it is now sought less by a demand for agreement over a dogmatic field than by concentration on one point. It rallies to one doctrine—the doctrine of the Church. For its unity the Church concentrates on the Church—with a certain egoism which makes a certain jar. But the principle is right enough. Concentrate. Let us also use the same tactics of concentration, but let us select differently. Let us find the unity of the Church not in itself ("He shall not speak of Himself") but in its message, in the unity of the Gospel that made the Church. To be sure of the one Gospel is to be secure of the one Church.

Let us not plead that variety is the sign of life. That

plea is a fossil relic of early Darwinism. It means by itself atomism and dissolution. For a Church founded on a positive Gospel, that way lies death. Variety does not indicate life but mere energy, mere vitality. Life is power, the power to hold variety together rather than to produce it. It is not a teeming life we have to do with in the Spirit but a sanctified, not an abundant vitality but a holy quality. Spiritual life is not exuberance. The Church is not a company of soul-adventurers. It is not made by moral experimenters or imaginative explorers. It is not for treasure-seeking; it has found the pearl of all pearls. It does not answer the call of the wild in the soul's unexplored interior, but the call of the Grace that finds it. It is committed not to a quest but to a faith. It only moves to a rich future because it has found a fertile, a creative finality. And let us not urge that to remain sects does not matter if we are not sectarian. To be content to remain sects is sectarian. The sects arose as gifts of God to the Church. They rose for a churchly need and purpose. They were appointed to recall the Church to this or that neglected point in the fulness of the Gospel. They were parts and servants of the Church, and should from the first have been so regarded. The medieval Church was often wise enough to do this and to make them orders. And that sense of the Church should grow in them. They need much to cultivate the ecumenical note. No sect ought to be content to call itself a sect, or to be so called. Either it is a Church (or an organism of Churches), or else it is a religious coterie, small or large. Nothing is a sect which was created by the Gospel, exists for it by Word and Sacrament, gauges the awful evil in the world, and takes the New Testament measure of the dimensions of that Gospel which copes with it, of that salvation, that Christ. Nothing is a sect which grasps a world-Grace, nothing which, measuring the man of sin, goes to the finality of the Gospel, the width of Humanity, and the range of Eternity.

But let us freely own to ourselves that we have been sectarian, and too often are, that we have either narrowed Grace, or reduced it to a form of God's general Fatherhood as mere kindness, a mere act of oblivion; just as Catholicism sank it on the other side to be an infusion of the divine essence into our souls through transubstantiated Sacraments.[1] We have starved ourselves of the rich treasury of Christian devotion in the profound and lovely liturgies of the long past, and of the wealth of example, inspiration, and guidance in the calendar of Christian sainthood.[2] Also (much as we have done for this country), we have not duly taken our national place, nor claimed the full national inheritance. There are whole strata of our intelligent youth that have no idea of the history of the Church as man's spiritual biography (they would not understand the phrase), nor of the national religious tradition—nothing except what is got from the press, the pieties, and the polemics, or from the evangelistic and individualist pulpit. We are not as deep in the national character and life as a Church should be—though at a supreme crisis we saved that life, when a Church meant more to us than it tends to do now. We have been as sectarian in our way as the Anglican Church, which owes its separate existence to one of the great schisms of Church History, and in certain cases keeps up that schismatic spirit—where it does not know, or care to know, or do other than despise, the religious life of one-half of the nation.[3] It is not even insular, it is but demi-insular.

My reference in speaking of the Anglican schism is to the Reformation. I am afraid this may sound offensive, but I do not mean to be offensive—only to interpret frankly and without animus a historic situation. It is the judgment of the chief branch of the Catholic family. If it is denied that there was a schism, how is it that the plea put with so much learning (whatever insight) fails to convince? It fails to

[1] "And that a higher (!) gift than Grace
Should flesh and blood refine—
God's presence and His very self,
And essence all divine."

We actually sing that—so blunt is our sense of religious meaning, our intelligence of our own faith.

[2] To keep the balance fair I wish to say that this loss of ours is smaller than the loss Catholicism suffers from its neglect and contempt for all that true Catholicism has gained from the Reformation and its train. It is a poor and partisan use to make of Aquinas to ignore Calvin ostentatiously.

[3] The Report of the Archbishop's Committee on Church and State does not once allude to the Nonconformity which is the Church of half the nation. (S.P.C.K., 1916.)

convince, on one side, Rome and the Greek Church (which know a good deal about schisms), and, on the other hand, ourselves (who are not ignorant of them). If the Anglican Church did not owe its existence to a schism from the Pope and, in connection therewith, to a schism from the great Church of the West, at least it came out there. By its detachment from European Christianity it acquired much of the insular spirit, which in a Church is the sectarian note. It seems extravagant, not to say harsh, to speak thus of a Church so great and even glorious. But I am only speaking the language it has taught us. Of course, it is a true Church and a noble, with a great glory both in past and future. Historically it is the mother of us all. And we should differ as Churches—respectfully, and not bitterly, like political parties or petty heretics. But, if it will insist on treating as sectaries and schismatics those outside itself in virtue of a succession now more than shaky to its own scholars—it must not be grieved if we interrogate its own history and explore it with the torch of the Gospel. It is a schism and a sect, which abjures the name because of its greatness—just as the Norman raid is dignified as the Conquest, and claims to be the beginning of the true England and of English nobility. But it is not size that parts a Church from a sect. Indeed, the larger the Church the greater is the risk of corruption into a sect, by the spirit of ascendancy; while quite small "sects" may be full of the faith and love that make a Church. Most of the sects were, in their inception, nearer the actual conditions of the New Testament Churches than the Churches were which they left. And, if the actual form, practice, and precedent of the New Testament Churches, as distinct from their Gospel, were decisive for all time, it is the sects that would be in the true succession, the true Churches. But, if a sect is the debasement of a Church, and if a Church is really debased only by moral faults, then the egoism, the pride, the spirit of ascendancy that gather these up is more likely to beset a great institution with a prerogative, a history, and vested interests. A Church becomes a sect when it develops the egoism which for the Church is moral marasmus and when it sees in its size, its splendour, and its domination the chief sign of its calling.

Yet, while we must teach the world, let us in relation to other Churches be very ready to learn. Do not suppose that this sectarian malady afflicts only the Churches which are a byword for lordly power and passionate prerogative. It infects us in our own way. We too become the victims of an outward pride, of Church statistics, of denominational egoisms and competitive numbers, of position instead of service, of a belief in machinery instead of faith. We trust devices more than majesties. We are more at home in discussing devices to increase membership than in acquiring the power from on high which makes a smaller Church a better Church. Our Churches are actually more interested in conferences than in colleges, and hope for more from them. We have often lost in a certain thin cosmopolitanism and fraternity the great ecumenical note, the great deep sense of words like Church and Catholic. We act as if the neighbour and the brother meant for the New Testament the same thing. Or we have come to rally upon what divides us from other Christians (and so far makes us feel superior) rather than on what unites us with them in the humility of repentant faith and humble hope. We have laid ourselves out for the victory of our differential dogma or rite. We have become, first, individualists, and then denominationalists, at the cost of the great corporate Church mind which so ruled our Puritans and fed their Puritanism.

It is quite true that the Church begins empirically, practically, with the individual, but it does not end there. And ideally, spiritually, it does not even begin there, for it was a race that Christ redeemed, and not a mere *bouquet* of believers. It was a Church He saved, and not a certain pale of souls. Each soul is saved in a universal and corporate salvation. To be a Christian is not to attach one's salvation to a grand individual, but it is to enter Christ; and to enter Christ is in the same act to enter the Church which is in Christ. Faith in Christ is faith in One Whose indwelling makes a Church, and Who carries a Church within His corporate Person. I mean this. Our individual salvation and our communion with all the Redeemed are not two separate functions of the soul, of which one is the cause and the other an effect, the one needful, the other optional. It is not as if individual religion, when it came to a certain pitch, produced cravings and sympathies which were to be satisfied only by fellowship with others of like mind. It is much otherwise. The very fact of being in Christ destroys already the barrier between soul and soul (Ephesians ii. 14). Our union with other Christians is not a matter of mere choice but of spiritual necessity. We are one, not in *consequence* of each being in Christ, but in the very fact that He is. Hence the Church was the body of Christ before it had anything that could be called organisation. It was a spiritual unity by the relation of each soul to the historic and corporate Spirit of Christ. To join a Church is simply to give outward expression and obedience to a fact existing as soon as we became Christ's by faith. The individualism must end where it really began, in the divine ideal, purpose, and fact of a community created by the most capacious soul that ever lived, the most cosmic and mighty personality that ever arose, and the greatest social act ever done. It was created by Christ's Cross, and then by His Holy Spirit individualising it. We never realise our true individuality but in communion. The ruling idea in a Church is not the individual but Christ. It is not love. For there is no entity or power called love *per se* apart from actual lovers (that were a mere abstraction), while there is such an entity, Christ; Whose atoning Person is not the supreme individual, nor the mere vehicle of a power or principle, but the organising unity which fills and binds, not to say constitutes, all Christian souls.

I do not sympathise with anti-denominationalism, nor believe in a Church of those who object to Churches. Congregationalism has been treated sometimes in that way—as if it were a colourless serum exuded from other Churches, a sweating of the legitimate ecclesiastical coinage, or a Cave of Adullam for the discontented, recalcitrant, and masterless, a creedless community of all the libertarian cranks. Such a plastic company is not a Church. It is but a form of crude clotted individualism. It means the total surrender of the Church idea for that of mere association, which might be but an association of antipathies. It yaws for want of a rudder. It has no steering way. It runs to any port where a cargo can be picked up. It has no route, and its compass needs adjusting. It has no Gospel to test newcomers by, no belief to crystallise on, no welding control to obey. If this were general instead of sectional we should have no divine reason to exist. Denominationalism can thus become but an extensive atomism. And, if that does not destroy the unity of the Church, it destroys any impression of it outside. Moreover, a Church without a positive belief and a consciousness to correspond succumbs to the Press, either vulgarly or pathetically.

§

But the idea of unity is not dead in the Free Churches. It is restless, and very restless. And that means recovery. And its invincible presentiment of itself takes the shape of *Federation.* As Humanity is a federation or family of nations, each with a personality of its own, and as it is not a chaotic sum of individuals, on the one hand, nor the empire of a single race on the other, so with the great Church. It is neither a cosmopolitan mass like democratic religion (with its loose sentiment always, and its moral failure at a world crisis), nor a universal polity like Rome; but it is the federation of living Churches, each with a history, but each also with a function and a loyalty in the whole.

I believe in the One, Holy, Catholic, and Apostolic Church. That, I often say, is to me like a great line of poetry, a great musical phrase. And it is part of our Christian duty not to allow those fine and venerable words to be monopolised by any one Church or section of the Church. The monopolist spirit is the sectarian spirit—however long it has lived. A sect is a matter of spirit and temper, rather than of majority or of antiquity.

We do not believe that the unity and catholicity of the Church are possible only on monarchical and canonical lines, on the line of a monarchical bishop and a canonical succession alone. The true catholicity and the true succession are the evangelical—the catholicity and continuity of the Gospel, in its creative, self-organising, and self-recuperative power. I have no objection to Episcopacy in itself. I could do my work happily under a bishop, and feel honoured under the episcopate of many. But part of my work would be to preach that in the first century he did not exist. Such an idea did not dominate the whole period of the undivided Church. We do protest, however, as Christians, against an Episcopal (as we do against a Presbyterian or a Congregational) monopoly of Church or Gospel, against polity as a condition of Church unity. If such an idea were carried out for the first century as some would carry it out for us, it would unchurch all the Christian communities of the New Testament.

The great external link between these was the moral influence and authority of the Apostolate; and the Apostle was not a monarchical bishop, nor indeed an official at all as official would be understood in a great institution to-day. And the Apostolate died out as the Apostles died, and as the Episcopate arose. The Episcopate replaced the Apostolate rather than prolonged it, taking some of its functions but not entitled to its prerogative. It was what the Church was driven to devise when it was slowly forced from that belief in the near return of Christ which prevented the Apostles from making provision for their work going on. It was a device where the Apostolate was a commission. Much writing on this subject suffers from a defect in method which already antiquates it—from what may be called the Oxford ban, from the tradition of the elders, from patristicism. It reads the New Testament through the coloured spectacles and horn rims of the Fathers. And its notion of the Apostolate seems accordingly to sit very tight to the institutions that held the Fathers, and very loose to the Gospel that made the Apostles. The mainstay of the Church, when State, Episcopate, and such ecclesiastical ideas fail it, is the Apostolate, whose one charter is the Gospel, and whose one suite is the evangelical succession, whatever may have happened to the canonical. Out of village Bethels God is always, by the word of His Gospel, raising up children to Abraham and successors to Peter and Paul, though bishops be ignorant of them and priests acknowledge them not.

§

We might put the matter of the Church and its unity thus, under the analogy of the State. The State is an institution at least as ancient as the Church, and *in its place* as divine. What would be thought of a publicist who refused the name, dignity, and reality of a State to any but the monarchical nations? Why, he could not get his article into any periodical intellectually respectable. It is the spirit and programme of Germany, which represents the last struggle of Feudalism. We all think Switzerland or America at least as high in the political scale as, say, Germany. But the ecclesiastical monopolist with his "No bishop, no Church" is in the same category as such an impossible writer. Let the polities all be on an equal footing. The Church which refuses the name and standing of a Church to all but the Episcopal bodies is in the same position as the State (say Germany) would be which refused the right to live to any communities except such as drew from it. Commerce alone would make such political monopoly impossible. And, if Christian faith and work, the commerce of the Christian heart and soul, were as keen as industrial commerce, the ecclesiastical absurdity would be very apparent.

We can never again identify the unity of the Church with one of its institutional forms, whether of polity or of rite. The real unity of the Church is of the kind which reflects the inner unity of the Gospel which created the Church. And the form of that unity is federate of various forms which serve that creative Gospel: it is not monarchical alone. The Church truly catholic is the anti-monopolist Church; it is not simply liberal inside a monopoly. Being catholic, it is generous, and repudiates monopoly—except the whole Church's monopoly of responsibility for the Gospel. That is the trust held by the Church. That was Christ's legacy. It was not a rite. The grand and new testament was not a Sacrament, but the Gospel. For a Sacrament does not save; it only edifies those saved by the Gospel. The only true catholicism is the evangelical. Its supreme Sacrament is that of the Word. And a sect is any Church, however old or large, that founds on prerogative, or on anything else than the Gospel in its Word and Sacrament. The Gospel, indeed, is monopolist. It is *the* religion. It is the monopolist Gospel of a catholic and manifold Church.

The ecclesiastical mission of the Free Churches is to stand for the Christian right and reality of the federal idea of Church Unity and Catholicity on the apostolic, *i.e.* the evangelic, basis of the Gospel. We may even say it is to give expression to the federal action of the Holy Spirit, Whose manifold operation of Grace makes the Church's life to be that of a community of communities. He fosters a unity controlling diversity, a diversity no greater than the unity of Grace can rule. The several Churches are members one of another on the way to the Kingdom of God. (This does not mean that the Church is but a means to the Kingdom. It is not a means but an end. It is the Kingdom in the making.) As the Church of the first century was one when empirically there were only Churches, so the true Church unity to-day is the federation of Churches, and not the monopoly of any one of them—not even its hegemony, except as a matter of courtesy and a *succès d'estime.* There is no form of Church institution with divine right, as there is none of human society. Christ was not a constitution-maker, and His Gospel was bound up with no ecclesiastical form or entail.

Are the Free Churches enough of Churches to realise this idea of federal unity which is going to work so powerfully in the Commonwealth? It is not a case of reunion, nor of amalgamation. It is a case of close co-operation while each keeps its own individuality. And it remains to be seen whether in the various bodies the Spirit of the Church is uppermost or that of the club, the sect, the chartered company—the sect more or less established, *i.e.*, settled into society, hedged in privilege, and entrenched in vested interests and egoist hopes. It remains to be seen whether the infection of a ruling sect has entered so deeply into the nature of them all, through their antagonism to it, as to make them incapable of anything but isolated and monopolist action. It is a misfortune for a nation to have a monopolist sect, instead of a truly Catholic Church, enthroned in social and political place, if only because it makes all the rest by their protest more of sects than they should be. And so it is harmful to the Kingdom of God.

The one true Church, therefore, is where the Gospel heartily is, where it is taken seriously as man's chief end; where that Gospel is lived for and worked for; where it is the source of our supreme action, namely, worship, common worship; where it takes its own native form in the existence of a Church speaking by Word and Sacrament; where it is the inspiration of all the energy and kindness that flow out toward men when we have really been dealing with God; and where it makes the Church the prophet of righteousness to nations and their States, bearding kings, sobering soldiers, and moralising finance. The true Church is where the Gospel creates its own institutions, prescribed by the situation, and flexible to it for God's purpose; and where the existence of a professional ministry witnesses that a Gospel for life must issue in a life for the Gospel. This true Church is in all the Churches. It is unseen, yet most manifest, like God Himself. It is unknown yet well known. In its purity it is everywhere to faith, nowhere to sight.

I will offer an illustration. When strangers come to Cambridge, and when they have seen the colleges, it would be natural to say, "Now take me to the University." It is a puzzling request. The Senate-House—it is not there. The Library—it is not there. The Schools—it is not there. If you say it is the aggregate of the colleges—it is not that either. It has a personality of its own; it is not a mere group, or sum, or amalgam. It has a history, a tradition, a life, a power, a spell, which is not simply the added-up history and influence of the colleges. To the curious stranger you cannot show the University—which yet is Cambridge. Who can deny the University? It is a great reality, a great spiritual reality, in which its colleges inhere. It gives the colleges their true value. It is that which they serve. It is the one spiritual corporation in which the palpable sodalities of the colleges hold together. It dignifies them all. It is the mother of them all from above.

So it is with the true Church. The universal Church is,

so to say, the University of the Churches. They are all, as it were, collegiate Churches in the great Church they express and serve. They are true Churches in proportion as they lay hold of this spiritual reality, which is their life. To ask to see the one Church among the Churches is like asking to see the University when you have done the colleges. And to refuse to believe in a true Church which is not identical with some visible company is like refusing to believe in the University because it cannot be shown you by your guides.

Let me offer another parable. I have seen, on a festive evening, as the illuminations came on, the outline in wire of a royal design which, when the darkness fell, was to be traced in light as an electric current made the wire to glow. But something went wrong with the fuses. Only fragments of the design shone out with poor suggestions of the whole. There were luminous patches, and these came and went. But in due course the hitch was arranged, the current flowed free, and the design spoke of the King. Each part had its place and meaning in the whole. And it was a whole invisible till the current passed—though you could see the supporting poles.

So with the Churches. They are contributory sections of the whole glorious Church, unseen in its royal ideal. For the time there is something wrong in the connections. But the engineers are at work. The scholars and the apostles of the divine unity are active. They wait on the divine design, and in due course they would make it stand out in light. The Holy Ghost will have free course through the mind of Christ, the Kingdom of God. One can see their work tell and grow, and the great Church emerge. In Rome,[1] on a festival night, St. Peter's is outlined in flaming patellas, which are lighted as dusk falls by men starting from different points. The areas of light grow and approach each other. Successive sections of the imposing fabric fill out. At last they meet; and the whole building stands forth like a constellation. All the sections fitly framed together grow into a temple of the Lord. So the Churches catch the flame of the servants of the Spirit, and gather into members of the great Church whose unity the garish day may even hide.

[1] Browning.

Such is the great Church subsisting in the many Churches, which only have their right to be in proportion as they contribute to its fulness. All the Churches draw their right from the Church which Christ created in His blood and equipped with His Gospel. A famous statesman once said of a great seaport which arose in the terrible commerce of the eighteenth century that its stones were cemented with the blood of slaves. What was bitterly meant of that city is gloriously true of the City of God. It was founded in a crime, and is built together in the outcast blood of the Son of God. But history has power by Grace to undo the past and erase the taint of origin. The spirit of commerce has outgrown the age of slavery. It is bad business as it is bad morals. And in the Church the blood of Christ is now the stream which flows fast by the living oracles of God, and makes one, and makes glad, the City of our King. That is the unity of the reconcilement which God makes and not man. And that is the life and secret of the One Holy Catholic and Apostolic Church.

The Church's one foundation is not simply Jesus Christ, but Him as crucified and atoning. The message and power of that at once creates the Church and moralises it. Without that it dies into moralist sterility and sentimental futility. A positive Gospel is the only base of an effective catholic, holy, and united Church, as it was its creator.

CHAPTER III

THE NEED OF A CHURCH THEORY FOR CHURCH UNITY

Church unity by federation can rest neither on fear nor on mere fraternity, but on a positive and creative theory of the Church. The analogy of the principle of nationality. The Church's advantage here over the State. The Church's foundation theological though not systematic. It rests on the Kingship of Christ. Which again rests on His work as Saviour and not on His person apart therefrom.

So (1) the basis of Church unity is not subjective in us but objective in our Redemption. (2) It is a creation of God and not a compact of men, and rests on the one act of Gospel, not on the several acts of Sacraments, nor on a second act or dispensation of the Spirit. (3) The faith with which we answer grace is therefore also an act. The same act that puts us "in Christ" also puts us in His Church. (4) The Church was one before it was many. Detail of this.

The local Church the outcrop of the whole great Church; the great Church not the agglutination of local Churches, but their *prius*.

A MOVEMENT, I have said, has arisen among the Free Churches which has for its object their federation into one Free Church of England. This would be the counterpart of the unity which is embodied in the Anglican Church with its parties, but which is there hampered by a tenacious connection with the State on the one hand and a monopolist view of the Episcopate on the other. The movement is one of federation and not fusion; and it deserves the greatest sympathy from all who yet believe in a Church but find current denominationalism to go stale. The ultimate unity of the Church, as well as its true relation to the State, would be much simplified and hastened if we had in this country but two great bodies to adjust. The issue would become much more ample and dignified; and the greatness of it would help to suppress or overshadow the trivial features and the petty men that so easily beset such a matter in a congeries of rival sects, and which at once confuse and debase it.

But for such an enterprise there is one signal requisite—a positive and effective theory of a Church from whose reality and the service of it each several Church draws its right to be. The object sought is not the kind of thing that can be won by sheer insistence. The inertia and the corporate egoism that have to be overcome may indeed by that urgency even be hardened. Nor is it to be done by a sagacious appeal to the fears of the Free Churches concerned. They are told, with insight and prudence, that they are losing public influence to such an extent that, if some thing of the kind does not happen, they will subside and die out. They are losing moral influence, weight, and impact, they are told, and told truly; and they are summoned to pull themselves together and recover it by a mass formation.

Now here is where the defect appears in the scheme proposed. The several Churches are urged to repair a loss of moral weight with the public by increasing their weight in bulk. More appeal is made to their fear than to their faith. That is to say, the movement lacks the inspiration of a positive idea of the Church, a formative core of ecclesiastical principle, and a dynamic of theological foundation. It is an ideal without a shaping idea, like warm intuition without moral intellect. It is but a movement, it has not enough in it of the nature of a reformation and its faith. If the appeal do rise above fear, it may not rise above a general Christian sympathy or fraternity. But we must go farther than either fear or fraternity. Though this federation does not aim at making a new Church, it is a Church matter, it is a matter of Churches, it is not a matter of mere religious fellowships. It is the unity of the Church it deals with, not at once of Christendom; for which large goal Church unity is the prerequisite. It is not fraternities that are to join, not sects, but Churches. And it can only be done by a Church principle of a positive and constructive kind.

Now that powerful principle can only flow from the thing that made the Church at the first; and, since the conscience is the real focus of human unity, it must flow from the moral message in that thing. Like the spiritual unity of the Churches altogether, it can but come from the reconciling nature of the Gospel, from its nature as social on the universal scale, and from a new insight into its inevitable Church-making principle. What we have to do with in the New Testament is the individualising of a corporate salvation, not the incorporation of an individual. The Church is the counterpart of a redemption primarily collective. It is the creation of such a gospel. Hence no one can be saved by a denomination as such, but only by what Church there is in it. As denominations settle in and grow egoist they lose their converting and saving power. So the appeal must be made to faith much more than fear, or even sympathy. Sympathy does not contain a principle, even piety does not, and faith does. And the Churches that rest on a subjective sanctity rather than on a real principle must be lukewarm to unity outside themselves and their organisation. To talk of unity being but a matter of brotherly love is not to gauge the problem.

The unity of the Churches can only rest on the unity, *i.e* the theology, of the Gospel that created them. An individual, or a fraternity, or a sect, can live on a vague and kindly sympathy, but a Church cannot. And the more a Church understands its destined unity, the less can it so live. It must have a common theology, not of the universe, but of faith's dynamic centre, a theology of the Gospel and its Redemption. A mere tradition, a denominational ethos, will not give it working unity, any more than a mere sympathy will. A vague Christocentricity will not. The mere rallying figure of Christ standing as a hospitable and impressive person at a point of history will not, how-ever vividly He is conceived; nor will the mere continuity of a Church through the course of history. For the unity of the Churches there must be, first, a formative theory, a principle of the Church, and, second, one that is forced on us, or inspired into us, by the positive nature of the creative Gospel of the Church's life. Cohesive affinities do their part, but they are not enough. It must be an evangelical principle. But certainly not an evangelical dogmatic.

§

Here an analogy may be useful from the political region, from political history, from the growth of the immense modern power of nationality. The great period for that growth has been the century since Waterloo. Long before that, since the close of the Middle Ages, the *thing* had been growing, and growing largely by the resistance of the minor nations to the attempts at world-empire by Spain, by the Sweden of Gustavus Adolphus, by the France of Louis the Fourteenth, and the France of Napoleon. But it was unsteady and precarious. It was a matter of aspiration and spasmodic effort, because it was based either on vague affinities or external pressures of an empirical kind. There was no *doctrine* of nationality. It was not a thing that could be preached by anything like a universal apostolate. It was not a public principle. But out of the whole revolutionary period there came the doctrine of nationality resting on the rights of man, the rights of the governed. It now began to be preached as a theory and a creed of a kindling kind. Mazzini came, and the great German historians and thinkers of the early period that admired and copied the national freedom of England, and led up to the revolutions of 1848. They dreamed of a family of free nations. The blight of the movement in Germany has been the fatal substitutions of mere racialism for nationality, which has grown ever since that date when the revolutionaries were violently suppressed. But on both sides the driving power has been a creed, a doctrine, a principle. "The years from 1820 to 1878 are in a peculiar and special degree the nationalist period in European history, the period in which the doctrine of nationality was preached as fervently as a religion, and became the dominant factor in the moulding of events" (Ramsay Muir). It must be so also with the unity of that great spiritual nation, the new Israel, the Church. From its source it spread at once as a κήρυγμα, a preachable theology. And the great Churches that influence nations are those which have a distinct and powerful idea of the Church, and have it not as an academic theory but as a driving and shaping doctrine. And so it must be with every effort to realise the unity of the Church as the reflection of the Kingdom of God, and as the spiritual nation impressing the kingdoms of the world.

§

Now in some of the Churches involved in this proposal there is more than the absence of such a theory; there is in parts of them an aversion to it; there is even a contempt for it. It is treated as a luxury when it is not taken as a lunacy. There is, in the woeful empiricism of current religion, a dislike to admit either a theory or the need of it. There is a notable revival of the mysticism which, in the sapping by criticism of so much that is historic, turns to seek rest in some form of inner light. But this inner light is individualist, and it is alien to a Church as more than a club of mystics without objective base or authority. There is a tendency to treat the theology of the matter at worst as a nuisance, and at best as collateral and not creative; it is valuable old furniture, but the house could be run without it on the hire system of the idealist firms. There is a disposition to rely on general sympathies and grandiose ideas, or on platforms, committees, and propaganda, when the chief need is the education of Church members and ministers in their own creative truths; which education is at the moment such that more bewilderment than welcome is often caused when the doctrine of a Church is pressed quite in earnest. The Church needs to pay more attention to itself than to the world—for the sake of acting on the world. But we can get on, it is said, without theories of the State; what need for theories of the Church? Now, could anything better show how politics has squatted on the ground of religion, imposed its notions and methods on the Christian tradition, and thrust in its own utilitarian ideas? The State is not founded on a revealed fact, act, or principle, but the Church is founded on all three. They create it. The State can do whatever seems expedient; the Church can be and do only what its Gospel inspires, prescribes, or allows. The State needs no theory for its action, because it has no charter. It goes sounding on its dim way, and steering according to the report. But the Church must be guided by its charter of principle given in the creating act of holy grace.

The Free Churches will not unite, it is doubtful if they will even federate, until they are more of Churches with an objective faith, and less of groups and denominations with but subjective affinities. Nothing but a Church theory, with the whole moral imperative of the Gospel behind it, can overcome denominational egoism enough for the purpose.

§

A theology and a Church stand or fall together. It is the decay or the vagrancy (not to say volatility) of theological faith in the ranks of some of the Churches (for I do not speak of their leaders) that is the real source of weakness which is alarming some of the wisest minds. I fear that the layman finds it hard to ascribe such effect to anything he does not understand (though he always may). It sounds nonsense to many laymen to be told that it was the Athanasian Creed that saved the life of Christianity for Europe, at a historic crisis, or that the Church ever owes its well-being and public effect to anything beyond what the simple soul can seize and be saved. That is an error quite parallel to the idea that a nation can live on exactly the same ethic as makes the cottager an honest man. But if these doctrines are true, Christian people should have the will to believe them and the power to measure them; if they are not true, we are in quest of another religion. The Churches cannot unite until they are more of Churches (it would not otherwise be Church union); and they will not be more of Churches until they are more of believers (without at the same time being less of sympathisers); and they will not be more of believers till they believe more, treat their theology with some of the respect it is fashionable to feel for economics, and view the ministry of the Gospel as more momentous than entering Parliament. They need more of the mind of Christ, in something else than the sympathetic sense of that phrase, in the sense of Christian truth and conviction, in the sense in which Paul meant it when in 1 Cor. ii. 16 he said he thought the thoughts of Christ,—they need that if their Churches are not to subside into mere friendly groups. The state of education has more to do than most see or allow with the state of religion and of the Churches. But that is not to say that faith is to be rationalised either in the way of orthodoxy or heresy. The climate of faith is not mere intelligence, but intelligence living as the will's action and transfused by the heart's love. "*Mentis ardor lux doctrinæ.*"

The Church's one foundation is a theological one, though not a systematic. It is the Word of a positive Gospel. A real reconciliation of hearts is founded on a real Atonement of the conscience. We miss the point if we say no more than that the foundation is Jesus Christ as head. That is not sufficiently dynamic. It leaves His personality too inert. What is it in Him that makes Him head? What is it in the nature of His headship that makes His company a real society, His society a real Kingdom, and His historic following a Church? Is He but the chief of a clan He inherits, the centre of a group He attracts; or is He King of a realm He creates? Are we but disciples of His person or are we confessors of His redemption? If He is a King, really and not poetically, as before Pilate He said He was, in virtue of what is He King? For this is the social, the Church-creating element in Him; otherwise the Church is a mere means and expedient for the Kingdom, it is not the Kingdom itself in the making; and to make the Church but a means is to bemean it. To answer that question is to go well into theology.

For a king, in those days when Christ died for the name, was not a spectacular person, he was not an æsthetic object. He was there not just to be seen on public occasions —indeed, he courted the majesty of aloofness and inaccessibility,—but to do something real in making his kingdom or keeping it going. His will was the realm's law. Also he was not simply a sheltering person, as if his people but dwelt quietly in the shadow of his broad wing. So the social element in a royal Christ, as He understood royalty, is not that He should be seen of many, and by many thronged or acclaimed; for they might do that but as atoms of a crowd, or as moths that desire a star. He was no mob-led King, nor mob-fed. That social thing is not His divine person alone, as the most capacious of all the living homes of the soul. That might but set us each in a quiet resting-place in Him to dwell in the House of the Lord for ever, where the Lamb is the temple, and each has a niche in Him as the Father's Son in Whom there are many mansions.

But that is not the fulness of Christ. It would not make Him our Lord *as* our Redeemer; He would be Redeemer among other things. His redemption would be but incidental to His Kingship. It would not give us a creative redemption as the one royal Gospel confronting a creative evolution, the one Word for the Church's unity. It would set up other words as well, and thereby perpetuate a variety of sects. It would not give us in Him a true and universal King, nor build us in Him into an everlasting Kingdom where souls are fitly joined together in a general hierarchy as active members one of another. That meant ethically an act of new creation—as in the æsthetic sense a cathedral was. A real king is one who does things—does royal things royally, but does things. He does not simply contain us and bless us; He rescues, and acquires, and makes us. The perfection of personality is action. The King of Kings is He Who does the one moral thing needful for the whole world. Truly we dwell in Him, but in His final crucial victory; we are not merely placed in His generous spacious person. We are not merely in Him, we are absolutely His. Christ is King in virtue of an Act into which all His divine person goes for the whole race, and by which alone we reach the deep interior of His person—in virtue of something done, and not merely said or shown, an Act universal and eternal, which changed everything, and leaves us with no right in ourselves but what comes from His redemption. It is this Act, corporate and universal, that creates the Church, and insists throughout history on its unity.

§

I should like to come to closer quarters with my subject and point out certain features in the Church's creative Gospel and its history which make unity imperative and not desirable only. They are principles whose insight makes a Church strong, whose action we cannot arrest by any stupidity (much as we might retard), and whose neglect dooms to impotence and extinction any sect or society that ignores them.

1. The unity of the Church rests on a basis not subjective but objective. It does not stand on Christian sympathies and affinities but on divine deed and purpose. It rests upon God's grace and Gospel, not on fraternal love—which God will see to if we see to His grace. Our love of each other is the effect and expression of our love of Him who gave Himself for us. This is in opposition to the modern desire for fellowship, comradeship, and brotherhood as the *direct* constituent of a Church. Of course there is no true Church without fellowship and brotherhood, but it is not on that that it rests, but on the Redemption, the new creation. Fellowship is a fruit and not a root, it is a duty even more than a joy, it is always a duty though not always a joy—as our youth should realise. The Spirit that unites the Church has its source in Christ's work on the Cross.

2. The great Church is primarily the result of an act of God. It is primarily a divine creation and not a voluntary association. It is not of man nor of the will of man. It was called and created by a divine Act of the Holy, which is continued by the Church in a mystic Gospel of moral action, and not in a sacrament. The Sacraments are not Christ's one legacy. They are not the kind of act in which the Church rises and rests. Its unity was created by the one Gospel and not by the several sacraments; these are but modes of the published Word, which is the sacred thing in all sacrament. It is that Gospel of moral Redemption that is the one gift of grace and the one source of the Spirit; which Spirit was not a second and superior gift. The one Act and Word of Gospel as the heart and source of the Church is thus against Catholicism with its sacramental basis, as well as against Quakerism with its pneumatic and sympathetic. Both throw to the rear the centrality, creativity, and cruciality of the Cross. This is specially the case with Quakerism. From Barclay's day till now it has never done full justice to the Atonement which lies at the root of all moral reconciliation, and therefore it is wrong and inept in great moral crises like a world war for public righteousness. It makes one of the cardinal mistakes of public life—

it mistakes the nature of God's righteousness in history. It is the fatal mistake of the Germans at the other extreme. It relies too much on movements of inner light, and too little on the eternal Act of power; on spiritual frames too much and on a final spiritual redemption too little. Its genius is too alien to crises, and therefore it is at some fault in a religon founded, like the Gospel, on the moral crisis of the race. It has founded on the Sermon rather than the Cross, and on the character of Christ in His life rather than on His person gathered into critical historic action in His death. And this is all of a piece with its depreciation of the Church idea and of its sacramental expression. It has realized the ethic that accompanies Christianity rather than that which constitutes it as the creative act of its life. It has seized the ethic of conduct rather than of atoning redemption, the ethic of our relation to man rather than that of our relation to holy God, the ethic of behaviour rather than faith. It has been more concerned with kindly sanctity in men than with the tragic holiness of love in God. It is upon a redemption atoning to that holiness that the Church and all its sanctity rests (I do not here speak of individual souls); upon an eternal self-atoning act of God rather than upon what is more vaguely called the spirit of Christ shed abroad in the heart; upon a regenerating redemption rather than a regeneration in the wake of redemption.

3. The act of God's grace provokes in us a response in kind. Our answer to it is also an act. It is an act which draws on the whole life—on the whole man in action, the whole race at last thus answering the whole God. It is an act of final self-committal to Christ. But to Christ not simply as the Founder of the Church, but as its Creator and its Life; to Christ with Whom the Church is united and not simply connected; in Whom it is integrated and not simply accommodated; to Christ Who has always within Him the whole Church by having the power which created and creates it; to Christ as a public and corporate person; to Christ Whose life, death, and glory, whose grace and love, the Church but writes large in history. Therefore *the same act which sets us in Christ sets us also in the society of Christ.* It does so *ipso facto*, and not by a mere consequence or sequel,

more or less optional. To be in Christ is in the same act to be in the Church. Anything we do in the way of joining the Church by a confession of faith is only making explicit in the statement what is already implicit in the fact. The act of faith which saves us from self would only have a negative meaning if it did not save us at the same moment into a society which is a centre of service and sympathy. It puts us into a relation with all saints which we may neglect to our bane but which we cannot destroy.

4. Historically the Church was one before it was many. For Jesus the kingdom come (in Himself) was before the kingdom coming in history, and the one was the ground and power of the other. And for modern anthropology the tribal self preceded and determined the personal self. The society created by the one God, the one Saviour, the one salvation was one as it left the divine hand. It was for a Church that Christ died, and we are saved by our share in that corporate salvation. It was one as the *vis-á-vis* of the one Redeemer, as His Bride, or His body. That fact is the charter of its historic unity. To the one God, the one Gospel, the one Christ, there can but answer the one Church. That unity was not put together by organisation. The Church is not an organisation but an organism. It was born one. The unity is not a matter of structure but of life, not of fabric but of faith. It is not an aggregate but a creation. These units themselves began as expression or outcrops of the unity created by God; otherwise the unity would be the workmanship of man's hands, and the Church would rest on a mere voluntarism. It would be a contractual thing, a matter of covenant, a thing of which the ecclesiastics would be the engineers and not the ministers.

It is upon this point that I would enlarge as a matter of historic fact.

§

There are in the New Testament but two ideas of the Church, and I wish to point out that these two are ultimately one.

There are but two ideas. They are the local community,

and the totality of believers in heaven and on earth—the totality of those who are in Christ.

And it is to the local that we must first attend. My point is that the local Church was not an isolated community, but a community whose isolation was modified in several ways, and really destroyed. The local or sectional Church in the New Testament was so far from being isolated that it was a community *plus* Christ, *plus* the Apostles, *plus* all Christians.

1. To begin with the first, it was a community plus Christ, who was never absent. The most real thing in the Church is not its democracy, but Christ's absolute monarchy. Christianity is a monarchy; and it is not a constitutional monarchy either, nor an elective, but an absolute. Our King is there not by our choice of Him, but by His choice of us; and He rules by no compact with us. We are absolutely His. We are not only His subjects, but His property. He is, indeed, no arbitrary King. He is King in righteousness. He is constitutional so far as that, and not arbitrary. But it is an absolute holy righteousness. He is absolute, so far as we are concerned, as King of Saints: "Ye are bought with a price; be not therefore servants of men." Ye are captives to one Christ; be not therefore distracted caterers to the public.

2. It was a community plus the Apostolate, and now the ministry in so far as based on the Bible, which was the real successor of the Apostolate as the precipitate and legacy of the message in their trust. The local Churches were ruled in their life and limited in their freedom by men whom they did not elect or control, by a body of such men, who made the Churches far more than the Churches made them—I mean the Apostles. Externally the first Churches cohered in the Apostles and their authority. It was an authority that rested upon their autopsy—they had seen and companied with the Lord, and were witnesses of His having risen. It rested, farther, upon the moral prestige of what Christ had taught them and committed to them, and of their own faith and spiritual character as His special agents. And, still farther, it rested on the way Christ in His Spirit opened their eyes to such meaning of His work as should be

normative for the whole Church always. But all the same there was no prerogative given them for transmission. Their authority took effect in positive injunctions, regulations, and revelations which were none the less weighty because they depended on a moral and not a hierarchical relation between Apostle and Church. It was a moral authority, but none the less regulative, in a way that every missionary with a young Church knows.

The more ethical and personal this authority was, the more unique it was and intransmissible. We must not minimise the apostolic authority for the sake of resisting the authority of those whose claim to be their only successors we contest. It is the succession we must challenge, not the authority. Their authority was real, but it died with them in its personal form. Of course the need of the Church for a living authority did not die, but the Apostolate did. It was put into the form of a living book, vital with the marrow of the Apostles' gospel. That precipitate of their message, that fixed capital of their divine industry, was their real successor. That living norm remained to rally and kindle the mind of the Church. The Bible and the Spirit remained. And when Cyprian set up his hierarchy he was not prolonging an old office, but creating a new machinery for an old function. The real successor of the Apostolate (as I have said) was not the hierarchy but the canon of Scripture written to prolong their voice and compiled to replace the vanished witness. The Episcopate grew up by election after the Apostolate had passed away. It did not grow out of the Apostolate by co-optation.

The Apostolate died with the Apostles, and with it died an essential factor in the Church life of the first century. What is to take its place? It may be said that the whole history of the Church since then has been an effort to answer that question. Something is needed over each Church to do for unity under Christ what is done in the New Testament by the Apostolate in interpreting the message. Something we need more real and effectual than the subjective feeling which flows upon the occasions when we fraternise and ebbs when we retire; something in the nature of a real authority; not absolute, yet objective, whose recognition should quell the self-will of the community, and provide not a subjection but still an obedience. And a part at least of that something is the office of the ministry. And another part is the organisation between the Churches.

3. The local Church was a community which was not self-contained, but which included spiritually all Christians elsewhere. In a word, the local Church was but the outcrop there of the total and continuous Church, one everywhere.[1] The total Church was not made up by adding the local Churches together, but the local Church was made a Church by representing there and then the total Church. It was just where the total Church looked out at one point. That is the divine ideal and norm to which all organisation and federation must work.

The ecclesia was the gathering of a *people*; Hort, completed by others, like Harnack (influenced by Sohm), makes this quite clear. It was not in the nature of a club, guild, or association. Hatch's line has not been adopted. It was the New Testament Israel, the Israel of God in Christ (Galatians vi. II), the New Testament *people* of God, the landless nation, God's *vis-à-vis* for the new age as Israel was for the old. It was the New Covenant people, resting, not on an act of association, but on a divine call and corporate creation. It was Christendom. It was the assembly of all Christians with God and before God. The local gathering, therefore, was not *a* Church but *the* Church seen as God sees it, Who sees all in one and the end in the beginning. It was the totality of Christians living, dead, and dispersed, flowing spiritually to a certain spot and emerging there in its indiscerptible unity.

But if that be so, how is it that the word can be used in the New Testament of local Churches at all? We read even of the Church in the house of So-and-so. How is it, indeed, that it is oftenest used in that local way?

The answer is that the word does not primarily describe the empirical meeting or society. For that purpose συναγωγή might be used, as in the Apocalypse, or in James. It has a

[1] I am describing the dominant idea of the New Testament, but I do not trace its genetic growth within the New Testament.

dogmatic meaning rather than a social or empirical. It means not the group there but the one community of faith everywhere which crops out there. Its reality is for faith and not sight. It is not a social unit but a facet of one solidary entity. It rests on Matthew xviii. 20. Where Christ is there is Christendom, there is the people of Christ. They are all in Him, and therefore where He comes He brings all Christendom. And He comes to two or three. With these, therefore, there is the whole Church. "*Ubi tres ibi ecclesia*," it was said. What did that mean? Not that three believing people made up *a* Church, but that where there are such a three there is *the* Church, that three with Christ draw thither spiritually the whole Church. To common sense, of course, that is nonsense. But the New Testament is not a common-sense book. And faith saw in each community not a distinct and self-contained Church but the whole Church, the people of God, the new spiritual Israel, as our Ambassador's house abroad is part of England, yea, is all England, if need and crisis bring all England to that spot. The whole Church as it were rushes to the spot touched by the presence of Christ, and makes the place of His crucified feet glorious. "Never, believe me, appear the Immortals bare and alone." So the community is a Church not because it is local, but in spite of being local. For Origen and Tertullian, in the gathered community Christ is present, and the angels, and the martyrs, and the faithful, living and dead. And this is the only idea that gives real meaning to that magnificent passage, Hebrews xii. 22: "Ye are come unto the city of the living God, the heavenly Jerusalem, and to innumerable hosts of angels, to the total assembly and church of the first-born, which are written in heaven, and to God the Judge of all, and to the spirits of just men made perfect, and to Jesus the mediator of the new covenant."

It was therefore *one* Church in many manifestations. It was not many Churches in one convention. The total Church was spiritually prior to the local, and it was spiritually entered by the same act that believed in Christ, that believed in Him as no individual but as a corporate personality, a personality with all the Church latent in Him as He was latent in every Church. The Church in the town, or in the house of So-and-so, means the total Church as emerging there, looking out there, taking effect there. The Church in the great sense is not composite, but organic. Its life is given to its members, not compiled from them. The Churches, no less than their souls, are members one of another.

My case would be that these considerations give us a basis in principle for Church union which makes it not only possible but imperative. It gives us the distinctive Christian idea of a Church which makes mere denominationalism intolerable. If the Churches grasped it there would be much less need for working up an enthusiasm which is bound to subside without such a principle as the Church's living leaven. Union is unity taking effect. It is the truth of the Church rising from its one Gospel and its one faith. To become a member of the one Christ Who is the Church's life is *ipso facto* to become a member of the one Church. And the one Church is to the many as England to her counties.

This idea of the Church, though not new, is so unfamiliar that I may be allowed to dwell on it. The New Testament time had no such idea as that of a Church, great or small, with a formal constitution and procedure adopted by covenant. It had not the idea of a local community formed by voluntary effort, by a Church contract, complete in itself, self-organised, and adequate in itself to all that a Church should be and do. It had but the idea of one Christian people in a dispersion, a Christendom as a purely religious thing without a prescribed constitution or a prerogative polity, but with purely spiritual methods and moral effect. It was called a Church, an Israel, a flock, a brotherhood; and all these terms mean the same thing—a chosen people of God, united in Christ, and living in His choice, His grace, His love, His Holy Spirit as each soul's new life. It was a sporadic unity in the world of that spiritual kind, an organism, not an organisation, the body of Christ—corporate but not a corporation. Sohm says that we might as well talk of a Christian rifle as of a Christian corporation in the legal sense; each is equally a contradiction in terms like a worldly Church or a mystic State. What makes the Church a living body is something entirely religious—the one faith, the one Lord, the one Spirit, the one life and conduct, the one regimen of free spiritual gifts exercised by each with due respect for those of the rest. The unity of the Church is purely supernatural and is an object of faith—it is not a matter of organisation, it is not any polity, even the Congregational. This destroys the idea of the Church being a Church only in so far as it is a corporation. Of course, in dealing with the law of the State it may present itself as a corporation, by way of talking the language of the natives; but that is not what makes it a Church. And the first age made no difference between the Church in this religious sense and Christendom as visible. The visible and empirical Christendom is the flock, people, and body of Christ, making a unity far beyond the region of law and ordinance, constitution or polity. The deadly thing that took place in Catholicism was the identification of the Church as religious with the Church as a statutory polity. It made organisation fundamental, and its action legal and coercive. Whereas the genius of the Church's life, unity, and action is not statutory but charismatic; it is less of prescription than of inspiration. And it is led by men who are chosen and endowed by God with certain gifts rather than appointed and authorised by men to a certain function. If appointed by men it is because of the possession of the divine gift. Such is the New Testament Church idea. And if the element of polity become necessary in history, it must always be in such a way as to keep this idea uppermost, and not smother it as Catholicism has done.

We must get rid of the notion that the great Church was composed by the coagulation of a certain number of single Churches, each of which was a Church in its own right, a Church organised at a spot or parish as we find our local communities to-day, and putting out processes or filaments to link up with others. That was not at all the case. It would be making the one Church to be of man and the will of man. What the Apostles planted was not Churches but stations of the Church. What the Gospel created was not a crowd of Churches but the one Church in various places. What we have everywhere is the one Church of Christ put down here and there, looking out in Corinth,

Ephesus, or Thessalonica. People did not go to a meeting which was on its way to become a Church; they went to the Church at a certain place of meeting. Wherever you went it did not matter, you went to *the one Church*. A member here was a member everywhere. Wherever you had the Word and Spirit of God you had not *a* Church but *the* Church. The localness was a mere matter of convenience, not of doctrine. Merely as local the Church had no Christian rights. There was no independency. If it had any rights at all they were those of the whole Church. They were not just parallel with the rights of other Churches. The gatherings were independent not as having the individual power to combine at will into a larger Church, but because the larger Church appeared equally at each. Where you had but two or three you had the whole Church on earth, and in heaven, which loved and worked in many companies in Christ. The Church as visible was but an appearance, an emergence of the Church as spiritual. It was a projection of it, not a constituent. The local cohesion was, as local, nothing; it drew all its churchliness and all its religious value from a communion supra-local. It had a right to exist only as a living occurrence of the one Church. It was all it was as a particular expression of an ecumenical Christianity. It is not *a* Church with sympathies with others, it was *the* Church, and there were no others—only similar outcrops of the one spiritual Church, not of the Episcopal Church, nor the Presbyterian, nor of any other form. The true Church but *occurs* locally, and in such a way that each appearance has equal rights and value as having equal part and lot in the Israel of God. All were one in being equally bound to the Word of God, and indeed due to it. Each is a vortex in the spiritual ocean, which appears at a spot but might disappear to another spot without damage to the Great Sea.

When the Christians at Rome write what seems to them God's Word on equal terms to the Christians at Corinth (1 Clement) it is only one room calling to another in the family home. It is not like one municipality negotiating with another. So that it is not strictly correct to speak of the Corinthian Church, but of the Church in Corinth, as it comes to the surface there. And the Church in a private house was as much *the* Church as the whole Christianity of Corinth. So that in one locality you might have a multitude of Churches with an equal place in the whole Church everywhere.

CHAPTER IV

THE CHURCH AND HISTORY

The Church is the creation of the historic Gospel, and it is therefore determined by it. But it succumbs to the civil society it set out to evangelise; and it cannot escape by mysticism. Charge against Protestantism that it fell between rationalism and pietism. Replies. The Reformation not yet done. It needs reforming. Return to the Bible—what is meant by that.

The Church and the State. Within the Church there is no hierarchy of prerogative, but only authority of function and convenience. So also the whole Church has no authority of prerogative to rule the State outside it. Its control is chiefly in the way of witness and guidance. But also it cannot be ruled by the State. The Church State and the State Church. There is no sacrosanct form of Church polity. But also let us have no rebellion against the past for rebellion's sake.

Is the historic Church the prolongation of the Incarnation? Consequences of that view and its impossibility. The Church is a creature, Christ is not. The outward and the inward must act and react in an interpenetration.

THE whole form and history of the Church is determined by the principle that creates the Church, namely, the Gospel, whose preached reality was Christ's supreme legacy to the world. The Lord is the Spirit—the creating Lord the quickening Spirit. And, conversely, the Church's form and history ought to be such as to reflect and preach its principle with growing power. If any Churches, or any heads of Churches, lose that principle and Gospel, their candlestick should be removed from its place. If no one else remove it, God will, and will draw down on them in due course the twilight of the false gods. Christ abides with those who by faith abide in Him. And if the old evangelical succession of the ministry were to fail, God is able out of stones to raise up children to faithful Abraham. He did in the Reformation. He did in the Independency which carried it to full effect. He will when Independency falls on its lees, and loses its Gospel in its liberty. There is hardly a Church that has not suffered from its success. And when I say suffered, I mean it has suffered in its power of witnessing the Gospel. It has gained comfort, affluence, and influence, but it has lost its prophetic soul, it has fallen from its apostolic insight and succession. And while this is true fatally of the dynastic and Byzantine Churches like Germany, it is also in its measure true of some Churches of the democracy which stand aloof from politics much more than from Mammon.

To be rid of politics is not to be free from the world. Indeed, in organising themselves the Churches have often organised themselves into the world. They have struck a pact with the dynasties at one end and with the causes at the other. They have become the victim either of uniformity at the aristocratic end or of what might be called platformity at the democratic. And of the two deadly things the former is the more irremediable and refuses resurrection. It means the mechanising of the Church, and its fall from Christ and grace and freedom. Where the Church has become most mechanical, so that the apostolic college waits on the Minister of State for Religion and becomes a mere chancellory or curia, there superstition flourishes, whether it be the superstition of reason or that of imagination. And it is then that mysticism rises as a protest—a protest with its own dangers, but a protest for life—with a depth and a power in it that had been stifled by the machine. The works were there but there was no faith to drive them. The Church could not go even slowly because of the world. The shell had absorbed the tortoise. And it does not matter whether it was the shell of a hierarchy or the shell of an orthodoxy. They both failed to keep or to rear true faith, and therefore they destroyed the root of true love. The outer unity of form killed the inner unity of life.

In such cases often the instinct of life, ceasing to be faith, becomes the mere passion for freedom in natures still energetic but still only natural. And from that arise all kinds of schisms and anarchies. It is the day then of the fruitless *franc-tireur*, the mere independent, the free-lance and the atomic weight, who, beginning sometimes as the amiable devotee of an inner light, may descend into the ecclesiastical adventurer, or, lower still, into the liberal bully. For every fad somebody is ready to raise a sect and call it conscience, or carry an irresponsible swagger and call it freedom. The air comes to teem with individualists who attract the Press and exploit the Church as a pedestal for their egoism; and they may be as religious in their superstition of freedom as the Calabrian peasant in his. They have a religion highly preachable, but they are the apostles of self-will more than of Christ. And where they do not come to grief morally they may spiritually—by substituting for the soul's redeemed liberty mere rational freedom, and wrapping it in the coloured paper of dainty sentiment as they vend it. They have nothing to say, and often say it like a gentleman. If they try to deepen their religion it takes the shape of a vague mysticism, so that the history of their career is no history but a mere chart of temperament. If they are tired of the vagueness they concentrate the mysticism by a plunge into the Sacraments. And so they return from their soul adventures to the point where they rebelled. The wheel comes full circle with nothing done and nothing won. The inveterate subjectivity has just revolved on its own axis. And once more rebellion is shown to be sterile when it is promoted for its own sake and follows its own gleam. It is the greatest mistake to confound the rebel and the reformer, the mere mutineer and the champion.

§

It has been charged against Protestantism that in falling from the true Church it fell at its own centre between two stools. It fell between rationalism and pietism; between a rational science of faith (whether orthodox or heterodox), which was detached from faith, and a pietist experience of faith, detached from any science of itself; between a theology to which faith was really otiose, and a faith to which theology was otiose—as for a Church it can never be. Whereon note:

First, the same thing took place in Catholicism. Many Catholics became victims of a theological system which had practically been drained of a living God. Before the Reformation the Church teemed with mystic sects of protest, which had no small part in preparing for the great revolt. Had it not been so the reaction would have been less violent, and the flame of revolution would not have blazed so fiercely as it has done in the Catholic lands. While, on the other hand, a pietism indifferent to its truth is at least as common in such lands as in Protestantism, though in a different form.

Second, pietism did preserve religion in almost the only way possible when the Church had become so hard and outward as it did. But then, as now, it was too individualist, and too alien to ideas, to preserve a Church. (For you cannot have a permanent Church unity without a due idea of a Church, provided from the Gospel that created it, and schooling the egoism both of souls and sects.) So that, without wishing or even knowing it, the mere Christian spirit or piety becomes a Church solvent, or else it becomes unable to resist the other solvents at work. It stops for a little in its deliquescence to coagulate into mere groups. And it leaves people hankering after that unity, catholicity, and authority which the old Church declared it alone could provide. Many therefore return to such a Church as being, with all its defects, better and more promising than the agglutinated atomism which a religion without a system offers.

Thirdly, during the last century a very powerful movement arose and spread in Protestantism which did begin with living and ethical faith of a truly evangelical kind, which based theology upon it, and which claimed the autonomy of theology on the ground that faith was an organ of real knowledge. This is a line which should have a real future as society becomes more sure of its ethical centre and demand.

And a fourth remark may be added. If it is doubtful whether Catholicism, as such, is perfectly sound and invincible at heart, it is also doubtful if the Reformation, so far as it has gone, is sufficient or final. The Reformation itself is in process of being reformed. And that it needs it is shown by the state of those Churches or parties in Churches that claim to have the special guardianship of the evangelical principle, but which have ruined the name of evangelical almost beyond recovery. But there are many reformed Catholics who would admit that Catholicism could not recover its health simply by a wave which swept Protestantism out of existence. The same banes which cried for the Reformation would soon reappear in new forms.

The disease in Mediævalism would break out in a new place. Yet whatever form the Church of the future may take, it must give due and better scope to the fundamental principle that the true Catholicism, the true Churchmanship, is there only to be the vehicle or agent of God's redeeming Word among human affairs. Which transfers the issue to the question: What precisely is that Word? What is the Gospel? Every answer is hopeless which seeks the unity of the Church in any mechanical, or even any institutional, uniformity, in any polity. A unity in an episcopate is quite hopeless, whether we regard Scripture on the one hand, or, on the other, the prospects offered in the present state of the Church or the age. The Church's unity is the unity of the moral, *i.e.* the evangelical, power which creates its inmost life where two or three meet with serious practical purpose in the name of Christ's Gospel. It may be a Church of conflict, which can exist only by the adjustments of warfare—changing its front, perhaps, but always keeping its ground. And it may be a Church which it is impossible in this life to mark off clearly from the world, while the difference is yet very real, as the warfare must be, and Zion must cope with Babylon to the end. The attempts to establish purity of communion by the vote of communicants, however worthily meant, have only issued in the formation of sects. And, while these have had their providential value for the Church, they tend, if they are left to themselves, to fall to pieces in a new Babel. For the exclusion of those deemed to be Babylonians does not destroy the Babel in the souls of those who are left within. Separation begins to divide the separate themselves, and reformation goes on to change the most reformed. So the Church can only be unified by that which makes the real unity of the soul. And that is the word of moral reconciliation.

And where is that to be sought? We must go back to the Bible. The Christian back to the Bible; the scholar, with all his splendid modern equipment, back to the Bible. But not to a miraculous code, nor to a Christian Koran, nor to a manual of saving theology. It is now back to that which makes the Bible the Bible. Back to that which is *au delà de l'intérieur de la Bible,* within and beyond the Bible.

Back to the Gospel of our moral redemption through faith in the pure grace and mercy of God in Christ crucified. That is the most certain thing in Christianity. That (and no dogmatic of it) is what must regather and merge the sects and Churches to the great Church which is identical with the Kingdom of God. The Bible must serve the Gospel as the Church does the Kingdom. That is the life that makes the sect die to its spirit of separation. No schemes of unity nor of doctrine can replace that. And till that is there they are in vain. Unity makes schemes, not schemes unity. No strategic coalition of Churches in the face of a common Antichrist can do it; for then we should be more scared than drawn into unity. Nor can it be done by sympathetic affinity. It needs a *creative* power to build the Churches into a holy temple. No consideration of economising our religious resources, and working our machine to the utmost effect, can do it. That is statesmanlike; but the Church does not live on such sagacity but on inspiration, or on something more creative still—on regeneration.

This return to the Bible is but beginning. The scholars clear the ground and show the way to the crucial point. And their work is more needed than most things. But it is not the one thing needful, which is a fresh realisation of the holy grace of God in the heart and conscience of a Church now distracted because devitalised. The chief problem of the Church is not in the world but in itself. And there it turns on its Gospel more than on what is called its spirit. It is devitalised because it is de-evangelised by orthodox and heterodox alike.

All this means something else than literary religion, enlightened views, charming addresses, and interesting sermons, nor sermons even impressive. It means far more than domestic piety with the light of a tender fancy playing on it, or ethical ardours and social programmes to which a moral regeneration is otiose. Not all the social idealisms in the world can do more for the Kingdom of God than German socialism or American democracy has done in the way of failure when a crisis in righteousness of the first rank burst upon history. It would serve us better than discussing what the Church is to do for the world after the war, to take more seriously and searchingly the question, what the Gospel has to do for the Church in the situation. We need an evangelical revival as much deeper than that of a century ago as the Reformation was greater than it. I know it is the standing refuge of the feeble to say we need a revival. But their feebleness is not in saying that, but in having no idea of what is meant by it. For in patting their hearts and petting their pieties their souls have lost any moral grasp adequate either to the first Gospel or to the public situation of our age.

§

The function of the Church to society is to lead it; it is certainly not neutral. Nor is it Byzantine; the Church is not to be dragged at the heels of the State. But we ought to be very clear that it is to lead in the sense of guidance and not in the sense of rule. Curialism and Ultramontanism are as foreign to the spirit of the Gospel at one end as Byzantinism (which is the superlative of Erastianism) is at the other. The Church is to the State neither neutral, erastian, nor imperial. The ideal relation is not that of the old Nonconformity, nor that of Hooker, nor is it the coarse Byzantinism of Germany; nor is it at the other extreme a lordly popery toward the Empire. It is a case of moral guidance flowing from spiritual positivity, and welcome, kindly light burning in reciprocal freedom.

Within the Church also there is no hierarchy of prerogative. There may be an authority of function and convenience, where the bishop is the choice of those he rules. The first form of the Church was corporative—a pneumatic fraternity. Christ forbade gradation of rank, however He recognised moral superiority and spiritual leadership among His disciples. The power of the keys He gave to all the apostles as representing the Church, and not to Peter only. The holy Spirit He bestowed on all disciples. His own regenerating presence is the being of a Church; and He promised it to any two or three met in His eternal and reconciling name. That supposes that they are not met out of strife, and that they do not simply cultivate Him as their saint, but they meet to reflect His eternity, and so, with serious purpose, to serve in such a Church for life; which distinguishes them from a casual gathering that dissolves with the occasion. Nothing was known in the early days of a prince of the apostles, nor of a vicar of Christ, nor of a monarchical bishop. And Christ did not found a Church here and a Church there, but *the* Church, which appeared here and there in facets of its vast polyhedral unity. To all these local but serious appearances of the one Church He promised equally His immediate presence, whether in Rome or in a desert; and it would be the possession of each remote Church none the less if Rome were swallowed by an earthquake, or the official succession broken for a hundred years. Whatever was given to Peter was given to his person, and not to his office, nor to his successors as such. It matters nothing whether he was ever in Rome or ever founded a Church there. Even had he passed the bishopric to Linus the legacy would have been quashed, and the succession extinguished, by the fact that succeeding bishops were chosen by the community of priests and laity, from, or through, whom the inspiration came. Indeed, there are no few spiritual and intellectual Catholics who say that the mechanical nature of the hierarchical headship, rising to autocracy, was the most powerful cause of the drop and the deadness which soon befell the Church.

All talk of a theocracy which should draw the secular power under the spiritual is foreign both to the Gospel and to the true Catholicism. The Church has been at its best when it did not mix with political transactions in the way of ruling prerogative or direct control. Its true influence is that of its apostolic Word and its moral character. When it sought first the righteousness of the Kingdom it had all that it needed of other things in tail. The chief example of theocracy—the Mosaic—was one that ended by slaying its Lord. To give either Church or State the rule over the other, in one and the same imperial sense, means one or another kind of despotism; their due independence of each other is the condition of freedom. For conscience to bow to a priest can be as slavish as to bow to a prince; but the free prince and the free priest can do much for each other.

It is not easy to say which has done more mischief, the State Church or the Church State. The original constitution of the Church, whatever it was, was not monarchical. It was corporative: until Cyprianism; and until the black years when first Constantine and then Charlemagne made it a State Church, and turned its officers into civil servants, and its government to a bureaucracy. And until, further, the spiritual autonomy and monopolism of Rome asserted itself in a form equally distorted and fatal, until a Roman bishop of genius turned the State Church into a Church State, whose officers not only refused service to the head of the State but forced the State into its service. Such was the Church of Hildebrand, Innocent, and Boniface. Its claims have not abated; and all its troubles since then have been due to that evil and unchristian principle.

No doubt the position had its advantages. It enabled the court of Rome to discuss on equal terms with other imperial courts. For it spoke the imperial language both in thought and idea. It was a great advantage for the Church in large affairs that its authority should be gathered into one point, and when it could act from that centre as an Emperor can. A court at Rome could deal with a like court at Aachen, a cabinet of Cardinals at the Vatican with a cabinet of Chancellors at Berlin, more easily than if the Foreign Office of the Empire confronted a society cohering as a spiritual organism only, with its powers scattered at centres all over the world. But the result to the Church in the way of moral debasement and spiritual declension has been unspeakable. It is fatal to any bishop when he gathers up all power from his Churches and his clergy into one point in himself; how much more when he is the bishop of all bishops, the Pope! Yet that is what was done by the infallibility dogma of 1870, and what had been growing for centuries to the Church's demoralisation. To what it has come we may mark in the attitude of the Roman see to this war[1], and its fatuous reply to sure proof of all the crimes and cruelties of the Germans in Belgium: "But then they deny it." The

[1] The First World War.

combination of the Christian bishop with the Pagan Pontifex Maximus began early, and it took long to ripen. For it wore several forms; and some of them were continued in Protestantism. It began with Constantine's State religion; and Luther placed the princes where Constantine or his successors had been. Little did he think that he was deposing the Pope only to produce a worse one in the Emperor, and exchanging the blight of Babylon for the blight of Berlin. Hence the moral paralysis of the German Church, as of the Roman, now that a call is made by the world-righteousness of the Kingdom of God upon the prophetic office of the Church and its duty to beard kings in God's name. It is a Church which has lost in learned servility or pietist sentiment the sense of what a Church is morally for the Kingdom of God. It has lost Christ and gone to Islam. God is on its Emperor's lips, like Allah, but never Christ. No doubt Luther meant to save the Church from the Church State, and restore it to its corporate freedom. But he has only succeeded in restoring the Byzantine State Church, with its religious parasitism. We had the like attempts with Luther's in the case of the Elizabethan Church, from which we were only saved by our Calvinist Puritans. It was the thorough Calvin that saved the Church from the State. Germany never had the blessing of regicide. It was only the Puritan execution of the King that saved us from what Germany became by the massacres of the Anabaptists (only now being expiated) and from what France became by the Bartholomew (expiated in the Revolution).

It grows clearer and clearer, as scholarship escapes from patristic prepossessions, that no form of constitution is sacrosanct; and none is undivine which gives scope to the word of the Gospel and the prophetic freedom of its redemption. The only divine Lord of the world is He who does not wish to rule it, but to bless it by way of service. (It is the inner secularisation of the Church to a polity that has been the chief cause of that outward secularisation of its revenues which takes place in revolutions from its despotism.) No form is sacrosanct. But also to discard form is suicidal. If an imperial Church is mischievous, sporadic Churches are futile. For a Church to live anyhow is to die. To abandon all noble forms of worship and to potter at it in dressing-gown and slippers, as it were, and to do this as a principle, in the name of independence, is to subside into hugger-mugger at the end in spite of any mysticism. Free prayer by all means, if you can keep it up. But few can pray in public, and they need help. No public body can afford to live in its shirt-sleeves, and pick up its meals, to disregard its social ritual and live casually. Certainly no Church can go on doing so with its creative spiritual wealth. Here the form can never be independent of the content. To abjure entirely Church authority and the solemn tradition of the worshipping dead in worship or doctrine is to slip down into a heap of sand. No authority, no Church. Loose procedure means slack belief. And slack belief means loss of public influence for the Kingdom of God. It is a mistake to think that a viscous belief appeals to the great public, or that mere mysticism is purer worship. Certainly no such sprawling and shambling type of Church can cope with the Catholicism of the day. That can only be done by a greater Catholicism, and not by a casual individualism. Without it the Church sinks either to be ruled by the world or to be eager to rule it; and in either case it is spiritual death. The Reformers found a Church dead one way; but they replaced it by a Church which, on the Lutheran side at least, was in another century dead in the other way. And it has never there regained, as a Church, spiritual life; while Calvin held the glorious West in fee.

§

There is a way of magnifying the dignity of the Church which, in seeming to glorify Christ in it, yet destroys the true relation with its Lord. Is the Church in history the *prolongation* of the Incarnation? It is an attractive imagination. It is the Catholic form of the engaging fallacy of liberalism that Christ is but the eternal God-in-man, supremely revealed and carried to a luminous head in Him, but forming always the spirit of Humanity and looking out in every great soul. But if the Church is this, can we also call it the Body of Christ? For when Christ became incarnate, His soul took a material body (the talk of a spiritual or astral body inside it is mere theosophy); whereas the Church in which Christ dwells is not a material body, but an organism of spirits. In the Incarnation Christ passed into a flesh distinct from Himself Who took the resolve so to pass. It was distinct from Himself because at the proper time He separated from it, and it became a corpse. But in the Church He passes into living souls capable of a moral reciprocity of which the body of His Incarnation was incapable. His earthly body could not love and trust Him as His Church does. Even if we speak of Him as having a celestial body now it does not do that. His body and His Church, indeed, have this in common—that in each He externalised Himself in some historic sense. And the externalising did not cease at His death and departure; it only took another form corresponding to the new creation which was His finished work. In taking human nature, even in its psychic sense, He externalised Himself; for human nature, though the creature and child of God, is yet not His only begotten uncreated Son, who emptied Himself to enter it. The Church He created cannot be a continuation of Him the increate. And that externalising went so far as that He took the body in which human nature itself is externalised. But the Church is not Christ's body in that material sense. Nor is human nature in its psychological sense the body of Christ; for it has to be reborn. It is regenerated human nature in which Christ dwells. But that cannot be a prolongation of His Incarnation, wherein there was no regeneration. His great spiritual work was not the result of a regeneration, but the source of it, as the Church cannot be. His externalisation in the Church took the form of souls outside Himself yet in Him newborn, and, though united with Him, not merged, as corporal substance might be. The interpenetrating personalities yet subsist as such. He is still outwardly present in Church and Sacraments, but present as He is not in nature, whether human or material. He is present as He can only be present in moral beings who have in grace left nature behind, and have risen from forces, and laws, and psychologies to become wills and consciences that baffle psychology. His presence with such units must be a very different thing from any divine presence of a material kind, where (as in the Elements) the contact *could not be* moral, or even of a psychic kind, where it is non-moral.

I have taken note of the fact that Christ's Incarnation was not simply His taking flesh but His entry on human nature, and especially on moral humanity, so as to become not only flesh but sin for us. I have said that that cannot be what the Church prolongs, because a Church must be reborn. That which owes itself to a rebirth cannot be a prolongation of the ever sinless. And there is the same impossibility in the Church's treatment of the Sacraments as part of the prolongation; where He is believed to dwell in matter, and not even in a psychic organism like human nature. I might have added that when He is said to prolong His Incarnation in the Church as a community of living souls, it surely cannot be said that the crisis of His death, resurrection, and life in the Spirit made no greater change in human history than is expressed in such a word as prolongation. That lends itself too readily to a view of the Church as the mere evolution of Christ, which squeezes the notion of a new creation outside. No. To express this second form of His outward presence, the Church, we need some other word than the prolongation of the Incarnation, and one that does more justice to the cruciality of the Cross and the reality of the New Creation. The doctrine of Redemption is signally absent from the creeds, yet the Church has a more direct connection with Redemption than with Incarnation. Only by experience of Redemption has it a religious knowledge of what Incarnation means. And if the meaning of Incarnation is only to be understood by the Church after passing through a moral crisis, then its intrinsic nature must be moral; *i.e.* it is not continued in the Church as a *process*, but reflected by the Church as an *act*. The Church is not the continuation of Christ, but His creation and His response. Moreover, it is a step too logical and inevitable from the Church as the prolongation of the Incarnation to the Eucharist as a prolongation of the Atonement, and to the treatment of it as a sacrifice offered instead of the acceptance, from a present Christ's hands, of His offering once for all. With such a theory as prolongation the Communion becomes logically the Mass;

and by the same process the Pope becomes the Vicar of Christ and the oracle of His protraction.

It is very useful that we should to-day dwell, with all the true aid of Bible, Church, and Sacrament, on the *real objectivity* of Christ's presence and action with His own. There is a tendency in the revival of *mysticism* and the flickering up of the *inner light* to despise the outward, whether in a Church or in a Sacrament. This soon grows to a view of history and its ethic as either bad and hostile, or else incapable of good and therefore negligible. Also the cultivator of the inner light soon finds not only that the several inner lights need an inmost light to keep them in order, but that it is not always forthcoming. He finds that he has evil waiting for him within, from which he must take refuge in the outer world. Hence the sound precept, "Pray *and* work." While conversely, from the infection of the evil without he must turn within, "work *and* pray." The real victory is both outward and inward. It is no victory to flee from an organised Church to silent groups; nor to escape again from the burden of silence into busy individual action to which a Church is unnecessary. As spirituality grows healthily it grows more moral; that is, it makes more of society, and especially the society of the Spirit; more therefore of those acts of the spiritual society which reflect the central morality of Redemption and are peculiar to the society (like Word and Sacrament) and not peripheral to it, (like the philanthropy in which many an agnostic shines). The more we moralise the spiritual, so much the more do we connect it with the effective life of the society it creates, and with its characteristic outward acts, especially in worship. We thus escape on the one hand from a religious materialism which is but mechanism and magic, and on the other from a religious spiritualism and rationalism which sit loose to history and to action. It is in the region of moral action and historic continuity that we find reality, not in being alone with the Alone. The great legacy of Christ was a reality neither mystic nor mechanical, but moral. It was a moral act, and the message of it to the conscience. It was the mysticism of redeeming action. It was the eternal Act and Deed of the redemption of the conscience from guilt—it was this Act externalised in the word, worship, and work of the Gospel, and functioning in a society it created and in sacraments it gave. So we rise from the theosophic notions coupled with "an immaterial corporeality"—notions for which sin is a disease curable by an infusion of divine essence, and righteousness is but a new quality or excellence inbreathed into the soul; we rise from such notions to the moral reality in which sin is guilt curable only by the forgiveness of atoning grace and eternal life, and righteousness a soul's relation of living faith to such a God.

CHAPTER V

THE KINGDOM OF GOD

Ideally the world needs a greater change than idealism can bring about. It is a change as deep as the Cross at least professes to produce, whether it can do it or not. It is the change from the realm of egoism to the Kingdom of God—and it is a gift to us, not an achievement.

The Kingdom of God has become more prominent in the theology of the last century than at any time since the Reformation, and the conception of it more ecumenical and less ecclesiastical or sectarian. The great service of Ritschl here. The criticism of him. His failure to appreciate the good in Pietism.

The Kingdom of grace and the family of love. The New Testament chooses the former. The Kingdom of God more than the spirit of sonship. As holy it has a moral centre and a royal constitution.

The Kingdom and the Church. The Church not a means to the Kingdom but the Kingdom in the making. The Kingdom of Evil is the foe of God's Kingdom in its moral kind. The historic aspect of the two kingdoms. The collision not that of light and darkness, but more radical—it is the holy and the sinful—the Messianic and the Satanic. It is a weak type of religion that fails to grasp the tragic reality of the Kingdom of Evil and of the conflict.

The Kingdom of God as the key of history. Its element is action more than truth. It is the goal of history, and not the arcanum of a Church. The Kingdom and what creates it gives the only teleology of history.

FROM the meliorist's point of view it is a world more or less satisfactory, for, fast or slow, it is moving on; but from the ideal standpoint it is a world so unsatisfactory that there is no hope except in a change greater than any idealism can bring about. To the morally earnest it is a world more lovely than good, and more interesting than hopeful. Towards the very good it is indifferent or hostile. An inch of moral progress costs a wealth of moral pains. It is a world of broad roads but narrow views, of rich ambitions but poor prospects, of full blood but meagre ideals, or its large ideals are of a low kind. It is uncertain about all the unseen, and not sure even of the seen in its constant flux. It has no charter even of this life, which is the horizon of all it thinks good. It is not happy when it looks back, and it is not comfortable when it looks forward. Sin, death, and judgment bulk differently to different people, but upon the race as a whole they lie as a load, and a frost, and a fear. Life is prosaic, except at a time like this, when it is tragic. It is aimless self-seeking in more or less protest against itself. And many have almost welcomed the tragedy of war to escape from the humdrum of peace, from the ennui, the vacuity, that makes them dread to be alone. Well, change is a divine instinct. The more that men are the victims of life's passing change, so much the more do they need a change fundamental. We need a radical change if life is to rise above its changes, or its monotony of change. The worst cross is the fear of crosses, and we need the Cross to save us from it. We need a change into the power, freedom, wealth, and poetry of life, a change from an atomism in which we wilt to an air in which we bud and bloom, from the final dreariness of self to the wealth of the sonship of God, from a drab and egoist religion to the religion of a world organised for grace and glory. That change means the change from the realm of egoism to the Kingdom of God; and this we do not attain, it is the gift of His grace in Jesus Christ and His Cross. To bring that Kingdom in, and set up the moral communion of man with God, man, and nature in history, is the task given to the Christian Church in being charged with the mystic Gospel of the Cross and its atonement as the moral basis of the Kingdom. It is, by a regeneration, to realise in man, his history, and his society, the image of God as his destiny from the first. But the process is very slow and very arduous. It needs the faith that it has been done to do it.

God was the Lord of creation on its very first day, and not only on the Sabbath, when all was done. And the New Creator is as much King to-day, when we are but at a stage of the new creation, as He was when He laid its foundation-stone in the Cross, or shall be when the completed Kingdom is given up to the Father. Father He is indeed. Yet royal Father. It is the Kingdom that fills the prayer which invokes the Father. And the Son always spoke of such a Kingdom rather than of a home. Nothing is more characteristic of the Bible than its sure faith, amid its deep sense of the world's evil, that the Lord God Omnipotent reigneth in holiness, and that His historic victory at last will not make His power or right but will only exercise it in a fulness of time. We are in the midst of the greater week of the New Creation by One to Whom a thousand years are always as one day.

§

It is only of late years that the Kingdom of God has taken a ruling place in theology. That is a striking and significant thing when we remember the place it took in the mind and action of Jesus Christ. The credit of restoring it to a corresponding place in the thinking of Christ's Church belongs largely to Ritschl. In the name of the Kingdom he made the supreme interest of theology ethical and social, and gave a place to the Church which it had not had since the break with Rome. Attention, he said, had been over-engrossed with the idea of personal redemption; whereas the system of belief should not be regarded as a circle, with that one centre, but as an ellipse, with the two foci of the Cross and the Kingdom. With such a position, of course, the temptation was strong to treat the Cross as the religious centre, and the Kingdom as the ethical, and so to divide the Gospel. But Ritschl did not fall into the danger in that blunt form, though he did not escape it altogether. For him the Kingdom was a religious idea, because, however ethical, it was wholly of grace, it was the gift of God rather than the attainment of man, and because it was entirely dependent on the forgiveness of sin.[1] It was founded by Jesus, in bringing the supreme gift of absolute grace and not merely of spiritual help—all that went before being but its dawn. But though that was so with Ritschl's theory, though it was at least as religious as ethical, in effect he did cast all the light on the ethical side, and the more religious and supernatural side fell into the shade. The ethic of the redemption did not rise to a real atonement. It was not mystic enough. The effect on man eclipsed the effect on God. The Kingdom became for him moral and social action inspired by love. This is all of a piece with his aversion to Pietism, his neglect of the doctrine

[1]This great point marks off his view from that of many who lay stress on the ethical nature of the idea. The centrality of forgiveness stamps redemption with a moral nature at its mystic source.

of the Spirit, and his evasion of the idea of the holy as the perfect harmony in God of the moral and the spiritual.

The disciples of Ritschl have in this, as in some other respects, gone forward by going back upon their master. It is recognised that in the teaching of Christ the Kingdom is spoken of as present no less than future. It is constituted by a final Presence and not only a final purpose. That is to say, on the one hand it is the *summum bonum* now. It is the soul's joy. It is the Christian's possession at every moment. Time is abolished in the Spirit. The believer already belongs in Christ to the future, and the future is already his. He has the redemption. But on the other hand it is also the Christian's *moral ideal.* It needs time to come home. Only by moral development is its perfection projected. Only by moral effort, discipline, and experience does the believer become the Christian he is. He must acquire his legacy. This, of course, is a paradox. But then paradox, where mystery is not only dark but aggressive, not only dim but absurd, is the very nature of Christianity as spiritual. Christ's is not the religion of common sense and mother-wit. The great practical problem of Christianity is to incarnate the paradox, and reconcile these two ideas of the Kingdom in a working fashion for experience. Every form of Christianity is to be judged by its spiritual success in so doing. If Ritschl did not succeed it was because he was too shy of the idea of atonement; and he was that because he did not give its due place in God to the idea of the holy, and especially the Holy Spirit. The holy is the Christian and ethical form of the mystic. The supreme and omnipotent thing is not mystic love but holy love. We have the two factors perfectly blended only in the revelation of holy love, of the holy (ethical) as the redeeming (religious) principle. But that is done only in the Cross as love's real atonement to the holy, as the Kingdom effected in a soul universal and eternal. And we return thus to the one centre which unites us, instead of two which distract and divide. If the supreme act of the moral world (and therefore of its Sovereign God and Father) was in the Cross of our redemption, then it was in that Cross that the Kingdom was set up. But that Cross was not simply the martyr height of Christ's moral fidelity, it was the crucial act of a present holy God Who in love deals morally and once for all with His own righteousness there. In that act we have the identity of the moral and spiritual; and we have it as a gift, for we could never effect it. It is singular that an ethical mind like Ritschl's did not make more of *holy* love than he did.

Ritschl's successors have corrected him in the moral stress they put upon the super-ethical side of the Reformation. If the issue is in the conscience, it is in the mystic conscience of the holy and not only of the just. Kaftan allows to Nietzsche that there is a region beyond good and bad (though it is not cut off from them), beyond good and bad in the matter of conduct or event—the region of personality, whence are the issues of good and evil. There is in the moral soul a holy of holies which we only reach through the holy place of ethic, but which is beyond it. The holy is the nature and destiny of the conscience, and at once its source and its superlative. There is in the soul, and in the revelation to it, that which the ethical alone does not meet, because ethic is too much modelled on the kind of relation that exists between man and man. It is the region of the love of God and of the peace and joy of it in our moral experience, the region of love as holy, the region of the Christ Whom having we possess all things. It is not true to say that the only way of serving God is to serve man. That cuts out worship. And without worship, passing into a communion with God, which is ethical unto holiness, even work for the Kingdom may cost a man his soul. The soul needs a worshipping Church to keep it alive and aloft. It is more true to say that the radical way of serving sinful man is serving a holy God, that the love and worship of God is the true self-love of mankind, and that the only effective way to the fellowship of man on any scale is the communion of Christ. We can only love man in a Christian way by loving Christ's God more. Work for man is dependent on the soul's supreme energy of worshipping God when we are not thinking about man, and when we forget our own soul and its prospects in our Saviour. Our Christian love of our fellow goes round by way of our Lord. The moral intercourse with God, centred in a real and holy atonement, is therefore the school in which love is saved from being mere spirituality, is reared to a true personality, and creates a society of persons living in the holy, and working together for the Kingdom and its righteousness. The most vital doctrine for the Church, and the mystic source of all Christian ethic, is a creative atonement. It lacks atmosphere, and all that atmosphere means for a Church, to say that the Kingdom is but the organisation of society in love. The Kingdom is not conduct, nor is it sympathy—for sympathy itself needs an atmosphere if it is to be spiritual, a finer glow in warmth. The Kingdom is not wholly public. In its root it is inward and holy, but, because holy, therefore inward, with love's bias to outward and social effect. Truly, it is sometimes necessary to protest against a type of pietism which can make piety silly, ridiculous, and feeble. But it is a mistake fatal for the Church's health and influence to ignore and depreciate that side and source of the Kingdom as Ritschl did. The fault of Pietism is when it cherishes a kind of religion without mind on the one hand or society on the other, when its love becomes either self-engrossed or even erotic, when it seeks to withdraw from social, national, and historic life, when it cossets a conscience introspective and scrupulous, cultivates spiritual sensibility more than moral personality, and acquires more religious taste than weight. But the whole history of that noblest of the sects, the Quakers, shows how unnecessary such seclusion is for justice to the inner light, and how a light that lighteth *every man* goes out into the love of men and the amelioration of society.

The Kingdom is therefore at once both a possession and a problem. It is that relation to God in which we have all things, yet in which also we have to win all things. It is a present relation and a future society. It is the society of the timeless and eternal. In the New Testament it is not only at once supernatural and ethical, nor only present and future at once, come and coming; it is also both a relation to God and a society of God. It means sometimes the relation of kingship (as in the Lord's Prayer) and sometimes a society of such relations (as when we are said to enter the Kingdom). It is there when we are filled in heart with the fulness of a holy God, and it is there when by historic process the fulness of the whole earth becomes His glory. It is the new love moving to be the new Humanity.

§

There is nothing so prominent in Christ's teaching as the Kingdom of God. And about that Kingdom there was nothing to His mind so sure as that it was the gift of God. It came to the world from His grace, and not from effort of ours. It was not man's achievement, it descended out of heaven from God. We put that in modern but inferior language when we say that the moral ideal, the social millenium, can only rest on religion. It rests not only on religion but on evangelical Christianity, *i.e.* on the faith that answers grace. We do not contribute to the Kingdom, we only work out a Kingdom which is ours wholly because our God works it in. The central thing in the Kingdom is not a state, nor a feeling, nor an act of ours, but it is an act and gift of God. To say that is not easy. It needs a real and thorough religion to say it. If we do not rise above ethic we cannot say it. Ethically we remain but Pelagian. Morality is bound to insist on that contribution of ours which religion that has risen to faith knows to be itself the gift of God at His moral height of holy love.

Christ was as sure as Paul was about the absoluteness of grace and the equal dependence of every man upon it. Such is the teaching in the parable of the labourers in the vineyard—so much abused by the Socialists. Christ was not thinking there of social conditions at all, of equal rights between man and man, but of equal dependence—the equal dependence of every man, however good, on the free gift and absolute grace of God. That is the only final equality between men—their absolute dependence on the grace of God. In the same way He spoke more than once of the childlike mind as the condition of entering the Kingdom "Of such is the kingdom of heaven," He said, caressing the children. But it was not as citizens of that Kingdom that He treated them, only as symbols of it. They might or might not become citizens. Now we are always prone to interpret Christ by our hearts instead of our hearts by Christ. And we are accustomed to think that Christ was making a remark of beautiful sentiment about the simplicity, or the docility, or the innocence of children (which are often less obvious to the nurses than to the parents). But it is the relation of the child rather than the sentiment that Christ would teach—treating the child as a parable rather than an instance. Whether they are engaging children or not, children they are. That is to say, they are entirely dependent on their parents. Everything their egoism desires or has comes from their father. It is his gift. That they may be little conscious of the fact does not alter it. That they may be more exacting than grateful does not affect the fact that they are but receptive; and they are the better children as they feel and own it. They do not owe themselves to themselves. It is another parable of absolute grace, as distinct from the Pharisaical synergism which thinks of claim and reward. In relation to the Kingdom we are all in the position of children. For everyone alike it is a gift of free love, something to be taken, as children but take and do not earn.

It is not enough to say that the Kingdom of God is identical with the spirit of sonship. For that might be compatible with a conception of Fatherhood which eliminates all the holy majesty of love that was most distinctive of Fatherhood in Christ's mind. His Father was the Father in Heaven in such a sense that the whole prayer that so invokes Him is preoccupied with His *Kingdom*. It is remarkable that Christ, who spoke so incessantly of the Father, spoke no less incessantly of His Kingdom and not of His family. Even the Lord's Prayer, with Father for its first note, goes off at once into the Kingdom and not the home, and there remains. That means that the vital thing in Fatherhood for Christ was that holiness which made the Father royal. If "Father" is the first note, "in Heaven" is the keynote—the Father of an infinite majesty. His grace makes Him more of a kingly Father than a kindly; so that His love, more holy than hearty, has not its due analogy in a happy father who is the comrade of his boys. That is to say, it was not a relation of love simply, but of love holy and yet gracious—which combination is a great miracle. The Father in Heaven meant for Christ the holy Father. The sonship is the sonship of *holy* love. Be perfect, be holy, said Christ, if you are to be the sons of the Father in Heaven. That is to say, the moral element in the love was of its essence, the ruling element and not only the sympathetic—thou *shalt* love. The sanctity was not a mere halo to the love but the texture of it. The idea of a realm's righteousness was more vital than that of family love, and more inseparable from love divine. It gave it its nerve and nature, so to say. And the citizenship of the Kingdom was not a response to love, and the return of its pure affection, but it was a response to grace and its forgiveness. It was a matter of receiving everything as a gift, our very souls as a prey, and of setting up no such claim upon God as made Israel Pharisaist, and turned the nation to be God's creditor instead of His servant and noble slave. The Kingdom, the Church, is more than the society of love. It is the society of grace, of love holy to wicked men. It is not a society that turns to cultivate a life of grace, but the society created by it, by a grace miraculous in being both holy and forgiving. The divine society rests on that moral miracle. Or have you not yet come to feel how miraculous it is?

The Kingdom therefore is set up by more than filial love. It has more than an affectional atmosphere; it has a moral constitution. Its King shall reign in righteousness. It is not simply the sense of sonship to the infinite benignity; it is not just the fine fellowship of the dear Father; it is the practical worship of the holy Father. It is not the response to love natural but to love wonderful and incredible, love which rises to grace and sovereignity. And it orders its goings by an ethic of grace, *i.e.* of the holy, not simply of the kind—of the holy which makes the love miraculous, and not simply of the paternal, which makes it just what we should expect.

§

All this is of great value when we come to ask what the relation is between the Kingdom and the Church. It is certain that Christ founded the Kingdom. He knew He was founding the New Covenant, the Kingdom as a relation.

He also founded, though not in just the same way, the Church. How do they stand to each other? If the Kingdom of God is only an ethical idea, then it is very different from the Church. It may by some be thought to be higher; it may be held to be the end for which the Church is but the means. It may go on as the converted State when the Church had ceased to exist. But we have seen that the Kingdom is more than ethical, that it is religious, holy with an absolute ethic; that it is a moral gift, *i.e.* that it is founded on the justifying grace which founds the Church, on Christ's fulfilment and satisfaction of the Father's holiness; that the hope of all its coming is the reality of it as come; that we can thus enter a heaven which has not yet arrived. Its foundation is the soul's relation of sheer faith, loving obedience, and close communion with God both in piety and practice. It rests on that kind of morality which regards the holy, and takes shape in forgiveness and eternal life. That is to say, it is created by that which created the Church—by the New Covenant. The real foundation of the Church was the founding of the New Covenant—the Gospel. Christ at the end was more engrossed with the founding of that Covenant than of the Church. That again is to say that what founded the Kingdom also founded the Church. Therefore they are the same.

The Church is not a means to the Kingdom, but the Kingdom in the making. It is the new relation, the kingship, in so far as that has become a distinct society. It is the family hearth or focus of the children of God. Truly the Kingdom's action is wider than the Church, for the kingship of God works outside that in a luminous penumbra. But in so far as the Kingdom of God is not just a holy relation but a holy society, the Church is the Kingdom of God. The mystic nature of the Kingdom is conserved in the Church, the moral nature of it conserves the Church itself. Inside the Church it works as holy love, outside it as holy righteousness. And the Church is made righteous by it as society is made holy. If the Kingdom were left without the Church it would become a moral pedantry. If the Church were left without the Kingdom, the moral, historic and social element would be lost from it in mystic spirituality of an individual kind, cumulative rather than creative. The Church would then fall to groups of people so minded, or clubs for mutual improvement of a religious kind. The public element, the element of righteousness, would be too otiose and pacific. The note of fraternal intimacy would submerge the world of public good, as the inferior Christianity tends so often to do.[1] The holiness would be lost in the love, and the love itself lost in society. But if the Kingdom is as supernatural in its possession of a holy God as it is practical for social righteousness, if it is as spiritual as it is moral, and as present as it is futurist, then the active Church, as distinguished from the pious group, is the Kingdom of God inchoate. And each several Church has its right as it partakes of this great Church.

The sin of man has not destroyed the power of God. It has only refused it; and, in refusing it, it has but changed its mode of action on man. It has not in the least weakened it. God is no less King because of man's sin. His kingship takes another shape. He has resources to deal even with that revolt. It is a delusion, even of religion, to think of the kingship of God at work in heaven only, and not on earth or in hell. He is Lord as absolute in all three as in one. His holy will is done not in heaven only but on earth. And the irresistible pressure of that holy will is as real in hell as in heaven, though it acts differently on His creatures' wills. His loving will is at work on earth without man's will, and in hell against man's will, as surely as it is in heaven with it. The kingship of God does not fail, and it is never weary. There is no doubt about its purpose, and none about its result.

There is no idea, no power, which it is so needful to carry home to either State or Church as the Kingdom of God, if only because it is the only power that opens our eyes to the Kingdom of Evil and the course to take with it. It is with an organisation, a conspiracy, of evil that we have to do, and not a mere bias. This Kingdom of God is the grand International, if our eyes could see it, since it gauges the whole

[1] As, for instance, when a minister makes kindness criminal by recommending a needy brother to a pulpit regardless of what his record shows this will mean for the Church.

moral situation of man and has no illusions. Amid all international changes it is the shaping power, whether we have vision to see it or not. And the number of those who do not see it makes as great a danger as the number ranged against it. The chief charge against popular religion is that it has blinded that eye, and taken that *flair* away. With the decline of faith goes the discernment of spirits. The Church, which is there for the Kingdom, which as I say is indeed the Kingdom inchoate, has yet done much to debase the idea of God's Kingdom into man's paradise, and simply to transfigure an egoism it ought to regenerate. It has made God's reign a mere auxiliary to man's glory or comfort.

Goodness is a realm; and there is a realm of evil. Each is spiritually against the other. If the other world has a King, there is also a prince of this world; and there can be no peace except in a complete victory, so that such a war shall never be again. Most people live in an armistice, and many only drag on with the war; but the High Command on both sides knows the only terms of the end. Yet we cannot sort men into their camps. As we cannot certainly decide in individual cases who is a subject of God, so we cannot say that so-and-so is naturalised under Satan. The two sides do not understand each other nor the campaign—only the heads do; for the good do not readily see into evil, nor do the evil understand the good. The victory must be left to Him Whose holiness gives Him the true measure and meaning of evil as the evil can never take the measure of good. The light shines into the darkness, but the darkness does not take it in; therefore it can neither escape nor defeat it. Its trickery is good, but its strategy is poor, and its diplomacy stupid at the last. And the power, which came in gleams of light, goes on to flashes of lightning; which are the judgments of God upon things civil and religious, on State and Church, on culture and crudity, on the progress and peace wherein the soul sinks and rots, and eternity is banished from the concern of time.

§

The more we dwell on the nature of the kingdom of heaven the more we are driven, by the very earnestness of the conflict, where Christ was driven—to the belief in a kingdom of evil very active and very intimate. To lose the sense of that kingdom of evil means, or it follows, the slackening of our sense of the Kingdom of God. And to grow in the knowledge of God's Kingdom is to grow in the insight into Satan's. The brooding of the dove with us is not yet the full presence of the Spirit if it extinguish the serpent wisdom of the Holy Ghost. It is an ineffective guilelessness that is not shrewd enough to know the world, nor passionate enough to feel its fires. There is an incarnation of the evil one as well as of the Holy One; though its king has neither the moral power nor the spiritual courage to appear as a historic person. For he cannot reduce himself to such limitation, nor empty himself to the form of a servant. He only acts in avatars and not incarnation, or he suborns picked servants full of the unholy ghost, or societies of culture which are the habitations of cruelty. The disbelief in Satan has much injured the belief in Christ; for of course to make light of the enemy is to make light of the Victor. We lower the whole level and tension of the conflict if we discard a war in heaven and think of God's antagonist as only human, or only a principle. The Lord has a controversy not with His people only but with a rival king and strategy. History, like Scripture, has suffered from piecemeal treatment without a conspectus or a plan. And the final conspectus is not in the compass of the philosophic historians who track tendencies and combine events, but it belongs to the apostles of a moral gospl which gives us the last teleology in a kingdom of moral souls won on the scale of the world by the conquest of its prince. For philosophic history, with all its power of insight and combination, yet does not, as such, realise evil or measure its final power. It does not gauge the grand conflict nor take home the victory; indeed, it shows some tendency to moral insouciance. The philosophic historian can grasp the idea of the untoward, or of the slow, or the sick, but not of evil. And yet we cannot grasp the notion of evil, as we cannot of good, apart from history and from the Cross in it. The sphere of history is the element in which the Kingdom of God acts. The idea of the Kingdom of God is not to be grasped without a sense of evil which flows from the sense of the holy, and from the experience of its salvation. The Kingdom of God is not civilisation. It is not even spiritual culture. The war has come, among other things, to destroy that ready fallacy of peace, as if the Kingdom could come (human nature being what is has sunk to be) by evolution, even by spiritual evolution or the culture of piety. It does not come by a Church of spiritual culture, but by a warfare with spiritual wickedness in eminent places, not to say in estimable people. Its foundation is in a crisis, not in an education—in a redemption and a repentance. Both Church and Kingdom owe more to conversion than to mere moral growth. So far the eschatological views of Christ's teaching are right. There is an organised power of disorganisation which wrecks all the organising power of culture, and the ordered methods of education; or it chains these things to its car. And it is with that power that the kingship of God alone can deal. The chief danger to organised civilisation is an organisation morally uncivilised; it is not mere disorganisation. It is not decay; it is positive hostility scientifically ranged. And salvation is the organisation of the holy; it is the Kingdom of God, of the Holy Father.

There is a type of inward religion—the mysticism of imagination or reflection rather than action—which has neither the taste nor the faculty for historic revelation, is without the national note, and shows small affinity for the Kingdom of God won on the Cross in a national issue. It is more concerned with its conventions, conferences, movements, and programmes than with the great orbits of the Lord's movement among affairs, or His righteous goings among the nations. Its saints have neither the national nor the ecumenical sense. They are sectary; not valueless—far from it—but still sectary. They are saints of a group in such a way that they are not citizens of the Kingdom, having more spiritual faculty than moral force, with soul but not moral soul, and more ready for martyrdom than choice in its occasions. They are without sacrificial sagacity. Truly the blood of Christ's martyrs is the seed of His Church. But all martyrs for conscience are not martyrs for Christ. All martyrs are not mules, but some mules are martyrs, and suffer for their self-will more than for God's will. That is because they have more spiritual interest than moral insight, and their conscience is more touchy than taught. Their cult tends to be sacrifice for its own sake. There is nothing the mystic should more study than history as the site and school of the Kingdom. For it was its vehicle. To dwell on the inner life and its devotion without an equal interest in its outer form and action is not the spirit either of the Incarnation or the Atonement. Truly the Kingdom of God comes not with observation—unless the observation is very deep. Yet it does come amid observable things, and we wait for the manifestation of the Sons of God. It is a long process, this redemptive evolution. If the evolution of creation is slow, the evolution of redemption is slower still. Moral progress is always slower than civilised; for each conscience has to start afresh, while each mind enters on the long legacy of device and culture. The Kingdom comes slowly, for it faces an Empire long and ably prepared. It has stage after stage. We begin with nature, or God over us. We go on with grace, or God with us. We end with glory, or God in us. We begin with the revelation of the Father and His power. We pass to the revelation of the Son and His love. We end in the revelation of the Spirit and His holiness. But these three are one. The revelation of the Father remains in that of His Son. And Father and Son remain within the revelation of the *Holy* Spirit, where the Kingdom covers all and pervades all. This is the theological way of putting it. There are other ways less deep. The historian of moral progress would put it in his way. He might appeal to the mentality of the present hour by tracing the development and refinement of human freedom. He might trace the ascent of the conflict with evil—with evil in nature, evil in the soul, and spiritual evil. But it would all be still the story of the coming of the Kingdom of the thrice holy God, the growing reign of

Father, Son, and Holy Spirit. The revelation with which the Church is charged carries in it the secret of the New Humanity, whether it come by grace or by judgment. But the chief victories for freedom have been won against an empire of tyranny.

§

The Kingdom of God in Christ is the key of all history, and the Church has the power of that key. It was the revelation which made both that first made a comprehensive view of history possible. The first to construct a philosophy of history was St. Paul, by his theology of universal redemption. The only final unity of man is objective in God's purpose of grace, not subjective in the touch of nature, which makes us often more kin than kind. Had that redemption by grace been but mystic illumination, and had the coming of Christ been but light, there would have been no such vision of universal history, and no such institution as a Church to correspond. For the inner light is but atomic; it lights each several soul; and its breadth is but multitudinous, it is not organic. It is cosmopolitan, it is not catholic. But the revelation in Christ was action much more than light. It was redemption, not illumination. It was power, and social power, it was not mere presence. It was therefore a matter of history, where men do act, and not of thought, where they do not. It intended not a new sect but a new Humanity, which was to put out on the stream and not preach from the shore. In so doing it was bound to make mistakes, but not such mistakes as if it did not.

Two great mistakes have certainly been made about revelation. First it has been treated as if its element were truth and not action. It has been offered as something to hold instead of something to obey. It has been thought to be a notional theology (or still worse a theosophy) instead of a moral energy of God. It has regarded Christ as the great theophany instead of the great—I wish the word theurgy had not been stolen for mean uses, it is what I want here. And the second mistake about revelation has been to treat it as the divine arcanum of a Church instead of the moral key to the whole of history, and the regeneration of the whole of Humanity. No wonder people do not care about redemption or regeneration when they have been made to regard such words as the technical terms for certain processes that were the secret of certain spiritual syndicates. How are we ever to reclaim words like these for their true Christian use? There are many thinking men who are driven to believe that *the* interest of Humanity is the historic and moral interest; how are we to convince them that the supreme interest of that conscience is that it should be redeemed? That is a question we cannot stop to discuss here. But this may be said. So long as the Cross is regarded as a device for the benefit of a few instead of the moral crisis of the race, so long will its advocates seem but sectaries without moral purchase on the race. So long as the Kingdom of God is regarded as but the extension of a private company's operations (as many view missions), so long also will it be an ineffectual thing. It will be regarded as one of many rival enterprises, all pushing to the front, instead of the suzerain and overlord of them all. And it will be left to its luck in the struggle. But it is not the extension of a private enterprise promoted to increase the shareholders of a joint-stock religion. It is the dominant power and final goal of history, if there be a God, if He has most to do with history, if His holy morality is the nature of things, if His Son is not simply the Head of the Church but the King of Humanity, if His cross is the turning-point of moral being. We can only get mankind to attend to the Kingdom of God if we can make it appear for what it is—the inmost core, the ruling principle, the moral ultimate, the spiritual dominant, the new creation, and the final purpose of Humanity. And the theology of the Church must be adjusted thereto, the message of the Church must be so delivered, the nature of the Church must be so defined. The regeneration it preaches is *the* moral issue of the world. Only thus can we change the German view of Humanity, as manure for the intensive culture of favoured races, to the Christian view of it as a family of nations to be loved, gospelled, and saved. The real organising principle of the race is what it is in

Christ—the life of the Kingdom of God. The coming of the Kingdom is the growing organisation of spiritual Humanity under the Church's moral gospel and King of holy love. It is the moralising of every affection, thought, and enterprise by the *Holy* Spirit—which, if it do reside in the Church, yet goes to business daily in the national world.

There are some moments when a vast and mixed audience are gathered critically round a rare man whose words are themselves deeds, and who has to make himself good with such a public. Which at last he does, and they are fired and lifted to forget wholly the things that part them in the moral passion of the things to which he makes them move as one soul. As he began his task it was as if he passed down the alley of one of those grim Safe Deposit buildings, where to right and left were but cells guarded and sealed. But as he went on the gates fell down and it was as if the very jewels in the cells were warmed to melt their caskets and pour out into the golden street. Such an occasion, or such an image, might offer us a symbol of that which one day will be the state of society, unless Christ has come and spoken in vain of His Kingdom.

The Word of the world's moral redemption by holy love must seize the conscience in the world's great heart.

> "And hell itself shall pass away
> And leave its dolorous mansions to the peering day."

CHAPTER VI

THE UNITED STATES—OF THE CHURCH

Current proposals of Church unity by federation. Instability of the present relation, or want of relation, in the Free Churches. The New Testament idea and the need of a new attempt to realise it. Comity is not unity. Federation the first step for abolishing sectarianism and its triviality. The Churches cover the world but they do not gauge it. Polity indifferent for faith and adjustment of the Church to democratic conditions. To bless the democracy the Church must be free in it. The note of spiritual aristocracy. The three ideal powers in society: Socialism, Romanism, Protestantism. Our immersion in commonplace motions and interests and lack of spiritual imagination. Hence a prosaic and uncontagious earnestness. We do not realise a saved *world*. What if democracy should attack the Church's freedom for lack of a note in us it could respect?

HAVING spoken of the Church and the Kingdom, I venture to return to my first chapter and speak farther of their action on a democratic world. And this time with special reference to the proposals of Free Church federation, which are attracting much attention as an instalment of the unity of the Church.

I begin with the actual state of things. Can we rest where we are? And I suggest we cannot, that the present relation of the Churches to each other is unstable and impermanent for several reasons. Because of—

1. The re-reading by modern scholarship of the ecclesiastical conditions in the New Testament—which is fatal both to monarchical Episcopacy and the old granular Independency.

2. The growing sense of the unity of that Gospel which makes the Church, and the inadequacy to it of a mere comity of Churches.

3. The consequent new arrangement and perspective of theological values in relation to the Gospel. Of course no Church unity is possible except on a doctrinal, *i.e.*, for us, an Evangelical, basis. Because no Church can otherwise exist. The sole unity of the Church is in the Gospel; and the Gospel must be stated; and it cannot be stated except in

doctrinal terms, as even John iii. 16 shows. But the theology of the Gospel has now fallen into a new scheme of values, which means the dogmatic disendowment and disarmament of the sects in so far as they went off upon doctrinal detail.

4. The Church's growing sense of the *vastness* of the problem to be met at home and abroad.

5. A new sense of the *nature* of the problem. The growing unity of pagan civilisation on the one hand, and of Humanity and Democracy on the other, calls for a great Church unity to cope with it.

6. The danger that the isolation of the Churches in a democratic society might entail the loss of their freedom at the hands of that society if it is not christianised. We shall lose our inner freedom at least, if it do not unite us more.

7. The growing sense in each denomination that its particularism is not a permanent stage makes it prudent not to stereotype arrangements as if it were.

Let me take these points in detail.

I

The meaning of the Church in the New Testament I have already discussed. May I repeat a little?

In the New Testament the one Lord, the one Word, the one Church go together; and especially the one Church. There is no such thing there as the Roman Church, the Lutheran Church, the Calvinist Church, no such thing as the Congregational, Baptist, Presbyterian, or Methodist or Episcopal Church. They do not exist in the New Testament. There is even no such thing as the Church of Judæa, of Asia, of Rome, of Corinth, far less of England or of Germany. Whatever the phraseology be, the meaning is the Church *in* these places, the one Church in these various places, the one Church, which was the direct object of Christ's redemption, looking out here or there. The one Church of the one Word and Lord, the Church of the firstborn and the yet unborn, spiritually continuous everywhere, emerges to the surface, like a stratum, at this point or that. Here or there it is in evidence; but it is in existence, with a subliminal continuity, through the intervals, and onward into heaven, as a spiritual and indiscerptible unity. *The* Church was not an aggregate, made up by piling local communities together, but it was, like the Humanity Adam shared, a direct and collective creation of God's Word. It descended and branched into these communities. It was not created by them, but realised in them. Each local or sectional Church is at the same moment an ecumenical community, whose largest part is out of sight, as in an iceberg. This and that Church are but the tips of a submerged continent representing the whole Church, present and future, on earth or in heaven. Each Church is an integer in the great Church, drawing its existence from it. The great Church is not organised *out of* the small ones but *into* them. Any individualism these may have is rooted in its unity, which they all represent and serve. The local officers are also ecumenical officers. An elder in one Church is an elder in the whole Church. That is the dominant New Testament idea; which alone makes disintegration intolerable, and our present position impermanent, and hence self-contradictory, and hence ineffective for the Church's one purpose on earth. Is it not the case that often the idea of a denomination, or of a national Church, or of a doctrinaire Church, or of a canonical Church, gets in front of the idea of the one Church of the World? And of course the Word suffers. The sect becomes the changeling or proxy of the real Church. It gathers to itself a passion which only the great Church deserves, as the trustee of the great Word. We ought to restore the New Testament perspective. It would make the denomination an integer of the Church, its surrogate and not its substitute. And it would make it so in practice and not only in theory.

II

The manifold, rich, and free unity of the New Testament Gospel calls for more unity of a similar kind in the Church.

We cannot preach peace among the classes or the nations so long as we are rivals among ourselves. Yet the one Lord and one Word gives the Church the instinct of unity and universality always, however dimly, even in the smallest sect. The one Gospel can only be presented effectually by a great Church, whose unity is (as now it is not) more striking than the diversities which it commands. Without a unity corresponding to our Gospel we are paralysed as a moral influence on the world. "Physician, heal thyself!" we are properly told. The one unseen Saviour inspires and requires a ruling faith in one unseen Church. Now most of the troubles of the past have arisen in connection with this unseen Church; and chiefly they have arisen from the identification of the Church invisible with some visible form of it, either by Rome or by a sect. For that is the fallacy of both extremes. Each practically says, "My visible circumference encloses the invisible Church. If my pale had might as it has right it would be the Christianity of the world." The claim is not actually and explicitly made save by the extremes of Catholicism and of sectarianism. But wherever it survives in any form it is a perversion of the true instinct —the instinct of the Church's unity and universality, which is as wide and sure as its Gospel.

Must we then go to Canossa? Must we wait at the gate of the traditional and imperial Churches, cap in hand? Must we return as penitent prodigals and be reabsorbed in some form of Catholicism, either Roman or Anglican? Nay, there is a more excellent way—the way of federation. No one visible organisation is identical with the true, invisible Church. No polity has the divine right to gather the rest under her wings for salvation. No one corporation can gather into itself the whole wealth of Christian tradition and promise. The Church's unity can never more be realised in one spiritual Empire to whose genial spell and imposing rule all the sects must return that it may cover the world. The note of the future, the true reunion, is federation, with a relative constitutional independence. It is no new monarchy, but *the United States of the Church.*

The present stage might be described as the comity of the Churches. But that cannot be a final stage. The fundamental unity of our Lord and Word cannot be duly met or expressed by a number of Churches which are but neighbourly, friendly, civil, and considerate. A street of decent neighbours, whose house is their castle, is not a temple of the Lord. All that comity of egoisms is well enough, but it is not yet Christianity, and we cannot stop there. It is too atomic and too subjective to be the real unity of Christ's Church. Such membership, whether *in* Churches or *between* them, is too much like a gloomy wood of self-contained pines each standing in his uprightness, with his hands in his pockets. It rests too much on the way the Churches *feel* to each other, and not enough on what Christ is and does for them all. It centres on Christians more than on Christ, on sympathy more than salvation. The objective unity of a common Lord and Word cannot take effect, it cannot act on the Word, without some form or measure of organic reunion. And reunion, as I say, can only take one of two lines. It may come either by reabsorption or by federation—either by a reabsorption under the old Catholicism reformed and made elastic, or by the federation of a variety of Churches entirely equal except in age. For the purpose of federation an absolute equality must be recognised. The word reordination must not be so much as named among us. "The first step to approximation," said Principal Rainy, "not to speak of reunion, is recognition." And, I add, recognition on both sides. For it costs us as much to admit Catholic orders as it costs them to admit ours.

§

No doubt there is here a great chance for Anglicanism. If it could, in any practicable time, discard as essential the Prelate, the Prince, and the Priest—the modern Episcopate, which its own scholars now remove from the New Testament; the Establishment, which a growing number, even in the Episcopate, would discard; and the sacrificing priesthood, which a vast number of its ministering priesthood would also renounce—then it would have a certain chance of gathering the other Churches round its historic hegemony, its venerable tradition, and its spiritual splendour, so long as no question of prerogative was raised.

But (though I venture to think the concessions are bound to arrive, especially by the great reconciling effect of modern scholarship in such questions) I am not sanguine about these inevitables arriving in time for the train. And therefore we may neglect the prospect for practical purposes, and meanwhile begin the process by federating as equals among ourselves. At least we may begin to prepare ourselves for doing so, by examining the idea frequently, till we cease to handle it like a loaded revolver. And let us do this, not for the ambitious sake either of mastering civilisation or winning the democracy, but for the sake of reflecting and glorifying our Saviour and our God.

But if the federation idea were to fail, and if Anglicanism should show signs of rising to the situation, many would be attracted by the Catholic note and spell (which we ought all to feel more than many do) to the idea of reabsorption. So that we are on our mettle. And do we realise how much we are on our mettle? Statistics go for little here as the mere counting of heads. It is weight that tells. There is no feature of our Church life more disquieting than the way we are losing the best people, men and women. By which, of course, I do not mean the rich people or the consequential people. I mean the people, whether in the ranks of Capital or of Labour, who are being made by modern affairs, education, culture, and opportunity. Are we keeping the educated women in particular, for instance? Are our interests and occasions too petty for such people? Is it the case, as one observer says, that popular religion in England is coming to the limits of its power by its pedestrian note, its engrossment with the trivial, the commonplace, the popular, the journalistic? Are the sects, robbed of their great theologies, settling on their gritty lees? Are they serving tables till they cannot serve Christ? Have we been neglecting the weighty consolidation of the Church for its thin extension, its quality for its quantity, its sanctity for its catholicity, its power for its area? And is this the reason why extension itself is arrested, why evangelistic work is discredited, and, in every Church, missions have taken a chill? Do let us get to the root of things. Do let us distrust the explanations anybody can offer in the train. It is only a deep and a weighty Church that can really be awide Church at last.

§

In the providence of God schism arose in the bosom of the great old Church, and it was led by some of its best and greatest. The sects came, to break up a unity hollow and outgrown. And they came to prepare for a unity much more flexible and free, and one, therefore, more permanent among free men. Of course the protest was extreme. It had to be so for its effect. It was attacking a very powerful and entrenched position. But now from sectarian extremes the pendulum settles to its steady mean. Yet we cannot relapse into the body that was abandoned, with all its prestige and resource. That Church made itself a sect when it made them go out; and sound union does not come by the mere absorption of one sect by another. The real contribution of each sect must be permanently recognised through the possession and service of an equal gospel. The sects have grown to Churches of equal right; and therefore union can only be by federation. The day of the sects as sects is over. The day of the denominations is passing. The commanding Church idea returns. We look forward to an ecumenical Christianity composed not of national Churches but of national types of Christianity; and, within each national type, a variety of cohesive and co-operated bodies, which shall be (what we are not now) at least as much concerned about their unity as about their variety. The federation of honoured equals should be the note. For reabsorption might involve some form of penance, or some confession of our fathers' sin. But it is impossible thus to compromise our famous men and the fathers that begat us in the great Gospel succession. The Apostolic succession has no meaning except as the Evangelical succession. It does not mean, at the one extreme, a historic line of valid ordinations unbroken from the Apostles to the last curate. Nor, at the other end, does it mean merely cultivating the spirit of the Apostles, or their precepts for sanctification. But it is the succession of those who experience and preach the Apostolic Gospel of a regenerating redemption. It is the grand preaching succession, the prophetic office of the

Church. The sects were made by apostles of God, to bring to their senses the priests of God. And a Church organised exclusively under the priest idea can never reabsorb the products of the prophetic, the apostolic, the preaching idea. But each has a note the other needs, so long as it does not claim sole dominance.

The final escape from sectarianism therefore is not absorption but federation. That is the religious solution, the solution prescribed by a common *faith*. The solution must be religious. It is not a matter of conscience only, but, still more, of faith, of evangelical religion. Do not let us deceive or flatter ourselves. The origination of our divisions was providential, and it was due to fidelity to conscience; but their divisive perpetuation may be gratuitous and due to poverty of creed or religion. It is as much the will of God that our divisions should cease to be divisive on the higher plane as it was that they should divide us at first on the lower. They were called into being to effect the transition from an imperial Church to a democratic; they came to modulate the change of key from a monarchical unity to a federal harmony. And if we resist this purpose, it will be to the cost of our Gospel and not to its glory. We shall peddle the Gospel round instead of preaching it abroad. We shall be allies from within of the rationalist culture without, whose effect is to break up the Evangelical faith and disintegrate the Church except as the harbour of religion in general. Is nothing to remain of Protestantism at last but the credit of having shaken hierarchy and of having referred religion to an inner but atomic experience of some feeble sort?

§

Both Catholicism and the sects have failed in respect of the unity of the Church. The Catholic Church created modern nationality, and the evangelical Churches, by their divine schisms, created modern liberty. But with all our liberty we have yet to show ourselves capable of providing a spiritual unity. And it is but another way of putting the same thing to say that we have yet to provide for the liberty we have created something much more important—

an authority; and an authority springing from the same source as the freedom, from the Gospel that set us free. We have yet to convince men that we have the secret that rules all Humanity and orders the destiny of all History. We do not yet reflect on them a Christ who redeemed *Humanity* and not merely a section of it. We have done great things, but here we surely have more or less disappointed the Holy Spirit. It does not matter if we disappoint human expectation, or even aspiration. It may not matter so much if we disappoint certain social ideas. And the *Zeitgeist* we must disappoint—the mere spirit of the age. But it does matter if we disappoint the Holy Spirit; for if the Church deny Him who is its life, it sins against its own soul. It does matter if, in failing to meet men's demands, we fail still more our own Gospel. We shall never satisfy men at last except by satisfying the Saviour first. It does matter if we give up to the sects what was meant for redeemed mankind. We hold every one of our resources in trust for Christ's word and Christ's world. We all confess that, and most of us try to realise it. Therefore let us *consolidate*. Let us consolidate that we may *extend* and extend to Divine purpose. For the Churches are not thinking ecumenically enough, but only imperially. They understand *covering the world* like the British Empire, but they are not as skilful in *penetrating Humanity*, in "finding" the soul, and moulding History by Christ. For that we need a new, deep, and piercing intelligence of the Gospel, and especially a new moral intelligence of it; not so much a new fervour, nor more of the Spirit (in the common use of that term), not of course less piety, but more faith; less occupation with meetings, committees, schedules, and conventional jingle from press or pulpit, and more immersion in a Bible brought up to date, more of the Word and its power, a new insight which is not a revival but a reformation. We need a reformation of faith, belief, and thought to make the Churches adequate to the nation, the world, and the age, a bracing up and a coupling up of our Churches, and a renovated theology as the expression of the Church's rich and corporate life. Is it not the case that we are more divided by poverty of religion than united by the power of it?

III

This new theology is on its way. As the Churches draw together the process is helped by the modern revision and new perspective of theological values. Some of the sects went off upon points which are now seen to be too peripheral to justify schism. They are not now central enough. They were sometimes points taken by people who knew their Bible in an illiterate way; but it will soon be true that they can only be maintained as divisive by people who do not know their Bible as the Spirit now unfolds it, as it is open to them to do, and imperative that they should. On the other hand, we see more and more clearly that the real differences between the Churches which are more than sects turn at last, not upon polity nor on theology as a fine art, but upon those doctrines of God and Salvation on which the great Church really rests. And those are the doctrines on which we draw more and more to an evangelical agreement. We concentrate on the Church-making truths as a positive Gospel takes the place of a correct creed. And we acquire the stability that such foundation gives. We grow more sure that Church unity can never be reached on an unsectarian and non-theological basis, on a basis of vague Christian sentiment, or genial fraternity, or common philanthropy. Years ago nothing impressed the Established Church with a sense of our unity and catholicity so much as the Free Church Catechism.

IV

On the fourth head I will just touch. We are all being driven together by the greatness of the work to be done at home and abroad. It can only be done collectively. We find it in our mission work abroad, and in our institutional work at home. It has to be co-operative. It is beyond separatist resources. If Protestantism could have taken at once to mission work, it would have been saved from the worst effects of that fissiparous tendency which we are now trying to repair to save our life. But here too we are on familiar ground, and I will not labour it.

V

While this sense of the *greatness* of our work unifies us in spirit, we must be unified in something more than spirit. A bodiless spirit of good will never master the well-organised spirit of the world. The Spirit of God, as it has a historic Word, must have a historic Church. We have to face a kingdom, and almost a church, of evil. Some organised and tangible unity is forced on us as we realise (beyond the vastness) the *nature* of the work we face; as we realise the nature of that unity which we have to encounter, the growing unity of civilisation, of democracy, of humanity, facilitated by the rapid means of transport, information, and culture. The earth shrinks and man swells. Mammonism, Paganism, Naturalism, Civilisation were never so organised as they are to-day. The war should put the power of the spiritual foe beyond dispute and beyond neglect, but as a rule our religion has not grasped the moral nature of the *debâcle*. And what is often called a "unity of spirit" can never cope with this collective Superman to any practical effect. Such merely spiritual unity has the weakness of our current subjectivity. It goes no farther than we feel. Often it does not survive the platform. And it is apt either to retire into coteries or convents or else, in attempting to influence the world, it is infected and captured by what it would convert. The tremendous pressure of the world, the flesh, the comfort and the pride of life is so great, its egoism, under the most plausible claims of religion, veracity, and liberty, is so mighty, that nothing can resist it but a supernatural and penetrative faith humiliating and kindling. And such faith can resist it only in a Church with some collective means of making God's will felt on the historic scale. I am thinking, for instance, of great public questions like those of war, and of social questions like those of sex in particular, involving marriage, divorce, and the family, with all their perils from sense (in licence of union) and from self-will (in insubordination of the children). The Churches are not equal to the *post-bellum* situation; and I mean the moral situation, for the social is not chiefly their concern.

As things are, I am more impressed with the Church's impotence in that world of morals and affairs than with its effect. I am troubled at its lack of self-respect. Both the Press and Labour venture to set up either as its patrons, its exploiters, or its censors. And I suppose we get what we deserve. Our own Free Churches are much too negligible in affairs, except for the mass of voting power they contain; they are too negligible as guides, except for the party whips. I am thinking of the *weight* of their moral word and their moral leaders on society. I mean their moral influence on the general public, which means more than their popularity with class or mass. I mean our power to leaven with Christian ideas the English nation as a section of human civilisation. Our religion may aim at Humanity—but our ethic is on a lower and smaller scale. But then we have been working with a double ethic, an Aristotelian and a Christian; which is one source of our reputation for hypocrisy. We lead a double life. We have two moral centres, because our theology is not moralised and our ethic is not theologised. It is class ethic, or sectarian ethic, or bourgeois ethic, or insular ethic, or socialist ethic; but it has not the catholic, imperial note of a power more than adequate to the moral redemption and leadership of Humanity. We have more sympathy with social ideals than insight into Christian ethic. We are properly ardent, for instance, in the cause of peace; but I have seen no single utterance from our Churches that realised and discussed the real point at issue and the real crux of war—the bearing of Christian ethic on national self-consciousness, and on national honour in particular.

I will not say anything about Catholicism, which I know less, but are we of the Free Churches equipped as we should be with guiding men who are abreast of the world's moral situation—rich as we are in preachers and pastors who are the idols of their circles? We were very well when it was a matter of local evangelising; less well when we had to face social questions such as labour or education; are we well now that it is a national question on the great scale; on the scale of Humanity and the deep righteousness of the whole Kingdom of God historic and moral? Are we afraid enough of our inadequacy to it? Do we duly dread a congeries of denominations with no Church feeling or force equal to the evil catholicity of the world spirit and the Church of the degenerate? Our type of religion is not false, but has it that note? If not, our Church idea so far fails the Kingdom of God and knows but a province of it—with the provincial and not the royal note.

§

We all agree outside Catholicism that the *form* of polity is indifferent for faith. It is utilitarian. The end shapes the means. Indeed, Catholicism itself with its Episcopacy we now see to have been only the form forced on faith in the first centuries by its struggle for life with paganism and Gnosticism. And to-day faith has to repeat that struggle on a scale and depth which has not been seen since the second century. We are at a far more critical juncture than the Reformation was. The Christian Church is in the first mortal battle since the early centuries against paganism in thought, conduct, and religion. And I am afraid the heavy artillery is not now as it was in the early centuries on the Christian side, for want of public intelligence and concern in the matter. I venture to think that this can only be denied by a lack of acquaintance with European conditions both of thought and life. Must we not, then, repeat the policy that saved the Church in those early days, must we not organise accordingly? The organisation of the Church must be adjusted to our antagonist, which then was (besides the pagan *Weltanschauung* that still faces us) the Roman Empire. Now there is no such Empire, and the old Catholicism is therefore out of date. We must reckon with the new phase of the old gnostic foe. We must be guided by whatever policy or polity best makes for the effect of the Gospel on the present world and the saving of salvation. Like Catholicism, we must unify in our own way to survive. The world has a powerful and unitary principle of its own, with which the grace of God cannot make terms. There is no compromise at last between the egoist spirit of the proud world and the sacrificial Gospel of holy love, between the obedience which is the first thing with Christ and the independence (rising to self-will) which is first with the world. It is war. And the social order evolved by egoism cannot surely be mightier in the end than the moral order and society of the Cross, if our clans do not fail it by ignoring and thwarting each other in the battle.

§

Do we realise that the various religious bodies have lived on into the midst of a solid democracy which was not there when they began? That means much for the Church's form and practice. As each new power arises in Society the Church is bound to revise its position in face of it. It is very flexible. It has adjusted itself to monarchy, aristocracy, and oligarchy of various kinds. But the forms it assumed under these do not suit with the new power, the democracy, in control. The Church must organise, it must change front, in face of that new fact. It confronts a very different society from what it saw in the days of the Commonwealth or of the Evangelical Movement. It confronts democracy in power, it faces the people not as a mere crowd of toiling millions, nor as a force in opposition for redress of grievances, but in power. And it must dispose its forces so as to be adequate for its task of sympathetic guidance for that power. Churches should realise the situation. The mark of a sect is that it never does. Its lens is too small for its landscape. It takes neither knowledge nor account of history. But we are Churches, not sects, if we will take it to heart.

Let us not lament that we have lost the democracy. We have never had it. The Evangelical Movement acted on the people in a way, but not on the people as *a power* in the State, to say nothing of *the* power. And it was not made by the people. Nor was the Reformation made by the people. It only began to reach the people in pietism, and then only in groups. Democracy as a power has risen but lately, when, unfortunately, the moral forces of the Reformation are more or less weak and spent in their old forms. And we have not lost this democracy, because we have never had it. We only go on to win it. We have not to retrieve, but to advance. A truce to much of our self-accusation. The Reformation conscience has yet to be tested for its power to win the democracy against a mere humanist religion and a natural Christianity.

The Church has to win the democracy, to guide it, to save it, and use it for the Kingdom of God. But it has therefore also to escape it. To lead the democracy the Church must be free of the democracy. It must have more self-respect before the democracy. The Church is not *a* democracy. It is certainly not *the* democracy on its religious side. That is but Hooker up to date. It is latter-day Erastianism. What is the difference? *Democracy will acknowledge no authority but what it creates whereas a Church has no authority but what creates it.* It is an infinite difference. The Church is not identical with the democracy or its organs. Nor is its cause to be identified with that of democracy offhand; and certainly not as a matter of faith, so that critics of the democratic ideal should be regarded as critics of Christ's cause. The Church is not the indiscriminate champion of the democracy but its benefactor, its faithful friend and prophet. It is not its tribune but its conscience. The Church is not there in the first instance to represent democracy, but to represent God to the democracy. It is not there to speak for it, but to speak to it. It is not there to champion it, but God's Kingdom through it. Has the Church a message for the democracy, for the people, when it is really clear what the people is, when it is the power? Has it a word of authority as well as sympathy for the sovereign democracy? Power reveals every man. It will reveal the democracy. Has the Church a word and an authority from God for the democracy as its power will develop it and reveal it to be? Yes, indeed. The Church so long as it has a God holy in His love has the note of eternal aristocracy, of Him whose right it is to reign in love. It has for its first duty to bring the democracy something which it does not have, something it must have, something which it can get nowhere else, and something that both blesses and commands it, a Judge, a Saviour, and a King. The Church has far more to give the democracy than to receive from it. And if with this gift it does not save the democracy one of them will be wrecked.

The democracy is not standing still. It is but coming to a sense of itself and its powers. It comes to feel powers which it missed in asserting its mere rights. And it is not easy to see how the Churches, working apart, or with a nominal unity, can make head against the growing unity and confidence of a non-Christian democracy. It will swallow them up in detail. In many cases already it is not a question of how the Church is to influence the world. Some of the Churches cannot even stand up to it. They have no notion of a world Gospel except in the way of missions. The Church must have a unity, a cause, a weight of its own, which can speak in the gate with organised civilisation, and confront it with something more than piety and philanthropy. It must have Christ's note of moral majesty; a unity drawn from its commanding universal Word, and one which reflects the Gospel instead of diffracting it. Divided Churches mean *for the world* a divided Christ, however they may feel and assert a Christ in common.

§

Think of the great ideal powers which are at work in the transformation of modern society. They are three. There is Socialism, which contemplates a *humanist organisation* of the world. There is Romanism, which aims at an *ecclesiastical hierarchical reconstitution* of the world. And there is Protestantism, which has in view an *evangelical re-creation* of the world, the moralising of it from its conscience outwards with a foundation in the conscience which is atoned by a Saviour to a holy God in a Church.

Now, leaving the first and second of these alone here (except to recognise that they do grasp the problem), do you think a mere concourse of Evangelical Churches, overlaying each other, and working past each other, will ever solve such a problem? Do they grasp it? Could such a mere concourse hold its own with those two other great powers and great unities in dealing with so great a world?

I would urge again that we should measure the greatness of our antagonist, and the cost of the warfare. There is a kingdom of evil as surely as a Kingdom of God. And the conversion of individuals, indispensable as it is, is not enough. For the world and its egoist passion is a unity, and it grows more and more organised as such. And it is only in some real and effective form of unity, both in action and impression, that the Church can cope with it. The security of the world lies in the partition of the Church. We divide, and it commands. Certainly the Free Churches will not overcome the world, even with the Gospel in their hands, till they provide that Gospel with an engine more effective than a number of clans armed with claymores, or of army corps acting at will. We do not believe enough in Christ because we do not believe enough in Satan.

Moreover, apart from the conquest of the world for Christ, the same thing is needed for the service of the world in Christ. How is that to be maintained? Mere fraternal service to the world does not yet secure Christ's purpose with the world. Christ the Helper is not yet Christ the Saviour. Merely to help and bless the world is not yet to secure it for the Kingdom of God. Humanity is there for the Kingdom rather than the Kingdom for Humanity. So that Christian service itself is only secured in perpetuity by what secures the Kingdom, by a Redemption and the message of it.

§

The Kingdom of God can only come by the Church of God, and only by a united, free, and independent Church. Some effective federation, therefore, is the only democratic form in which the Churches can be independent enough of the democracy truly to bless it while yet local enough to interest it. Only so are they equally free to inspire the democracy or to control it in a spiritual way. Only so can they be strong enough spiritually to convert its ideals, and not only smile upon them. The democracy welcomes our smile on its ideals; but we are not so welcome when we are the apostles of Christ's criticism and control of these ideals. The democracy has no quarrel with the humane Jesus, but it has with the supernatural Christ, the reigning, humiliating, regenerating Christ who makes the Church. And this lies very near the root of the decline in Church-going. But we are also unwelcome for less noble reasons. And partly because we do not judge democratic ideals with an utterance or a vision as large as their own. What is the use of going to an ideal democracy with a prosaic Christ, of approaching Humanity with a sect? It is only by some such means as I suggest that we can appeal to the imagination as well as the faith of men, and do it in a democratic way parallel to the wonderful monarchic spell of Rome. We must have a unity that appeals to the spiritual imagination.

"One of the reasons," says Professor Granger, "why popular religion in England seems to be coming to the limits of its power is that it has contented itself so largely with the commonplace motives which, after all, find sufficient exercise in the ordinary duties of life. Unless God is presented under the attributes of the Divine Majesty in such a way as to summon forth an heroic effort of the soul to come to its own in Him, religion is degraded to a level below the ordinary standard of honour, and does not appeal to the higher spirit which is the natural temper of a free citizen in a free state."

Our type of religion does sometimes lack this one thing—imagination, idealism, especially of a historic and ecumenical kind. We have social sympathies, but not historic imagination nor moral insight of that scale and kind. We know the history and the principles of the Puritan succession more or less, but we do not know the history or principles of the whole Church as they knew them. We lose the great historic sense and the world note. It is true, the romance of a sect's struggle upward into a Church can be a very stirring thing. But chiefly to those already sympathetic, not to the public. In the face of world questions, such as now fascinate the democracy, it motives are apt to be too pedestrian, too provincial and parliamentary—too limited to the things voters can press and a Government can do.

We have, indeed, had a great outlet for the imagination in our missions. They have fed the romance of faith, as Catholicism feeds it on the splendours of the Church's history, belief, and ritual. And this romance is a great source of the wonderful success of these missions in one century.

They filled an imagination starved by the eighteenth century and its type of piety. But the mental quality of the eighteenth century—its mere common sense, its rationalism, its moralism, its matter-of-factness, its bias to humdrumness—though it has gone from the levels of culture, survives in masses of our people. Of course some of these things have their value in their place. But only there, only in their place, only in the context of some great unity and power which dignifies the daily round, floats the sectional soul, and keeps it from sinking into sand. This power we have had in our missions.

But do we not lack something of the imaginative appeal which does this in connection with our home work and influence? Look at Democracy, at Socialism. They exert an ideal spell in which we widely fail. They make apostles, canvassers, propagandists even at street corners, as we do not. Compare the ideal and intellectual note of the street-corner socialist and the street-corner evangelist. How near the one gets to life compared with the other—who gets to close quarters neither with the problems of time nor with the powers of eternity. Like much speaking it makes plenty of lather but it does not cleanse. And yet the socialists have at their call neither an ideal nor a power comparable to that of the Church, with its way to the soul, its secret of the new Humanity, and its supernatural unity, majesty, promise, and glory. Their motive-power is an imaginative idealism on the basis of a natural fraternity. Their kindling conception is a socialised Humanity of the future, working with man's natural resources and his intrinsic divinity. So, in another way, with Romanism and Anglicanism. There the imagination of faith is fed by the constant spectacle and ideal of a Church of the past, not only great but grand, with an imposing unity, a historic splendour, a spiritual spell, and the most magnificent and beautiful worship ever devised.

What are we setting over against those idealisms of the past and the future? And remember that Democracy at heart is very idealist about the limited realities it does apprehend. We have resources far more ideal than we seem to know, if we will claim them and acclimatise them. The great Church of the past is still the Church of *our* faith, and the new

Humanity of the Future is also *our* responsibility and our hope. We have been made Christians, not by the peculiar differentia of our denomination, but by what makes the great Church in them all. But are we never bald, and flat, and petty; with a tradition of eighteenth-century orthodoxy or of sentimental religion rather than Reformation faith and evangelical power? Are we never tempted to cultivate a pretty piety at the cost of an imaginative creed which is poetry and architecture in one? Well do I know how deep and devoted our piety can be; but the idea of the Kingdom and City of God has often been overlaid and stifled by minor phases and childish devices of an unintelligent piety; or, when it is regained, it is regained as a scholarly idea, or it is thought of as a new social order, outside the Church and more or less indifferent to it.

Our Church does much to educate our sympathies, and to concentrate our effort, but it does not do enough always to foster our imagination on the New Testament scale, or raise us to the measure of a Church adequate to the Christ of our belief. The Church of Ephesians we are tempted to regard as a piece of theological poetry, not to say rhapsody. Or it is valuable as a sermonic theme rather than as a vast reality energising in every true Church, and an integral and commanding element of our personal faith. Our personal piety, sincere as it may be, is not always adequate to the Catholic faith. Our corporate life does not do justice to the Catholic Church. And so people are apt to gather in groups, or dream in coteries, to talk sentiment about faith, and nonsense against theology; and we suspect and denounce Catholicism when we might learn from such an opponent. In our Church idea we have less than we might have to meet and rival the effect on the imagination, either of the splendid Church of Catholicism which we must often oppose, or of the grand, resourceful, teeming, and organised world that we must finally master. Why do we allow Rome to run away with the Catholic idea?

The social interests that grow up in our Churches are very useful, and we could not dispense with them. But for some they are a jungle where they are lost, or a thicket where they hide, rather than a garden where God walks and talks

Eternity among the trees. The trivialities of life, and even of faith, are certainly to be regarded. But all depends on their relation to its great course. Either they are runnels on a wide gathering ground, which are being collected into the mighty stream; or they are the threads in which the same stream trickles to its death in a desert, and is frayed out to be lost in sand. Faith can be lost among the very energies of faith, and men grow small as work grows busy. These social activities are apt to grow narrower than the real interests of the human society we live in, or the corporate affairs of a great Church. And what happens then? Some (ministers even) seek outlet for the larger sympathies in the social problems of the hour outside the Church; and they put into these an enthusiasm and service which belong first of all to their Church.

Surely the society which has the first claim on Christians is the society directly made by the faith which is their life—namely the Church. A Church which has lost its practical recognition of membership in the great Church is open to this danger—it may provide within itself social interests too small for the social sympathies that its own faith creates, and so they go outside. That may be all right in the case of the lay and citizen members of the Church, and it should oftener be done; but it would be a misfortune if it became the rule for all the ablest and most active representatives of the Church—if they were driven into social politics for the lack of any social opportunity large enough for their generous minds in the Church where their first service was due.

Let us not approach the great catholic problem with a sectarian mind, or handle universal issues in the spirit of a religious group.

§

It is only by an ideal like this that we can exhibit a universal society which does not represent the supreme sovereignty of the people, but of Christ over the people. Only so have we a society with the same word of Christ to present to the monarch or the multitude, and the same

Christocracy to offer to aristocracy or democracy. You are aware it is one of the great political problems of the hour whether a democracy, such as Britain has become, is capable of ruling an Empire such as Britain inherits. It is a problem which will become acute after the war.[1] Time will show. And at last it will show this also in one form or another—that democracy can be safely imperial only if it own, in an evangelical experience which is the base of ethical practice, the sole monarchy of the Eternal Redeemer, and if it stand for that sovereignty of God's grace which we used to call the Kingdom of Heaven. To that the democracy will not come except through the Church, with the note in its faith of absolute surrender and obedience to Christ in His world salvation. But it is a result beyond Churches which are too weak to be more than sporadic in their action, small in their ethic, and only suggestive with their Gospel. The Church that is to do that great thing for society must be in a position to impress the spiritual imagination of the world, capture its moral idealism, and have a word in its great affairs, as well as convert its souls. And such is the note of the great Church, to which the actual state of the several Churches still does some injustice. We may convert any number of souls, but is it sound work if, by the same power, we are not slowly printing the marriage law of Christ, or His principle of peace by His national righteousness, on the society about us?

§

To say that such an ideal is far off is only to say in other words what I have been saying all along, that it is on the scale of the world. All universal ideals are far off. It is part of their greatness. But they are made near in Christ, who is not far from any one of us. This ideal is nearer than when we or our fathers first believed. For our view of the world has changed since then. The object of the Gospel is no longer to save a group out of the world, but to save the world itself. That is felt to have been its original purpose. Souls, sects, and Churches are saved in a universal, a racial,

[1] The First World War.

salvation. The world is no longer an area from which the Church is gathered, a broad soil from which a small barn is filled. It is the raw material of the Kingdom. History is no mere preparation for the Kingdom, it is the Kingdom in the making. The actual world is not only the workshop of God. It is His building in process. Therefore the Church has a world policy. I do not say it has a world programme. That would be too curial, too papal, too socialist. But it has at least a world passion and a world ideal, and a world power to which our ecclesiastical sectionalism does not do justice. All the Churches are in their isolation too provincial for the City of God.

We have great room and need for a figure that we are too much given to despise—the ecclesiastical statesman. We have paid all due honour to the political tribune, and more than enough to the popular preacher. But, if we have some more positive object than the redress of grievances growing yearly less, we need among ourselves the ecclesiastical statesman, to enable us to adjust our Gospel practically to the social need, to the commerce, science, and culture, the ignorance, misery, and sin of the world, without succumbing as a disintegrated Church must do. He ought to be as much at home in the Christian ethic which should stiffen Christian sentiment as he is in public affairs. The old Puritans believed, with the New Testament, that all the world and its policies were there for the saints or the good. And I wish we did. I wish we believed it. It is quite true—if only we realise that true sainthood is the calling and destiny of every soul, that it has a native historic and civic effect, as it had in Catholicism and Calvinism, and that the Church of the saints must be great enough not to falsify the divine vocation of the races.

It is a universal, social, and solidary Gospel that descends on us. It is for the whole soul as for every soul, and for the public as for the individual. We may evangelise individual souls, we may politicise certain issues, but our work as Churches of the Kingdom of God demands that we do what we are not doing as we should—moralise faith, society and affairs. If we moralise society with our Gospel its politics will not fail our Gospel. It is a poor exchange, if we gain the political world and lose the moral soul, or if we take the note of our negations instead of our Gospel. We cannot live as Churches upon protests, whether against Establishment, or against Pope, or against other and smaller abuses. Crusades and protests, *on due occasion*, by all means; but unless we have behind them the weight, volume, and dignity of some union more real, positive, and palpable than our differences, our protests may seem but red flares, and our crusades but turbulent broils.

VI

As to my sixth point. There is a risk that if we do not consolidate our freedom we may lose it. A natural democracy, full of its own power, will welcome the Church so long as it smiles upon the people's ideals and gives them the benefit of its immense social resources and spiritual sanctions. But the real pinch and test will come if ever the Church has to act the prophet to the new king, and bring his ideals and projects to book with God and His Kingdom. The young monarch might then show signs of so much impatience as would seriously curtail the Church's liberties, were the spiritual democracy in no position to make its rights real. Sooner or later the collision is bound to come. It is more than doubtful if the isolated Churches can really Christianise the democracy; and an unevangelised democracy may pay but hasty heed to spiritual freedom, and give it but the toleration of contempt.

In that case, there is another risk, still more real—lest by our isolation from each other we lose the note and experience of an inward freedom. That we should preach democratically to a whole democracy, that the soul of Calvin should preach to Rousseau, and Puritanism to the Revolution—it means the largest utterance of the living God, the redeeming God, and His costly right to reign. To do that the Church must be independent of the democracy, and come to the free with the air of the free. But if our life become straitened by disintegration, and our communities do not endure in the faith of the great Church, we shall not carry to free men the air of freedom that goes with impressive power won in unworldly realms. Our speech will be smaller than History or Humanity. We shall be below the level of our Word, and short of its range. We shall be martyrs who do not secure respect; for martyrdom tha misses fire is a jest. We shall speak to parliaments like pacifists instead of prophets. We shall have the strained and strident mood which betokens a deeper sense of the problem than of the answer. Is that not what weakens many to-day? They speak as if they were more at home in the problem than in the answer. We may shrink in our certainty, even when we are free enough in our thought; we may develop more freedom to devise our questions than to follow God's solution. We may become as high-pitched as a piccolo in our very claim and boast of ample liberty. We may be bound in soul, while brain and tongue are free. But as Churches have we not in our hands and hearts the secret of all human development? In Christ's Gospel have we or have we not at once the goal and the ground of all human destiny? We have what is at once its aim, its secret, and its power, its way, truth, and life. And that possession comports not with the small word and the little liberties of spiritual amateurs and free-lances. The condition of our great liberty in this possession is not isolation or rivalry, but mutuality, reciprocity, co-operation.

It may well enough be asked whether in closer union there is not danger to local liberty. To which two answers. First, Christian liberty is less concerned for itself than for the freedom of God's cause and reign. If we look to His freedom, He will see to ours. And, second, liberty worth the noble name is better secured in a great Church than in a small body, so long as it is a Church of the Word, which cares little for orthodoxy and everything for the Gospel. Truly we do not shrink from persecution, if ever our liberty were curtailed and we were persecuted by the public we had to address for God. But we do shrink, I hope, from being straitened in ourselves and from losing an influence and a leverage with that public because of our weakness instead of our strength. We should shrink from letting it pass to those who have a poorer Gospel in a more effective form.

All detailed and programmatic things, all the items of a scheme, will come of themselves as the great corporate idea spreads. Let us only come down from vague and fruitless talk about our spiritual unity, the sinking of differences, and so on. We do not want differences sunk. We want them to be developed, if only they are made complementary, and if they serve to enrich what were otherwise a colourless, feckless charity. They cannot be abolished, but they must blend. The two forms of Baptism, for instance, and their ministers, should be equally valid at choice in Churches of the same polity, each filling out a hemisphere of the whole truth on that subject. There are questions, I know, of property, of historic tradition, of a separate existence dearly bought, of dear denominational ties which no scheme must despise, or override, or treat with anything but respect. But they will all fall into place by consent as the passion and ideal of evangelical unity comes to work like a fire in our bones. Let us commit ourselves to nothing that would make this harder.

The present stage is not permanent because it represents a development not yet done. We have gathered individuals into a community, and taught them they are members one of another in it. We have gathered the communities into a denomination, and taught them to be members, one of another there. What is yet to be done is to federate, but not to lose, the denominations, to unite them really and not sentimentally, in the great Church and its organic action.

The religious future is with those who believe in their Church. But they must believe in it for the sake of the great Church, and not the other way round—not believing in the great Church for the sake of their own. That is what makes all the difference between the Churchman and the sectary.

CHAPTER VII

THE MINISTRY SACRAMENTAL

The first effectiveness of the ministry is its effectiveness for the Church, not for the public. It is world-reforming, but it is Church-making. It does not so much act on the world as provide a Church that does. The ministry is effective as it is creative and develops the new birth. The minister not the talking brother but the divine messenger and trustee of the Church's Gospel—sacramental and not merely functional. He is an apostle, not a mere disciple. His relation to the unity of the Church. The apostle made the Church more than he was made by it. The ministry as an office was appointed by Christ, its *personnel* by the Church. The New Testament the real successor of the Apostles. The ministers are first called by its action on their soul. The minister is surrogate of the apostle rather than successor. The first Apostolate incommunicable. The continuity in this message and not in the order. The ministry effective only as it is sacramental. What are Means of Grace? Four functions of the ministry examined:—1. Preaching; 2. Pastoral; 3. Liturgical; 4. Philanthropic or social. The effectiveness of the people essential for that of the ministry. The pulpit not a pedestal for a genius but service to a flock of Christ. The ministry has to make Churches more than impress the public.

THE ecclesiastical question of the hour is not that of the laity (as at the Reformation) but that of the ministry. Have Nonconformist Churches in their ministry an equal right with Rome or Anglicanism? Are we ministers by a title equally good with that of Pope or Archbishop? If a Church, therefore, wishes to show its self-respect, it will go out of its way to be respectful to its ministry—to its ministry as such, and not merely to its lions. It will tend its lamps and not merely worship its stars. It is not well to idolise the genius and despise the office, nor to esteem only those whom it pays to push. If the ministers do not rise to the level of the ministry it is for the Church to see that they are better selected and trained. And it is for the laity to see that there is a due supply from their midst of such candidates as can take the training, and earn the respect.

The Church will be what its ministry makes it. That stands to reason. The Church is made by its gospel, and the gospel is the special trust of the ministry within the Church, as it is of the Church within the world. What follows?

This surely, that the first test of an effective ministry is its effectiveness on the Church; effectiveness on the world is a test of the Church which the ministry makes. Neither the public nor the Press has the material for a judgment of what an effective ministry should be. Its appeal is to the Church; it is not to the public that it stands or falls.

The ministry, therefore, has not to be directly effective on the world so much as to make a Church that is. It has not to reform the world, but to create a Church for the world's reformation. For this we are not to look to single ministers but to the ministry. Free-lances are apt to be final failures, as the Church will be that trusts them. Evangelisation is the work of the Church through its preachers, not of preachers who may but use the Church, and grow egoistic in doing it. There is no small uncertainty in the ministry about the range of its proper work. There is some tendency in it to be acting directly on the world with the Church for a platform, instead of acting directly on the Church, and on the world through it. The ministers are tempted to exchange slow deep influence on the world for swift power over it. It is part of the impatience which is the bane of the democracy. It is the Kingdom in a hurry. But it is demoralising. And it is ineffectual at the end. Radicalism, root measures, must be slow where the root is deep. You cannot hustle conscience. And a true ministry of the gospel, to a Church and through it, is a more radical matter than to be a social reformer to the public; therefore it does not go so fast. For the gospel of God's reign carries social reform with it, but social reform does not carry with it the gospel. Truly the State is real, great, and divine; but the Church is more real, more great, and more divine still. It is a greater dynamic than the State. And this wholly in virtue of its thorough gospel. By which word gospel, once for all be it said, I mean neither an orthodoxy, a talisman, a mascot, a shibboleth, nor a magic spell, but the grace of God in historic, moral, mystic action always upon racial guilt. It is theological at the core, but susceptible of constant theological change to meet the mind of each moving age, with a public ethic equally large, subtle, sensitive and impressive.

§

What, then, is the precise right and function of the ministry in the Church, and how is it effective? In a word, it is effective as it is *creative*. It is a productive industry in the highest sense. It is creative more even than consoling, cheering, or reforming. For it wields the new-creating Word. It first makes the Church, and then it shapes the world. In one sense it is created by the Church, but in a far greater sense it creates it. For it handles God's re-creative Word. The Church can appoint ministers, but the ministry, as an institution, is God's gift to His Church, like the preacher's power. No power of men can make any man the oracle of God. "There is no Shekinah but by divine assignation."

I am lingering on this word creative. I am pressing it. It is often said that the ministry is there for the sake of decency and order in the Church. That is, it is a matter of convenience. But this view is only partial. If it is made the whole it is a levelling and unworthy view—like the Zwinglianism which makes the Supper a mere memorial, or like the historicism which reduces the Bible from a sacrament to a document. No wonder the ministry is lightly treated if it is viewed as a mere convenience, like a chairman, as the proposer of the adoption of the divine report. And in quarters it is so viewed. Some preaching is like proposing the health of the gospel. Some prayer is like moving a vote of thanks to the Almighty, with a request for favours to come. Some ministry is but a facility. There are those who look on the minister simply as one of the members of the Church—the talking or the presiding member. They think anything else spoils him as a brother. They believe a Church could go on without a minister, only not so well, with less decency and order.

That is all wrong. The minister is much more than a leading brother as the Church itself is more than a fraternity. He is neither the mouthpiece of the Church, nor its chairman, nor its secretary. He is not the servant, not the employee, of the Church. He is an apostle to it, the mouthpiece of Christ's gospel to it, the servant of the Word and not of the Church; he serves the Church only for that sake. The ministry is a prophetic and sacramental office; it is not a secretarial, it is not merely presidential. It is sacramental and not merely functional. It is the outward and visible agent of the inward gospel Grace. It is more sacramental than the elements. It is a living host, produced by a conversion that goes deeper than transubstantiation. It is the trustee of the one sacrament of the Word, the Word of New Creation. An effective ministry is creative—nothing less; and a creative ministry is a sacramental. The Church needs men more than rites, movements, or money; but for her ministry it is sacramental men more than brilliant that she needs.

§

Such a ministry has a special effectiveness in connection with the unity of the Church. For the question of Church unity is the question of the ministry, of an effective ministry, of a ministry practically valid. And what does effective or valid mean? It means sacramental. That word is my keynote. The ministry is sacramental to the Church as the Church itself is sacramental to the world. For the Church is sacramental as a living element and vehicle of Christ's redeeming grace, though not in the sense in which the host is held to incarnate Christ. It is not sacramental in the sense that it is Christ as incarnate in a society as He was in an individual. The Incarnation was perfected in his corporate person, not in a quasi-personal corporation. As its organ the ministry is sacramental of the last Reality, which gives the soul any reality it has, and religion any value. It conveys that Reality. That is what I go on to explain.

The more we think of the unity of the Church, I say, the more we must make of the significance of the ministry. Where does the unity of the Church lie? If we go to the very root of the matter, it lies in its theology. It lies not in its mere religion, its spirituality, its mystic ideality, its humanitarianism, its propagandism, its common sympathy, its hearty fraternity, or even its beneficent work, but objectively in its positive and historic gospel of a felt Redemption. If a man hate theology he must abjure Redemption (which has no meaning but a theological one) and be cool to the Church. It is the one gospel that makes the one Church. The Church is where that gospel is. If the Churches are not greatly exercised about their separation, it is because they have sunk into sects which may be negligent of belief (except when there is a *fracas*), and which tend therefore to be more to themselves than they are to the gospel. In the absence of a common, intelligent, and active creed, they have a collective egoism, and their collective egoism filters down to individual. And so they are too much at home in an egoist and competitive economic. They are on too good terms with such a world. That is a perversion and a debasement, which the ministers must remedy. The evangelical ministry is a protest against it. It is the trustee specially charged with this one positive gospel; therefore, it is the most effective agent of the one Church. With the loosely organised Congregationalists the ministry is perhaps the greatest bond. For the one ordination of the minister to his first church is accepted by all other churches to which he may remove. He is not ordained afresh to each, as strict theory would require. This mutual eligibility should obtain in all the Free Churches. So it is because the gospel is the creator of the Church, and the ministry is the official trustee of the gospel, that I call the place and function of the ministry creative. It is sacramental of the new creation. And it is specially creative for Church union, because it is the gospel of reconciliation.

§

It is not enough to say that the ministry *represents* the unity of the Church. It does that, but unless it does more it is not effective; it is only symbolic, only indicative; whereas its gospel is donative and imperative. Its gospel *gives* something, it does not *just exhibit* it. And the gift is also a demand, which itself creates the power to meet it. "*Dat quod jubet.*" So it *creates* Church unity by carrying home with sacramental power the reconciling and regenerating gospel of the One Lord. This action of the ministry sets *up* the Church's unity, and not only sets it *forth*. It does not only show a unity that is there, it creates a unity that was not there, between God and man, between members, and between Churches. It is not only the symbol of the unity of the Church but its source.

God's Word of the gospel created the Apostolate—the word of the Cross and its salvation. Before that they had only been apostles designate, they were only disciples, students. But that Cross made them ministers; that gave them their ordination, unction, and freedom; they were neophites no more; they forsook no more, they betrayed no more, when the Resurrection gave them the insight of the true Cross.

In the course of this work the Apostles created the Church; or rather, they were the living organs of the Word that did create it. The same positive and supernatural gospel that made them made the Church through them. It is more true to say that they made the Church than that the Church made them. It certainly did not appoint them, nor did it equip them. And when they passed away no doubt those they trusted, those they converted first, had much prestige in the Church, and, if they were otherwise fit, they became the leaders and ministers of the Church. But they were not planted on the Church by any prerogative of the Apostles. For such a belief the evidence is of the poorest.

Again, the Word created a class of apostolic men outside those few Apostles whose prerogative was that they had been in personal contact with Christ. It created the class of prophets, enthusiastic and inspired preachers, who were treated both by Apostle and Church with great respect as vehicles of the Spirit. This respect was so great that many facile religionists coveted it—not always insincerely, only temperamentally; their native spiritual make-up gave them great facilities for it. Some of them were mobile in constitution, with the mystic knack, religious sensibility, and a bias to utterance; they were fluent of speech, journalistic, quick to exploit current notions in popular phrase; and they could polish up the *clichés* and *Stichwörter* of their public till it could see its own face in them with delight. And the crude young Church had no Bible, or did not use it; and the great Apostles could not be everywhere; so that it had no standard to judge these ready preachers. But such a test the

Apostles had to provide before their death. And the epistles of John show that they did it. But they show also that they did not do it by referring the new visitors to the judgment of a bishop whom they had appointed to carry on their own prerogative. They sent them to the Church *of the gospel*, and left the responsibility there. They told the Church it had a right and duty to test these candidates for reverence and to apply to their easy inspiration (especially when it was in semi-philosophic vein very fine and large) the standard of revelation.

This, according to John, was the authentic Word, the new creative Word, the apostle-making, Church-making Word of the gospel of forgiveness and eternal life in the historic Jesus and His atoning, redeeming work. It was the historic Redemption of the conscience in the Cross of the only Son of God. The Apostles credited the Church's faith with the *flair* for that, the power of discerning that. If it had not such discernment it was no Church. The Church had, in that "anointing", the duty and the power to recognise or refuse the new message as a God-given charisma of evangelical truth. It was not to succumb at once to the gifted preacher but to discern first the apostolic note. The first requisite of the minister is not the preaching gift, but the gospel within it. There have been many ministers who had not pulpit gifts of a striking kind, but who, in a steady lifetime of work not only faithful but deeply spiritual, have become fountains of rich life, while meteoric hierophants slew their thousands every week.

§

The Church has therefore selective power in respect of the ministry, but not creative. It did not institute the function of preaching; the irrepressible nature of the Word did that. Nor could it equip a man with the message; the Spirit did that. But it could and must discriminate between the clamants to prophetic respect and scope. It could not give divine authority but only social opportunity. That is ordination, which no single congregation has power to give, but only the greater Church. The Church did not create the ministry but only filled its ranks. It could license individuals to represent it, but not equip them. It could own the Spirit but not command it nor bestow. The case was one of recognition of the Spirit and not investiture with it. The Church did not institute the ministry as an office (for that was God's gift to the Church, along with a Word that mystically chose its own organs), but after a careful test it could ordain men to the office. We must certainly not say that the ministry creates the ministry in a co-optative way. The Apostles did not appoint Apostles in any such sense as is often pressed. Their first attempt in that way was but a lottery, and it was swept aside by the Spirit's selection of Paul—in whose case the Apostles did not even recognise an apostle when they saw one. And later, when the apostolate died out, the method was by election. In so far as we can speak of men creating the ministry, it is the Church that creates the ministry. But we must be careful in what sense. In the second century, it did greatly alter the form of the ministry; but that was to carry on the work of apostles who were made such neither by the Church nor each other. And, when the ministry had been thus established as an office by the existence of the first Apostles (though not entailed), it was part of the trust committed to the Church, so far at least as the provision of its incumbents went, and probably at first the regulation of their functions.

The Church provided and provides the *personnel* for an institution already created for it by God's Spirit. And it modified its form. It did this as the need arose for filling a place that could strictly never be filled again—the place of the Apostles, whose companying with Christ, and their gifts of normative revelation from Him, had been quite original, unique, and historically intransmissible. The strict successor of the Apostle is the New Testament, as containing the precipitate of their standard preaching. It is not the ministry that is the successor of the Apostolate, but the ministry *plus* the true apostolic legacy of the Bible—the ministry *of the Word*. The ministry is the successor of the Apostles only as the prolongation of their Bible—as the nervous system spreads the brain. The ministry of the Word is, therefore, not a projection or creation of the Church. The authority of the ministry is not drawn from the Church—only its opportunity is—else the message of the Word would be no message to the Church but only its soliloquy, the Church calling to its own soul, "Bless the Lord, O my soul"; and not the Church receiving the call and Word of God. What does come from the Church is the recognition of an authority it cannot confer, and the provision of opportunity. The word authority is ambiguous. It may mean the ultimate equipment, commission, and *élan* by the Spirit, or it may mean the licence given by the Church, and its call to exercise the gift in its midst—especially for life. In ordination the two things must meet—the man's call (not by religious sensibility but *by the gospel*) and the Church's seal of it—the authority of the Spirit in the man, and the recognition of it by the Church. There is the creative and sacramental authority, and there is the judicial and licensing authority.

The Protestant minister is a surrogate of the Apostles rather than their successor. But it *is* in the wake of Apostles that he stands, with their soul in his as the Bible is in his hand. His effectiveness is therefore apostolic in its kind. It lies in what made an apostle an apostle—in the gospel as an act and power of person on person. It is evangelical. He is a successor of such apostles functionally if not canonically, evangelically if not statutorily. The Apostles appointed no canonical successors. They could not. They were unique. Through personal contact, they had been trained by the earthly Christ for witness, and dowered with a fontal power of interpreting Him. That was their prerogative. But the Apostolate in that limited sense died with the last of them. It was by its nature incommunicable. Christ gave no canon for its perpetuation. The ministry was an ordinance of Christ rather than an institution, with the atmosphere of a gift rather than the regulations of a fiat. Christ ordained a ministry, the Church ordains ministers. And the expectation of a near *parousia* made a scrupulous provision for successors to the Apostles seem unnecessary; the necessity only arose when that expectation died away, and some substitute had to be found for Apostles now gone. The Apostles could not send as they had been sent by Christ.

The ministry is, therefore, not the canonical prolongation of the Apostolate any more than the Church is the prolongation of the Incarnation. The Church is the product of the Incarnation, and the ministry is a gift to the Church. It is not the prolongation of the Apostolate but a substitute, with a like end, and on its base. The prolongation of the Apostolate and the legatee of its unique authority (I have said) is the New Testament, as the precipitate of the apostolic preaching at first hand. This is the minister's charter. The apostolic continuity is in the function, not in the entail; in the Eternal Word proclaimed, not in the unbroken chain prolonged. It is in the message,[1] not in the order of men. A hitch in the conveyancing therefore matters nothing. The Apostles were not chosen by the Church, but when they died out a ministry arose which was; and which, under different conditions, performed the like function of preaching, spreading, and consolidating the gospel as interpreted by the Apostles once for all. Christ chose the Apostles directly, the ministers He chose and chooses through the Church. The Church does not always choose right; but then Judas was in the twelve. The Apostolate was not perpetuated, and certainly not self-perpetuated; but it was replaced by another instrument for the same purpose at the motion of the same Spirit. It was replaced not by a prolongation but by a mandatory to administer its trust—by the minister of the Word. For that Word the Apostles had authority by a unique call direct from Christ, the ministry had function by a call truly from Christ but mediated through the Church and repeated generation after generation—the function of being the living sacraments of a gospel the Apostles gave.

What the ministry had was a functional continuity in preaching the Word revealed to the Apostles, administering its Sacraments, and applying its principles in a Christian ethic. The Apostolic succession is the Evangelical succession. Its continuity lies not in a due devolution but in a common inspiration, a common ministration of God's grace as mercy. It is (so to say) not a vertical continuity descending

[1] The Apostolic succession was at first a succession of truth rather than of persons, till in time the depositories became more than the deposit. The Church fell to a bureaucracy in the sense that the officers vouched for the matter more than the matter for the officers. The *charisma veritatis* was planted on the bishop.

in a line, but a solidary, spreading through a mass; not a chain on which the Church is hung, but a nervous system pervading it and, by the Word, continually creating it. This ministry took the place of the Apostolate in the second century. The Ignatian bishop is a congregational minister. The Church changed and corrected the form of the ministry then, as it did at the Reformation, as it has always power to do. The Apostles had a commission from God by Christ's endowment. They descended on the Church, they did not rise from it. But the ministry had also a mandate from men, from a Church who, by spiritual discernment, recognised in certain of their number Christ's gift of gospelling in some form. It did arise from the Church—though the trust it ministered, the gospel that made it, did not. The Apostolate was not instituted by the Churches, the ministry was. But the trust was in common, and the function was alike. It was to convey (not merely to announce but sacramentally to convey) the grace of God to men. And that is the nature of ministerial effectiveness, in various forms.

I deliberately avoid speaking of the effectiveness of the ministry in the sense in which the phrase would be most promptly understood, where people are ceasing to believe in the Church, and coming to believe in congregations, agencies, movements, fabrics, and funds. The effectiveness of the ministry is to be found in its sacramental quality as I have explained it, its conveying quality, its moral, life-giving, life-deepening quality. We can never sever that great impressive idea of a real Sacrament from the idea of the ministry. Without that conveying power in the end it is nothing. We hear much question raised whether our ministry is a *valid* ministry. It is absurd. God alone can really know if a ministry is valid. He alone can search the chief results. Only that gospel validates the ministry which created it. And if the work of the Free Churches for the gospel during three centuries in this country be invalid, we must revise the whole New Testament idea of apostolic value and the Spirit's work.

Sometimes, however, the word valid is deprecated, modified, and we are only *irregular*. Again, there is but one thing that regularises the ministry. It is the gospel and a Church of the gospel. Christianity began in an irregular ministry. It was disowned by every religious authority of the day. It began as a sect. And it burst and broke the Church in which it arose. The ministry is valid or regular according as it is effective as a sacrament of the gospel to our experience in a church. It is what makes the gospel, and Christ as the gospel, a real presence for life. The great sacrament of Christianity is the sacrament of the living and preached Word of Reconciliation, whether by speech, rite, or work. The elements may be anything; the Word is everything, the active Word of God's Act, Christ's personal Act met by His Church's.

That sacrament of the Word is what gives value to all other sacraments. They are not ends, they are but means to that grace. They are but visible, tangible modes of conveying the same gospel which is audible in the Word. In the sacrament of the Word the ministers are themselves the living elements in Christ's hands—broken and poured out in soul, even unto death; so that they may not only witness Christ, or symbolise Him, but by the sacrament of personality actually convey Him crucified and risen. This cannot be done officially. It cannot be done without travail. A Mother Church must die daily in bringing the gospel into the world—and especially in her ministry must she die. There is indeed a real change in these true elements. Their transubstantiation is a constantly renewed conversion. It is the passage of the preacher's soul from death to life incessantly. The Apostles were greater sacraments than those they administered, as Man is more than the Sabbath, Christ than the Temple.

For the true sacrament is holy personality. The body and blood of Christ is the heart and soul of Christ, the broken heart, the soul made a libation. A soul elect to the Cross of the gospel conveys Christ as bread, wine, or water cannot. In like manner we say that, in strictness, a book cannot be inspired, but only the soul that wrote it: and the Apostles were more inspired than the Bible. A Church cannot, indeed, live without sacraments, which are "essential means"; but still less can it live without sacramental souls, which are also ends in themselves. There then lies the prime effectiveness of the ministry. It is its sacramental power, not to change elements but to change souls, to regenerate personality. Let us rise above the idea that the preached Word of God is a mere message warmly told. It is a creative sacrament by the medium of a consecrated personality. It is more than good news fervently spoken, it is a soul's life and power from God. Ardour is not life. And the Word's bearer is more than a herald; he is a hierophant from the holiest place. He is, as gospelling, more than a herald God sent, he is a living oracle of God.

§

We use a phrase sometimes which is indispensable but is not without its dangers. When we allude to the channel that conveys grace to us we speak of a Means of Grace. But there is a tendency in the expression to fix attention on things as the organs of grace, or upon institutions, or ordinances. But things or even institutions play but a subordinate part in the mediation of grace as the gospel understands grace. Grace is not a force. It is not among natural causes, quantities, or infusions, nor is it due to natural effects. It is nothing corporeal or emanative. It is a Person's will, the freest of all objects in the compass of our knowledge. And the freedom of grace not only sits loose to things, but it is something that Christians are bound to consider before any freedom of man—an order this, that we have subverted in our passion for freedom as an end in itself. It aims, therefore at the production of a certain type of free personal life in those to whom it comes. It aims at their will and its recreation to a new freedom. It is the action of will on will, of soul on soul. In strictness, therefore, it cannot really work with things for means. Things are but under-agents. It works with wills, with persons—whatever the elements may be that these employ as machinery of the soul, whether they be things or institutions. Grace makes its own prime instruments out of the souls that receive it. They are its great sacraments. It is by men of grace that Christ spreads and confirms His grace in men. It works by putting into the service of Christ everyone it brings to Christ.

The gift of grace, therefore, is nothing distinct from grace's own saving function in the soul, the soul-activity, the new life it stirs. The effects of grace are personal activities, emotions, worships, sympathies, to which Christ rouses us in the gospel of His Word and the gift of His Spirit—faith, repentance, hope, love, the passion for souls in a great loving-kindness. These are the gift of grace, and the Spirit's great work in us. It has nothing to do with magical, subliminal, metaphysical powers residing in the substance of things or elements and passing into the substance of souls. Those spiritual energies in us are not the sequels to some infusion of essence and substance all divine, which is treated as God's true gift and great work in us, a higher gift than grace, and more refining,[1] as is supposed in sacramentarian doctrine. The real intimate means of grace are sacramental souls and not sacramentarian elements. Conversion, regeneration, is the true Transubstantiation. The ordinances are therefore not the action of functionaries but of believers, men of grace.

One bane of the whole question of the Sacraments is the obtrusion of the material elements. I wish to speak very respectfully of what is by many so deeply revered. But I shall have to show later that this provokes a jungle of metaphysical issues that are not religious, nor even theological, but only theosophic, insoluble, too often demoralising. But do not let us by such deflections and perversions be robbed of the sacramental idea and its vast Christian effects. The sacramental rite is an occasion of sacramental souls round Christ crucified, and not of a magical action or entail. Let us be outdone by none in reverence for the Sacraments. It is an attitude we much need to cherish. But let it be a real reverence for the personal Christ in donative action in our midst. What metaphysic may be behind it belongs to the metaphysic of personality and of energy and not of substance. The Sacraments will never become the symbol of a united Church till the whole tissue of thought, speech, and practice in connection with a metaphysic or magic of the

[1] Nothing shows more strikingly the loss from popular religion of intelligence of itself than the spectacle of a hearty Protestant congregation taking Newman's verse *sans gêne* in its stride through the great hymn. To this and other points here touched I shall return later.

elements as substances has been converted and transfigured, and they are construed as acts of Christ in person through the corporate personality of the Church, embodying the gospel's action in and by sacramental souls.

§

In urging the sacramentalism of the ministry as its true effectiveness, let me be more concrete.

The ministerial office has four functions in which it must be effective.

(1) *Preaching.*—This is prime for the genius of the office with us, whether it be prime for each minister or not (and there are diversities of gifts). The ministry represents God. It carries the Word of His mercy to the Church and the world. The Church is in trust of the gospel to the world, the ministry is in trust of the gospel to the Church. Nay, more, it *conveys* God in His grace. It is a living sacrament, for there is a soul of truth in the Roman idea of orders as a sacrament. The ministry is a living sacrament which not only shows something, but by word and prayer does something in the spiritual world, confers something, changes much, regenerates all. Preaching the gospel is a great sacramental deed, whatever preaching sermons may be. It is not Apostles that people are tired of, but the pulpit. It is sermons that weary them, not the gospel. Preaching the gospel is far more truly a deed, an act of the personality, than the priest's in the Mass. It effects more in the unseen. And in the case of the minister, as with the Apostle, it is a life-deed. The whole of the minister's life is given up to it. Life and Word are identified. His Word engrosses his life, his life is consecrated to His Word. He is a sacrament of grace (would that he oftener knew it!) always meaning by grace not the substance of Christ assimilated in bread and wine, but Christ as the living Word, appropriated in personality, in the Spirit and in power. It may be clear that I am most concerned about preaching as real, and less about it as eloquent, artistic, or impressive.

(2) *Pastoral Work.*—This is but a special aspect of the other. It is bringing God's grace to men in another way,

for which some are more fitted than they are to preach. It brings the gospel to each door. The pastor's work is not merely to go about among the people with human sympathy and kindly help, but to do this confessedly in the name and for the sake of something greater—in the way of carrying Christ to the people individually, sacramentally, not for humane objects only, but for the sake of the Kingdom of God. The pastor is only the preacher in retail. The cure of souls! No mere assiduity can really cure souls, only a gospel of grace working through a subject of grace.

(3) *Liturgical Work—and especially leading in Public Prayer.*—Now, this puts us at a point of view quite different and secondary, since man's faith is second to God's grace. Here the minister is no more prophet but priest. His effectiveness is not prophetic but priestly. His voice does not now come to the Church, but rises from it. He is the organ of the common priesthood of the Church. When he speaks in God's name to men, he properly speaks down to the people from a pulpit; but, speaking in man's name to God, he speaks properly from the floor, and from among the people. If acoustics permitted it, he should have his back to the people; because he and they are all on one level, and all face one way, and all bend to one Godward wind. He is here what as preacher he is not—the mouthpiece of the people, of their sin, confession, need, and praise, all of which he shares. Here his effectiveness rests in his call by the people rather than in God's call. The people commission him to express them. He speaks for men, not for God. He is not here God's sacrament to men, he stands for man's sacrifice to God, man's oblation of himself in Christ. He is here the organ of the essential priestliness of the Church. As the officer of the Church he is sacerdotal, as the organ of God he is sacramental. The Church is a great priest, the ministry is a great prophet. The Church confesses for the world, intercedes, suffers, is offered for it. It is, under Christ, the world's High-Priest. But the ministry speaks even to the Church, and to the world through it. It conveys God in His Grace to living faith. It has the secret and sacrament of the ever-regenerating Word. It prophesies, it testifies, it wrestles with men rather than for them, it is despised and

rejected, and, it may be, dies at their hands and for their sake. It is over the Church in the gospel (but only in the gospel, not in thought, and not in action). As priest, the ministry offers to God the Church's soul, as prophet it offers to it the salvation of God. In the minister's one person, the human spirit speaks to God, and the Holy Spirit speaks to men. No wonder he is often rent asunder. No wonder he snaps in such tension. It broke the heart of Christ. But it let out in the act the heart of God.

But with us one of these two functions of the minister is prime. His chief effect and calling with us is as the channel of the Holy Ghost. He is God's human sacrament to man. He is sacramental, therefore, more than sacerdotal. For he is chiefly what he is for God. And for God he is agent of His Christ, the vehicle of His Word. And it is only God's Word to us that makes possible our word to God. Our safety, therefore, if Protestantism be the Church's salvation, is that the ministry be more sacramental than sacerdotal, and sacerdotal only as sacramental—because the gift of grace creates the Church's answering sacrifice of faith and prayer and Eucharistic praise.

(4) *The Ministry has Other Functions—it is social and philanthropic.*—These belong to another group, also sacramental in their way: which, however, receives so much attention at present that it threatens the greater functions. And that releases me from saying much about it, except that here also the minister is the channel of God's grace, love, and help. Yet it can easily distract from the ministry of the Word and the unique witness of the Church. It can make the Church but a waiter on the State, and no Church at all, but only a religious society lacking the Holy Ghost. It is not good for the minister to be an almoner. And it takes work away from the laity. This whole side of things is passing more and more from the Christian Church to the Christian State; so that it becomes more and more difficult, with the spiritual demands of such an age, to be both minister and statesman. Or, if social interests and reforms do not pass to the State, they are, in the care of the Church's members, banded in free societies for a special purpose. These, however, should have their spiritual force and cheer

in the Church. And a Church meeting could not be better spent than in hearing from the members accounts of their Christian work in the world, whether it be by societies of the Church or not, and praying for both workers and work.

§

But now to express the whole truth, there is another pole. The effectiveness of the ministry is not possible without that of the people. A sacrament is a sacrament to faith, to a real recipient. Effectual calling implies effectual hearing. In the case of a stranger speaking, that means that the Church starts with active criticism; but criticism of the preacher, not the gospel. For Paul and John that was certainly so. The prophet, the preacher had to *win* confidence. The wandering preacher's gift of uttering the word must be met and matched by the hearer's gift of evangelical discernment. Religious judgment precedes religious sympathy. We ministers ought not to expect new men to believe in us upon our word till we make them. Of old the prophet on arrival offered himself to the spiritual judgment of the Church. And it is to the men of the Spirit, men regenerate, that the prophet of the Spirit appeals. The world has not the test for the effectiveness of the ministry. "The spiritual voice needs the spiritual ear."

And this ear must be cultivated. But how cultivated, you ask me? Is it not for the ministry to cultivate the ear of the people? Yes, when it has been won. But how is the ministry to win the ear, the confidence of the people? In the New Testament age the critical right of recognising prophets when they appeared lay with the Church. And how? By bringing them to the test neither of eloquence, nor impressiveness, nor idealism, nor mere liking, but to the test of the historic gospel, to the evangelical test, as the Apostles had put it into their hands. (What a pity it has been confounded with Orthodoxy!) That is, as we should now say, the test must be applied—not of our whims, prejudices, views, tastes, or hobbies, but of the redemption as the New Testament puts it. Paul said, if prophet, apostle, or angel preached another than that gospel, he was to be disregarded.

No matter how magnetic the man may be, how charming, how spiritual, how impressive, how powerful, how popular the speaker may be with a mere congregation, he has not his right to a pulpit in a Church in virtue of any of these things. He has his right according as he serves sincerely, capably, and heartily the New Testament Gospel. He is to be received not for his temperament, but for his message; not as he may be a poet, a saint, an oracle, or a capital fellow, but as he is a sacrament of the Word of the Cross and its regeneration. The test of an effective ministry is not impression but regeneration. And to discern that regenerative note in him, the Christian people must tune their ear not at the minister, but at the same source as the minister—at the Bible.

But then, if the personal use of the Bible die out of our laity, if they decay in their sense of that gospel which makes the Bible the Bible, how is the ear for the true apostolate to be cultivated? Has the membership of our Churches the ear for the gospel, the ear which detects in much spirituality the false note and the wrong key? Or has it become vulgarised by orthodoxy, the Press, or democracy? How is the gift then to be acquired which distinguishes the living Word from a mere live man, or from mere mystic religiosity on which no Church can live? Does the Church's right of choosing a minister remain if it lose this gift, this supernatural *flair* for the authentic gospel? Mistakes are often made in calling a minister, through the lack of this spiritual discernment in Churches that do not feed their souls on their Bible, nor will go for guidance to those who do. They take up what costs them least effort to take in. If a man seems *spirituel*, easy, and interesting, they do not ask if he is effective where the preacher's effectiveness begins—with God, if he is accessible to God, and so, effective as an apostle. The ministry of the Word and prayer go together. The man who prays as much as he preaches will not be an ineffective preacher. And he will be very effective with those who do not preach at all but pray much. Gifts do not make a preacher; brilliancy does not; but there is a seal that does. And it is not a rapt nor a magnetic soul, nor a subjective facility for religion, nor even a devoted life; but the apostolic note, lived in and lived out.

Again, the Christian ministry is not effective, however active and influential, except as it makes and builds up Churches. I have said its true feature is not impressionist, but creative and regenerative. That means one or two things. The true ministry creates personality rather than creates a *furore*. It first builds up the preacher's personality, and protects it from his vogue. And it rears personality *in the flock*. It is less concerned in stirring stray heroisms than in making men, less given to lead crusades than to make Churches. That is the great seal to a ministry—not enterprise, not vogue, nor even conversions, but Churches. It is not an effective ministry when the crowds the preacher drew melt whenever he goes, when they gather about an interesting or a bizarre personality rather than about the Church's Word. The idolatry of such preachers tends to reduce the general estimate of the ministry rather than to raise it. Besides, there is a corporate personality that belongs to a Church and its history; and a Church with a history should not sink to be a mere rostrum for a reputation. The business of the effective ministry is to develop the Church, to raise it above the denomination, to turn audiences into Churches, and sects into the Church.

We come round again to what I said about the ministry and unity. Unity is a question of the ministry, both of its status and its effect. We shall not get a union of the Churches except through a Church-making gospel, except as we produce real Churches to unite, bodies with a real Church-consciousness, and not watered down to be mere religious groups, pleased audiences, benevolent societies, or fraternal clubs. We can reach the union of all the Churches only by developing the Church-consciousness of each. It is strong personalities that make up real communities. It is strong Churches that make real union, Churches that believe in themselves and look also on the things of others. The ministry is most effective which makes the most effective Church, which teaches people that the Church of Christ is the greatest society on earth, that it is the society which is to save society. Its gospel is the one power to overcome Egoism, and an Egoism not overcome means anarchy. The saved soul wakes up to realise that it is only saved by a gospel which saves a world. And the saved Church is the earnest of a saved Humanity; it is the New Humanity in the making. The ministry cannot solve the social problems, but the Church it makes by its gospel of life can. And it is a sterile mistake for a preacher to despise the doctrine that makes a Church, and then fill his yawning intelligence with the dreary dogmas of sociology, the prescriptions of eugenics, or even the evolution of the Absolute Idea.

If the wrong form of sacrament could make Rome the greatest single power the world has ever seen, what would the right form not do for the Church, if it were as thoroughly realised? But if we surrender to Rome the mighty sacramental idea, if we spend our time in a jangle of attack on that idea, and if our ministry have nothing sacramental in its note with which to go to the world, if our living sacraments do not exceed in real effect the sacraments of a legalist Church, then we cannot hope to cope with the influence of Catholicism on the world and its mighty use of the sacramental note. We have ourselves to blame for much of the sacramentalism we object to, because we have not taken our true sacramentalism in earnest. Our religious type grows so flat, stale, and trivial, that we need Nietzsches to scourge it. As I have said, there is a great truth underlying the false Roman view of the sacrament of orders. And the humblest minister who was as sure of his grace as the poorest priest is of *his* would be a power among the people and over them more sacred than brilliant gifts or imposing personality.

I have been more moved and blessed by the word and prayer of a Scottish peasant or an East Coast fisherman with the sacramental experience, than by High Mass in Cologne, *Parsifal* on the stage, or pulpit genius at home—and I have been deeply affected by them all. Let us be less concerned to denounce a false sacrament than to realise the true. There is nothing that can so uplift the ministry, and secure its dignity against the swarm of religious trivialities that fly upon it like a cloud of locusts to eat its life. It is enough to sober any light man, tame the rude man, and exalt the meek to know and feel that he is ordained to be a sacrament to his Church, to be, through his own soul's faith, the living channel of the creative Word of Grace.

PART II

THE SACRAMENTS

CHAPTER VIII

THE PLACE OF THE SACRAMENTS IN THE TEACHING OF ST. PAUL

The new trend of modern criticism in the interpretation of the sacramental passages in St. Paul. An examination of the symbolical theory of Baptism. Its inadequacy in view of St. Paul's statements. The implication of St. Paul's doctrine of the Eucharist. Verification of the conclusion from other passages in the New Testament. The two alternatives: (1) to revise our doctrine of the sacraments; (2) to explain the Pauline position as an intrusion of foreign elements from the current thought of the time. The decision must be left to theology.

THIS chapter is not mine. My colleague Professor Andrews has recently written in the *Expositor*, and (with its editor's courteous consent) has most kindly let me include here one of the most valuable of recent articles on the sacraments, from the point of view of a New Testament scholar who keeps his eye on modern results. These are things which cannot be ignored. They may seem to some to make a present too handsome to the sacramentarians. Such a consideration, however, should not deflect our desire to get at the real truth of this or of other matters. Perhaps the present may amount to less if we treat the Bible in its proper relation to the Gospel, and are ready to correct the view even of an apostle by the principle of his central faith. Dr. Andrews speaks but as the scholar, and he expressly leaves further developments to the theologians. What I have tried to do is to evaluate the sacraments by the principle of faith in the light of the scientific knowledge of Scripture, to start with such results as Dr. Andrews' in my mind, and to point out that even were they accepted we are still not thrown into any sacramentalism fatal to the evangelical principle, or more than we have much need to recover.

One great misgiving I do have. After Dr. Andrews' lucid and *ligato* style, I fear that many will be very impatient of mine.

I

THE tendency of modern Free Church theologians has been either to ignore the sacramental elements in the teaching of St. Paul or to assume that his views were in accord with their own. Bruce, for instance, attacked with the utmost vigour the position of Weiss that "baptism is the second great principle of salvation not less indispensable for regeneration or the reception of the Holy

Spirit than faith is for justification," and maintained that "it is not necessary, in order to do full justice to the Apostle's argument, to assign to baptism more than a symbolical significance."

In recent years, however, the pendulum of criticism has swung in the opposite direction, and the position represented by Bruce has been challenged from many quarters. The attack is all the more significant because it has come from scholars who cannot be suspected of the slightest bias towards sacramentarianism. We may take as illustrations of the new movement the following statements.

Wernle, in his *Beginnings of Christianity*,[1] says: "It was Paul who first created the conception of a sacrament. . . . He would have baptism regarded as a miracle and a mystery. The baptized convert should believe that he steps forth from the water a different person from what he was when he entered it. . . . It appears to us to-day exceedingly strange that the hero of the word should at the same time have become the creator of the sacrament."

Pfleiderer, in his *Primitive Christianity*,[2] is equally definite in his statement that in the theology of St. Paul "baptism appears as the foundation of the life in the Spirit and at the same time as the *means* by which He is communicated."

Kirsopp Lake, in his *Earlier Epistles of St. Paul*,[3] regards this interpretation of St. Paul's teaching as absolutely incontrovertible. "Baptism is for St. Paul and his readers universally and unquestioningly accepted as a 'mystery' or sacrament which works *ex opere operato*: and from the unhesitating manner in which St. Paul uses this fact as a basis for argument, as if it were a point on which Christian opinion did not vary, it would seem as though this sacramental teaching is central in the primitive Christianity to which the Roman Empire began to be converted."

The same conclusion has been reached by scholars of such diverse outlook as Weinel, Feine, Titius, Heitmüller, and Schweitzer (to mention but a few), all of whom—some of them with extreme reluctance—have come to the decision that the sacramental principle is a vital element in the teaching of St. Paul.

[1] Eng. transl., i. pp. 273, 274 [2] Ibid i. p. 387. [3] p. 385.

If there is any sound basis for this new movement, it is perfectly clear that a very serious problem will be raised for Free Church theology—or at any rate for that section of it which has been in the habit of regarding the sacraments as merely symbolical. The whole question of the doctrine of the sacraments will need to be re-examined in the light of modern criticism and "the comparative method" of investigation.

II

Let us examine the case upon which the sacramental interpretation of Paulinism rests, and let us deal first of all with the question of baptism.

At first sight the arguments in support of the position of Bruce and Holtzmann, who deny that baptism was anything more than a symbol to the mind of St. Paul and his converts, appear to be very weighty.

(1) In the first place, Paul never works out in detail his doctrine of baptism as he does his doctrine of justification by faith. His position has to be determined from incidental allusions and stray references, and there are less than a dozen of these in the whole of the Epistles that bear his name. If baptism was as fundamental to Paul as modern critics assume, how are we to explain the paucity of his references to the subject? If he regarded it as an essential factor in the process of regeneration, why is there no reference to it in the first five chapters of the Epistle to the Romans which explain his doctrine of salvation?

(2) On one occasion, in writing to the Corinthians (1 Cor. i. 14-17), Paul makes the definite statement: "I thank God that I baptized none of you save Crispus and Gaius . . . for Christ sent me not to baptize, but to preach the Gospel." Now if baptism was regarded by St. Paul as the vehicle by means of which Divine grace was communicated to the recipient, could the Apostle have written a sentence of this sort? Would he not have been bound to feel that in refusing baptism he was depriving his Corinthian converts of a necessary means of grace? Does not the very form of the sentence—"to preach and *not* to baptize"—imply a dis-

paragement of the rite of baptism, as being something of altogether secondary and subordinate importance?

(3) The famous *locus classicus* in Romans vi., on which such stress is laid by the modern exponents of Pauline sacramentarianism—"We who were baptized into Christ Jesus were baptized into his death," need not necessarily bear the construction that is put upon it. We must not forget the strain of poetry in the temperament of St. Paul. As Bruce puts it: "It cannot be shown that baptism is for the Apostle more than a familiar Christian institution which he used *in transitu* to state his view of the Christian life in vivid, concrete terms which appeal to the religious imagination. He employs it in his free poetic way as an aid to thought, just as elsewhere he employs the veil of Moses and the allegory of Sarah and Hagar."

(4) The sacramentarian interpretation of baptism seems to be absolutely opposed to the general tenor of St. Paul's theology taken as a whole. Weinel admits the discrepancy between the two halves of Paulinism—the spiritual and the sacramental. "In St. Paul's writings we have the two forms of religion—the sacramental and the purely spiritual—standing side by side without any attempt at co-ordination. At one time it is faith that brings the Spirit, at another time baptism; sometimes it is faith that unites with Christ, sometimes the Lord's Supper. These two series of conceptions have not as yet been united under any one system. They cannot be harmonised." But is it possible to assume such a hopeless antinomy in the thought of the Apostle? Does not Weinel's inability to discover a *modus vivendi* between the two elements in Paulinism throw suspicion upon his interpretation of the sacraments? Moreover, are we to suppose that Paul, who attacked so stoutly the rite of circumcision and entirely denied its religious value, would have allowed himself or anybody else to substitute another ordinance, equally external and equally physical, in its place? Is there any argument which Paul urged against circumcision which does not *mutatis mutandis* apply to the sacramentarian conceptions which these modern writers read into his statements about baptism?

III

These arguments, however, though *prima facie* they appear to be weighty, are nothing like so convincing when we come to examine them. In the first place, it is not a sound canon of criticism to assume that there is any *ratio* between the importance of a subject and the amount of space devoted to it in the Epistles. The paucity of the references to baptism need imply no more than the fact that it was not a subject of controversy, and that it was not therefore necessary for St. Paul to write at length about a matter upon which all sections of the Church were unanimous. There were so many points of disagreement which needed discussion and argument that it need occasion no surprise that the Apostle passes lightly over such a topic as baptism, upon which there is no indication that any difference of opinion existed.

In the second place, Paul's statement, "Christ sent me not to baptize but to preach," must be read in the light of the context. Paul is protesting against the party spirit in the Church of Corinth, and rejoices that he himself had never done anything to create or accentuate it. If Paul refused to baptize his converts at Corinth with his own hands, the explanation may be, not that he undervalued the rite, but that he wished to avoid the possibility that the Corinthian Church might regard itself "as baptized in the name of Paul," and so consciously or unconsciously place him on the throne which only Christ had the right to occupy. Paul's refusal may simply have been his way of safeguarding the "crown rights of the Redeemer."

The third argument begs the question altogether. Poetry and mysticism are undoubtedly blended in the opening paragraph of the sixth chapter of Romans, but it is pure assumption to state without further proof that the phrase "as many as were baptized into Christ Jesus" is merely a poetical expression.

There is much more force in the fourth argument. The discrepancy between the spiritual and sacramentarian elements in Paulinism seems at the first view to be fatal. There are two considerations, however, which may serve to mitigate the force of the argument. Are we quite sure that the Apostle Paul ever wrought out his theology into a harmonious system? Are there not other indications in the Epistles of theological impulses which are not always co-ordinated? Do we not sometimes find other cases of antinomy in Pauline thought? Is it much more easy to relate the juridical and the mystical sides of Paulinism than it is to find a place for the sacramentarian in relation to the other two elements in his theology? Or again, we may adopt an alternative explanation. We may say that the apparent discrepancy between the sacramentarian and the spiritual sides of Paulinism may be due to the limitations of our own understanding. It exists for us, but it did not exist for Paul. We may yet be able to discover the higher unity in which the seeming antinomies are resolved. There are three facets which gleam from the crystal of Paulinism —the juridical, the mystical, and the sacramental. Some men see only one facet, and very few see all three, and these few are lost in wonder that three such different rays of light can emanate from the same source.

IV

So far we have only shown that the arguments which can be marshalled in support of the contention of Bruce and Holtzmann are not necessarily final. The real weakness of these arguments, however, lies in the fact that they do not explain the whole of the data. There are some statements in the Epistles which seem to make it abolutely impossible to suppose that the Apostle Paul regarded the rite of baptism as nothing more than a beautiful symbol.

Let us take, for instance, the reference to baptism in 1 Corinthians vi. 11: "Be not deceived; neither fornicators nor idolaters . . . shall inherit the kingdom of God. And such were some of you: but *ye were washed* (or *ye washed yourselves*), ye were sanctified, ye were justified." The best commentary on the phrase "ye were washed" is to be found in Acts xxii. 16, where Ananias is represented as saying to Paul on the day of his conversion, "Arise and be baptized and wash away thy sins." In both these statements there seems to be a very definite nexus between baptism and the forgiveness of sins. It would rob the statement in Corinthians of all its force if we paraphrased the phrase "ye were washed" into "ye were baptized as a symbol of your conversion."

Then there is the remarkable and much-debated expression in I Corinthians xv. 29, "Those who are baptized for the dead" (οἱ βαπτιζόμενοι ὑπὲρ τῶν νέκρων). There is probably no text in the New Testament which has been so violently wrested by exegetes in their efforts to evade the plain meaning of the words. Thirty-six different interpretations of this clause have been enumerated, and thirty-five of them are ingenious attempts to pervert the clear sense of a perfectly unambiguous Greek phrase. There is no reasonable doubt that St. Paul is referring to the practice of vicarious baptism by living Christians on behalf of those who had died in an unbaptized condition. But if baptism is merely a symbol, how are we to explain the existence of this practice? The only ground for the origin of such a custom is to be found in the fact that baptism was believed to confer some spiritual endowment which could not be obtained in any other way, and it was hoped that vicarious baptism might remedy the defect for those who had died without it—a defect which otherwise seemed irremediable.

But it is in the Epistle to the Ephesians (which, in spite of the arguments of Dr. Moffatt and other modern scholars, I still hold to be Pauline) that the most indubitable evidence is to be found. Take for instance the great passage in the fourth chapter, where Paul appeals to Christians to maintain the unity of the spirit in the bond of peace on the ground that there is "one body, one spirit, one Lord, one faith, one baptism, one God and Father of all." Why is baptism assigned a place in this great hierarchy of spiritual realities? There is no mention of the Eucharist. There is no reference to the Apostolate. If baptism was merely a symbol and nothing more, it is difficult to find the reason which led St. Paul to set it on so high a pinnacle. But the clearest and most incontrovertible statement is to be found in v. 26: "Christ loved the Church and gave himself for it, that he might sanctify it, *cleansing it by the washing of water* with the word." These words are perfectly categorical and definite. No amount of ingenuity can eviscerate their clear meaning and significance. They are corroborated by the Epistle to Titus (which, though it was not written by Paul, certainly emanated from the Pauline School), where it is written (iii. 5): "He saved us through the washing of regeneration (διὰ λουτροῦ παλινγενεσίας), and the renewing of the Holy Spirit."

In the light of these statements it is difficult to believe that the more neutral phrases, *e.g.* "baptized into Christ," "baptized into one body," imply a merely symbolical interpretation of baptism.

With this evidence before us, it seems very hard to resist the conclusion (however little we may like it) that if the Epistles of St. Paul do not enunciate the ecclesiastical doctrine of Baptismal Regeneration, they at any rate approximate very closely to it—with this difference, of course, that there is no shred of real proof that baptism was ever administered to infants in the Apostolic age.

Nor is our impression of the significance of baptism in St. Paul's conception of Christianity lessened when we come to consider the functions which the sacrament discharges. It seems to play a part in all the initial stages of the Christian experience. It cleanses from the defilement of sin (1 Corinthians vi. 11; Ephesians v. 26). It creates the mystical union between the believer and Christ (Romans vi. 3; Galatians iii. 26), and it is the means by which he is incorporated into the Church as the body of Christ (1 Corinthians xii. 13).

V

We come now to the question of the Eucharist. We are not concerned with any of the critical problems with which this subject bristles. We need not, for instance, stay to discuss the relation between St. Paul's account of the origin of the sacrament and the parallel accounts of the synoptic gospels. The only issue which is at all relevant to our investigation is this: "What import did Paul attach to the sacrament, and what function did he assign to it in the creation and maintenance of the Christian life?"

That he regarded it as a memorial feast and related it to his eschatological conception of the Parousia of Christ is of course patent to the most casual reader of 1 Corinthians: "This do in remembrance of me, for as often as ye eat this bread and drink this cup, ye proclaim the Lord's death till he come." Now if the great passage in 1 Corinthians xi. were all that Paul said upon the subject, and if it ended at verse 27, we should have some justification for maintaining that the commemorative theory represented his view as to the right interpretation of the sacrament. But there are other statements which seem to make it absolutely certain that such an interpretation does not exhaust the significance which Paul attaches to the Eucharist.

There is, for instance, a passage which is far more important for determining St. Paul's doctrine of the Eucharist than the *locus classicus* in 1 Corinthians xi. It is the remarkable paragraph in the previous chapter (1 Corinthians x. 16-21), which commenced with the significant words, "The cup of blessing which we bless, is it not a participation in the blood of Christ? The bread which we break, is it not a participation in the body of Christ?" The importance of this statement lies in the fact that the reference to the Eucharist is introduced incidentally, and forms part of the argument which Paul uses in the discussion of another question. It may therefore be assumed that these words represent not merely the Apostle's own view, but the theory which was universally accepted and regarded as axiomatic by the Christian Church in his day. Another interesting point about this paragraph is the analogy which is drawn between the Christian Eucharist and the feasts in the pagan temples. "The things which the Gentiles sacrifice they sacrifice to demons and not unto God; and I would not that ye should have any participation (or communion) with demons. Ye cannot drink the cup of the Lord and the cup of demons; ye cannot partake of the table of the Lord and the table of demons." The assumption which clearly underlies these words is the belief that to participate either in the Eucharist or the pagan religious festivals involved also the participation in the nature of the particular deities in whose honour the festival was held. In some mysterious way the life of the God is conveyed into the life of the worshipper through the medium of the material elements which are consumed in the course of the meal. To St. Paul, therefore, the bread and the wine of the Eucharist are not merely emblems of the sacrifice that was once offered for the sins of the world; they are the vehicle by means of which the virtue of that sacrifice is appropriated by the participant.

Kirsopp Lake is quite right when he sums up the gist of the passage in the words: "St. Paul clearly means that the Corinthians knew quite well that the Eucharist is a rite which really conveys that which the heathen erroneously thought to obtain in their sacrificial meals—that is, participation in the Divine Nature"—but he exaggerates the results which follow from this conclusion when he says: "The Catholic doctrine of the Eucharist is much more primitive than the Protestant."

Turning back now to the *locus classicus* in chapter xi., it becomes obvious that we must read the passage in the light of Paul's statements in the previous chapter. In the first part of this paragraph there is nothing that is inconsistent with the Zwinglian theory, as it is called. But when we reach the closing verses, ideas are found which seem to transcend that view entirely. Verse 29 is perhaps the strongest illustration of this: "He that eateth and drinketh, eateth and drinketh judgment to himself if he discern not the body." The last phrase—"if he discern not the body" (μὴ διακρίνων τὸ σῶμα)—had always been a serious stumbling-block to Protestant commentators. The usual interpretation "if he distinguish not between the sacramental elements and common food," is too loose a paraphrase to have any claim to be regarded as a fair rendering of the Greek words; it introduces ideas which are not found in the text, and, what is more important still, it leaves out of account the ideas that are there. If Paul had wished to say this, he would have said it in a perfectly clear and unambiguous way. Honest exegesis requires us to say that the phrase "not discerning the body" must be interpreted in the light of Paul's previous statement, "The bread which we break, is it not a participation in the body of Christ?" There are many commentators who regard the body of Christ, in which the Christian participates at the Eucharist, as the heavenly spiritual body which Christ assumed after the Resurrection, and by this means they try to evade the Catholic and Lutheran doctrine of the Sacrament. But the words which Paul puts into the mouth of Christ, at the moment when He was instituting the sacrament, "This is my body, which is [broken] for you," seem to render it unlikely that such a view was really what was in Paul's mind when he wrote the words "not discerning the body."

There is another point, too, which is often overlooked or glossed over by exegetes. St. Paul states most explicitly that the Eucharist produces physical as well as spiritual effects upon the communicant. Speaking of the abuses which existed in the Church at Corinth, he says: "For this cause many among you are weak and sickly, and not a few sleep" (verse 30, πολλοὶ ἀσθενεῖς καὶ ἄρρωστοι καὶ κοιμῶνται ἱκανο). These words cannot possibly refer to moral and spiritual deterioration. The two adjectives are frequently used in the New Testament to denote physical maladies, and the second is never used in any other sense. The verb is a technical term employed in the New Testament to describe the sleep of death. The text, therefore, admits of only one interpretation. St. Paul definitely attributes a large number of cases of illness among the Corinthian Christians (many of which had proved fatal) to the misuse of the sacrament of the Eucharist. We can scarcely argue, as Ellicott and some other commentators do, that St. Paul is here describing a unique experience which was peculiar to the Apostolic age. We have no right to suppose that the ordinary laws of cause and effect were modified in the Apolostic age in order that swifter and more spectacular forms of punishment might be meted out to offenders. There is no evidence to prove that the principle of divine retribution adopted a distinctive *modus operandi* in the Apostolic age. We are shut up to the conclusion that St. Paul held that the health of the body no less than the health of the soul is absolutely dependent upon the right use of the sacrament of the Eucharist.

Taking all these facts together, it becomes very doubtful whether any theory that falls short of the Lutheran doctrine of Consubstantiation will adequately explain the utterance of St. Paul in reference to the Eucharist.

VI

The conclusions which we have reached with regard to the sacramental teaching of St. Paul are corroborated by the scanty references to the subject which we find in the other books of the New Testament. In the appendix to Mark (xvi. 16) Jesus is represented as saying, "He that believeth and is baptized shall be saved." According to this statement there are two conditions necessary to salvation—Faith and Baptism, and we have no warrant for saying that the one is less essential than the other. In the crucial passage in 1 Peter iii. 21, after a reference to the eight souls in the ark who were saved "through water," the writer goes on to add the significant words "which (*i.e.* water) also in the antitype doth now save you, even baptism." The force of this expression is not cancelled by the sentence which follows, "not the putting away of the flesh, but the interrogation of a good conscience toward God." This latter clause deals simply with the mode in which baptism works, and states that its efficacy consists not in the physical effect produced by the water in cleansing the body, but in "the interrogation of a good conscience," whatever this much-debated phrase may mean (a point which does not concern us at this stage of our inquiry). The essential point in the passage is the categorical statement that baptism is an agency by means of which salvation is rendered possible. The climax of the New Testament statements about baptism, however, is reached in the words which the author of the Fourth Gospel puts into the mouth of Jesus in the course of his conversation with Nicodemus: "Verily, verily, I say unto thee, except a man be born of water and the Spirit he cannot enter into the kingdom of God." There seems to be no way of avoiding the decision that what these words signify is this: Baptism is essential not merely to the *bene esse* (to use a time-honoured expression), but to the very *esse* of the Christian life.

In the light of the reference to baptism, it seems to be

almost impossible not to see an allusion to the Eucharist in the sixth chapter of St. John's Gospel. The arguments which are used by Westcott and others against such an interpretation of the passage do not seem to me to be very convincing. The crucial phrases, "Except ye eat the flesh of the Son of Man ye have not life in yourselves," and "He that eateth my flesh and drinketh my blood hath eternal life," "My flesh is meat indeed and my blood is drink indeed," seem to be too definite to denote a purely spiritual process. And, moreover, they do not seem to arise naturally out of the situation described in the chapter. We shall not be far wrong if we regard them as the writer's summary of the Eucharistic doctrine which prevailed in his day. To what extent he is correct in assuming that this doctrine goes back to the teaching of Jesus is another problem which lies altogether outside the province of our present discussion. The only point which we are making now is the argument that the sixth chapter of St. John bears out the interpretation which we have placed on the Eucharistics utterance of St. Paul.

VII

If these arguments are sound, we are forced to admit that as far as exegesis is concerned the sacramentarian interpretation of Paulinism has won a decisive victory, and the Symbolical school has been driven off the field. There can be no doubt whatever that baptism and the Eucharist stood for far more in the life of the Apostolic Church than they do in the estimation of the bulk of the members of the Free Churches to-day. The evidence seems to me to be so clear upon this point as to amount almost to demonstrative proof.

Now if this be the case, the problem at once arises, What is to be our attitude towards the situation which has been created for us by the new and more scientific study of Paulinism? There is little hope to be looked for from the renewal of hostilities on the field of exegesis. We might perhaps ease the pressure a little as far as baptism is concerned if we surrendered the Pauline authorship of Ephesians, but even this would not really restore the position. Sacramentarian ideas are too strongly entrenched in 1 Corinthians, the authenticity of which is unassailable, to make it possible for the sacrifice of Ephesians to bring any real relief. Whether exegesis has spoken its last word upon this subject must of course be a matter of opinion, but as things stand at present there seems little prospect that a new campaign against sacramentarian exegesis would be attended with any considerable success, and modern scholarship will no longer tolerate the subterfuges and devices which used to be employed.

There seem, therefore, to be only two alternatives left open to us. The first alternative is that we should revise our own conceptions of the sacraments. There is a feeling in some quarters that the Free Churches have never yet entered into the full sacramental heritage, and that to that extent their spiritual life has been beggared and impoverished. No one can read the biographies of the great mediæval saints without realizing that there are whole regions of spiritual experience which are a *terra incognita* to ordinary Free Churchmen. What an infinite gulf, for instance, there is between the religious life of St. Catherine of Genoa, the heroine of Baron von Hügel's book on *The Mystical Element in Religion*, and the normal Christian experience of the majority of the members of our Churches to-day! St. Catherine seems to live in one hemisphere and we in another, and the difference is not so much due to her mysticism as to the place which the sacrament holds in her devotional life. May it not be that in the fervour of our protest against sacerdotalism and a merely mechanical view of religion (a protest that was divinely inspired and has been abundantly justified by its works) we have allowed our iconoclasm to carry us too far, and as a result we have attached too light a value to ordinances which to other Christians have been not merely "the medicine of immortality and the antidote against corruption," as Ignatius put it, but the mainstay of the faith of the soul in the life that now is?

The first course open to us, therefore, is to advocate a return to the sacramentarian teaching of St. Paul and the other writers of the New Testament. There are two serious difficulties, however, that confront us in this direction. The first is this—we cannot acquiesce in a theological position that involves the dualism which Weinel finds in the antinomy between the spiritual and sacramental elements of Paulinism. We cannot live on a faith that is split up into two unconnected halves. We cannot travel at one and the same time along two parallel roads that never meet. We can never abandon the spiritual side of Paulinism. It is "bone of our bone and flesh of our flesh." It is woven into the very tissue of our spiritual life. It is the faith in which we "live and move and have our being." Before we can accept the sacramentarian position, we must accomplish what Weinel regards as an absolute impossibility, we must discover the higher unity which combines the two apparently antagonistic strains of thought into an intelligible harmony. But there is a second difficulty equally serious. Is it possible for us to go the length to which Paulinism seems to carry us? We could very easily accept Calvin's interpretation of the Eucharist (which as a matter of fact many of us have always held)—but can we accept Luther's? We can easily appreciate the spiritual value of baptism as a means of grace, but to maintain that it is one of the essential conditions of regeneration is a different matter altogether and one that would prove a serious stumbling-block to many of us. If Pauline sacramentarianism is indeed all that it seems to be, and if it really involves, as it appears to do, an *ex opere operato* theory of baptism and a doctrine of the Eucharist that is practically equivalent to Luther's consubstantiationism, it will be very difficult for us to come to terms with it, since it seems to traverse the fundamental principles and convictions which have made us what we are and which seem to us to be the very truth of God.

VIII

But there is a second alternative open to us, which offers a way of escape from the dilemma. We may argue, as a large number of scholars do to-day, that Pauline sacramentarianism in its more extreme forms is not native to the soil of Christianity, but is one of those alien elements which have filtered into his thought from the atmosphere of the age. Its origin is to be traced, not to the teaching of Jesus or the inspiration of the Holy Spirit, but rather to current beliefs and practices which prevailed in certain pagan forms of religion at the time. Sacramentarianism arose not as the natural evolution of the primal seed of Gospel Truth, which was revealed to the world in the teaching and work of Jesus Christ, but rather as an "involution" or product of its environment.

There is abundant evidence that sacramental ideas analogous to those which we find in St. Paul existed in connection with the Greek Mysteries and other forms of contemporary religion. Apuleius and Tertullian tell us that a rite of baptism formed the means of entrance into the pagan religious societies connected with the worship of Mithras and Isis and the Mysteries of Eleusis. The poet Ovid protests against the common belief that water could wash away the stain of sin:

> "Ah, nimium faciles, qui tristia crimina cædis
> Fluminea tolli posse putetis aqua!"

One of the best illustrations of the prevailing belief in the efficacy of baptism is to be found in the famous liturgy of Mithras, edited by Dieterich, though there is some doubt whether the document is really a liturgy and whether it is connected with Mithras worship at all. The significant words for our purpose are these, "Hail to thee, Lord of Water, Founder of the Earth, Ruler of the Spirit . . . born with the birth that begets life, I am redeemed unto death, and go the way which thou hast appointed, as thou hast ordained and instituted the sacrament." We must be on our guard, however, against attaching too much importance to this statement. The origin and character of the document are obscure, and it is quite possible that some of the ideas which it contains may be due to the reflex influence of Christianity itself. Still there seems to be no doubt that a belief akin to the doctrine of Baptismal Regeneration was very widely spread at the time when Christianity was formulating itself. There can be little doubt that large numbers of pagans would have subscribed to the view of

Tertullian: "With the increase of the grace of God water also acquired more power: that which once healed ills of the body now restores the soul: that which once worked only temporal good now renews to eternal life!"

The same phenomenon is also seen in the case of the Lord's Supper, though the analogies are not so close or striking. St. Paul himself suggests the parallel which existed between the Christian Eucharist and the feasts in the heathen temples. And Justin Martyr was so impressed by the resemblance between the Christian and pagan Mysteries that he accused the latter of plagiarising.

It would take too long to go into the details of the evidence, but enough has been said to prove that the atmosphere of the age was charged with sacramental ideas. We know that at a later stage in its history Christianity was very susceptible to the influences of current thought and philosophy. This has been clearly demonstrated in Hatch's *Hibbert Lectures*. May not the infiltration of the environment have commenced at an earlier stage than Hatch supposed, and may not the sacramentarianism of St. Paul be one of its products? There seems no reason to doubt the probability that this was actually the case.

But we have not settled the question (as most people seem to think we have), when we have shown that Paul's sacramental ideas (or at any rate the extreme form which they sometimes assume) penetrated into Christianity from foreign sources. The origin of an idea is no criterion as to its worth. Many of the categories which were used for the interpretation of Christianity in the later creeds were borrowed from Greek philosophy, but that does not in itself prove that the interpretation is unsound. The fact that Paul borrowed from the Greek Mysteries for the construction which he put upon the Christian sacraments is by no means fatal to the truth of his doctrines. The Greek Mysteries themselves may have been, nay in so far as they represent a genuine quest for God must have been, part of the *Preparatio Evangelica*. It would be no discredit to the author of the Fourth Gospel nor to his theology, if it could be proved that his Prologue was based upon the teaching of Philo; and it is no discredit to the Apostle Paul (nor to his theology) if he borrowed the categories of Greek religion to explain the meaning of the Christian sacraments.

The battle of the sacraments can be settled neither by exegesis nor the historico-critical method of investigation. A decision can only be attained in the higher regions of theology. And we have now reached the point at which a New Testament scholar must hand over the problem to the theologian. The data which have been gathered are (1) the theology of St. Paul involves certain very definite sacramental positions; (2) analogies to these positions are to be found in the current religious circles of the time. The problem is—Does the second proposition cancel the first? If it does, what are the grounds upon which such a result is attained? This last question can only be answered when we have settled the larger issue, "What is the seat of authority for the Christian Faith?"

CHAPTER IX

DEBASED TREATMENT OF BAPTISM

Indifference rather than contempt of Baptism in the Free Churches. Synchronism of this indifference with modern child worship. Does it matter to the child? Should it take place before we have a voice? Illustrations. Plea that people feel the benefit in attending Communion but not in attending Baptism. The felt benefit is not the measure of our duty to the Church, or even to the Gospel. Every infant Baptism should be sympathetically an adult Baptism. The Church not the spectator but the actor in the rite. To leave it to the minister is sacerdotal. The real rallying-points of the Church are its services, and especially its Sacraments.

THERE are in some of the Churches people who are more or less indifferent about Baptism; or they are disposed to regard it not as a Sacrament, but as a mere interesting act of dedication. They certainly have not the superstition that christening makes a Christian by subliminal magic, or that the unbaptized babe is in peril if it die. But they think the parents are the chief people concerned, and that they are only concerned as parents. For the majority the interesting thing is the baby, and not the Word of life and cleansing enacted by the Lord through His Church. And some conscientious Christian people, who really prize the Communion, do not hesitate to say that they find no such value in Baptism. They can share the one sacrament, the other they have to leave, and are willing to leave, to the minister and the parents. And they would not complain if the minister always administered it in the home.

The Congregationalists do not believe in Baptism as much as the Baptists do. They are not as much in earnest about it. For Baptists, as for Catholics, the Church is the company of the baptized. But surely it should not be a reason for preferring infant Baptism that we need not spend so much interest on it? If it be equally right with the other, that cannot mean that it may be believed less or honoured less—by breach rather than by observance.

We neglect Baptism and we cosset the child. When I think of the decay of interest in Baptism alongside of the unprecedented interest which the modern world, and especially the present century, has in the child, more suggestions crowd in on me than there is place for here. Many of the child-lovers are among the careless about Baptism. This is only one of several current indications how the cult of the child in the Church may destroy the worship of the Gospel; how natural religion drives out spiritual, and especially evangelical. I have been at many Sunday School anniversaries, and I have found the same thing shown; when all the singing, even of the morning service, was on these occasions given up to children's, not to say babies', hymns, with music to correspond, while Baptism was of little moment, or was hidden away in the home.

It is so easy to let a precious rite die, and it is so hard to restore it. It is dropped through misconception or indifference, and it can only be restored by something so hard as the revival of principle, something like a Reformation or a Revolution, the renewal of conviction and the return of earnestness not in one or a few but in a whole community.

If we probed the reasons for the different treatment of the two Sacraments, we should probably be told that people feel they get good from the Communion in which they partake, but they do not feel that they get any special benefit from being present at Baptism. They just make a "house." It is like a Mass to a Protestant eye, where the congregation are simply spectators. They say it is really their act in the one case; it is not in the other. This is a point which I will deal with later.

Some again will say that, so far as they can see, the child gets no good from Baptism either. There is no difference in after life between baptized children and non-baptized. But I do not believe that it makes no difference to a child's growth whether it be regarded as a child of the Church or not. If it do make no difference, that is a censure on the Church. The Church should see that it does, and that what is begun in Baptism is completed in vital membership. Baptism is at least a formal introduction of the child to these influences of a loving Church and a Church of grace which are meant to surround the growing life with a Christian atmosphere of sympathy and instruction. And it should be easier to grow up a Christian inside the Church than outside of it as so many children are.

Is it not the case that many of the things that are of most value to us are done for us (and done by us even) before we are able to appreciate their value? This is true of all our earliest education. We were made Britons by an act we do not remember—our birth into a British home and tradition—which we certainly did not make, whether we think of our home or of our country. And is it not true of our very Redemption itself? Was it not done for us ages before we were born—God calling things that were not as though they were? If you object that Baptism can mean nothing to the child because he knows nothing of it, must you not object that the Cross means nothing to him because, while he was even without life, Christ died for his ungodliness? Yet to remember and take home the Cross is salvation. And to remember our Baptism and what it means would be a great means of grace if we would seriously use it, and if parents would periodically recall it. The following illustration has been given.

"A child receives, when an infant, a gift from some loving friend—a Bible, say. It is of no immediate use to him. It will be some time before he can feel that it is a gift of love, a keepsake to be valued for the giver and his affection. But the child can ere long understand and feel this; and he will feel the giver's love with a certain inquisitive wonder because it was shown before he could value or use it. Instead of taking away from the gift, does it not enhance it to know that the giver cared so little for appreciation, and was so full of love, that his gift was not kept till it could be understood, but given long before, and as early as possible? So Baptism testifies of an overflowing love, what used to be called 'a prevenient grace,' that met us at the very outset of life, of a Saviour waiting for us thanklessly ever since we had a being." Let me put it differently. The child's grandmother makes him the common present of a christening mug, which he uses as soon as he begins to sit at table. For a long time it is taken as a matter of course, signifying nothing more than a pretty dish would. But a day comes when he begins to ask (if he has not often been told) who gave him the mug. He is answered that it was his grandmother, because she loved him as a child. "Where is she?" "She is dead. You can't remember seeing her." "And she loved me before I could speak?" "Yes." "As soon as I was born?" "Yes." So love comes home to the child as a beautiful thing, an unseen mysterious thing, a thing that was about his very beginning, and yet a thing that goes with him every day.

A later day comes perhaps when he is idly gazing into the water it holds. For the first time perhaps he dimly feels what poets write about the glamour in the heart of water. He feels the spell of it. Already he has felt how sweet it is to the thirsty, how good it is for cleanliness. If he then ask where it came from, he is told that what the mug holds did not come from the hand that gave it him, but from a higher hand, the same hand as sent grandma's love. So his thoughts are raised to the love from which love flows. And he is made to feel that that old, old love too was about his cradle, and meant to bless him, and to call him into the mystic society of Christian souls. The mug and its contents speak to him of something that knew him, chose him, blessed him, and transfigures life for him, just for love's sake, before he could make any return, or as much as say Thank you.

Let this be a parable. The gift of the mug is Baptism, the water is the Spirit of God in Baptism. The gift of love came to him before he could know, and its contents were meant to follow him all the days of his life, like the river which makes glad the City of God. And, as he grows in power to learn, and is truly taught, the primal gift is borne in on his soul with deeper suggestion. And as he sees other such gifts given, his childish associations with the gift expand into an adult sense of the preciousness of these prevenient boons. The tradition of unremembered things becomes a power over him that works mightily, and grows he knows not how. And, as his mature affection might tenderly prize his childhood's gift, so his man's faith, dwelling on his infant Baptism, finds it to broaden and deepen in spiritual suggestion, as the seal on him of God's watchful grace. It says to him, like an inverted psalm coming down from Heaven instead of rising from earth, "O child, thou art my child, early will I seek thee."

Again, some will say that there is so much superstition connected with baptismal regeneration that their gorge rises at the whole ceremony. Of course that is a wild revolt, whose logic means sweeping away both the Sacraments as well as the Church. You would abolish Communion because of the Mass. And you would desert the Church because the great Churches of history have offered such homes for what you call off-hand superstition. For Christ's treatment of superstition read Mark v. 25 ff.

And again some will say that it is not clear that Christ instituted Baptism. There is no distinct express foundation of it, as there is of the Lord's Supper. And "Jesus himself baptized not, but his disciples." The answer to that is that Christ submitted to Baptism, not as needing it, but to put Himself in order; in the order of redemption; that the disciples would not have baptized except at the Lord's wish; and it would not have been a rite of the very earliest Church in Jerusalem had it not been understood to be His will. We never hear of a Church without it, going back to the very contact with Christ Himself.

§

These are points I will deal with later. Here let me go back and speak to the objection of those who say they get good from Communion and none from Baptism, that they go from the one impressed and helped but not from the other. I am speaking chiefly to members of the Church, because the Sacraments belong to the Church. They are part of its trust from Christ. Their meaning is in its faith wholly. They are its badges. It is their trustee. And I answer this objection briefly by saying that membership of the Church means that you have passed into a higher stage than impressions. You leave to a casual public the kind of religion where everything turns on impressions, and people run after the preachers who produce them. You may welcome impressions, but they have ceased to be your guides, your principles of action, your supreme considerations. As a member of the Church you are guided by the will of Christ, the mind of the Spirit, the regeneration. Also as members you have assumed Church duties. You do not go to Church just for what you get by it, even in spiritual benefit. You have accepted Church trusts. You have to transmit to posterity the treasures of the Church preserved at the cost of thought, prayer, life, and suffering by those who passed them on to you. Among those treasures are the Sacraments. They are not the inventions of the Church, but gifts to the Church from Him who created it. They are second in value only to the Word of the Gospel itself. And together they mean more for the Church than anything else it does.

The Word and the Sacraments are the two great expressions of the Gospel in worship. The Sacraments are the acted Word—variants of the preached Word. They are signs, but they are more than signs. They are the Word, the Gospel itself, visible, as in preaching the Word is audible. But in either case it is an act. It is Christ in a real presence giving us anew His Redemption. The Sacraments used to be called seals. A seal is something distinctive of the person who uses it, and of an act of his. Being dead he yet speaks. It is not simply a sign or relic of him, which might be unconscious, unmeant, like his footprint or the smoke of his fire. It means an act in which he intends to convey *himself*, his mind, his will, his act.

The Sacraments are not only signs or symptoms, but deliberate seals of the loving will and work of Christ for us. They bring Him to the spot in His crucial significance. They are love-tokens to the Church—but love-tokens different, for instance, from a ring. The same ring might serve for a token between *any* lovers. It has nothing characteristic of either. But if it has a name and a motto on it, or if a lover compose a poem or a piece of music to his mistress, that conveys his inmost self, and is both a sign of love and a seal. It is much more than a memorial. A child again is not so much a sign of love as a seal of it, and a means of deepening it. In this sense the Sacraments are Christ's love-tokens to His Body, the Church. They not only suggest Him, but they convey Himself to the Church. They deepen the relation between them. They have a positive meaning which He intended. They are not accidental suggestions. They are connected with Him by much more than association. They are more than souvenirs, keepsakes. They are bequests. They are conveyances. And what they mean and bring is of the very essence of what He was and is and willed to be to the Church—its Redeemer and Sanctifier.

These love-tokens, these heirlooms, the Church has to guard and use. She has to keep them bright, and not by care only but by use. She must so use them that they shine with their message and not merely by a polish. Like rails, they gleam with traffic which carries value to the soul.

Every member of a Church has a duty by these Sacraments, apart from the personal religious profit they may bring him in a conscious way. To think always of that alone may be too egoist for Christian faith. We come together in Church not simply, nor indeed primarily, to get good from God, but to confess God, to aid the Church's worship, confession, and preaching of His grace. For each member the Sacraments are part of the confession. They are one way of owning and declaring the Church's word. Each member has to do his part to give them effect. He has to do his share in the Church's sacramental act as a worshipper—in the energy of common worship, and not as a spectator.

These Sacraments are not primarily *individual* acts. They are corporate acts, acts *of the Church*. It is the Church that does the sacramental act. Nay, more, they are the acts *of Christ* really present by His Holy Spirit in the Church. It is Christ doing something through the Church as His body. It is only after these two higher senses are met that they are the acts of an individual. In the Communion individual administration is against its nature. Baptism is not primarily an act of the parent nor of the child, but of the Church, and of Christ in the Church. It is our individualism that has done most to ruin the sacrament of Baptism among us. We get a wrong answer because we do not put the right question. We ask, What good does Baptism do me or that child? instead of, What is the active witness and service the Church renders to the active Word of Christ's Gospel in the Baptism of young or old? Baptism is not there primarily for the individual, nor for the family, but for the Church, to confess before God and man the Word of Regeneration. It is not a domestic occasion but an ecclesiastical. Like a great theology, or a great psalm, it belongs to the Church rather than to an individual. To claim private property in a hymn is to sell the Holy Spirit. Baptism, therefore, should not be private in the house but public in the Church.

And the next thing for the Christian, after taking his part in the act of his Church, after keeping its treasure intact and using it, is to see that it does not lose its meaning but remains rich for himself. If Baptism have no result for you who take part in it, is that not because you have somehow lost sight or sense of the truth for which Baptism stands—the cleansing of the soul not by a growth in purity simply but by the regeneration of the Holy Ghost, the baptism not into Christ merely but into Christ's death, not simply by self-sacrifice but by the burial with Him, and the rising with Him to newness of life?

§

You say perhaps that the children of believing parents need not be baptized at all. But is that not to say that the cleansing from sin and regeneration by the Spirit, which are symbolised in Baptism, are not needed by such children? If you believe they need such regeneration, and that the new life of the Spirit is not transmitted by natural parentage, why not use so expressive a symbol of it as Baptism, and one so impressive besides? You may of course prefer a Christianity which has no symbol at all, no sacrament, like the Society of Friends. Well, that raises another issue, and means parting with the Lord's Supper as well. I cannot pursue that issue here. I rather speak to those who do believe in so much symbolism, so much action, as may be in the Communion, but who treat Baptism less seriously than they do the Communion. To such I say Baptism is not a mere form. It is not just dedication. It is not an empty ceremony. It has a meaning, a Christian meaning, a church meaning. What is that meaning? It has a function. It is effective, it does something or conveys something. What is it? Well, among other things it means what I have said—that every soul needs, and may have, regeneration by the Spirit through the Church. Do you not hold with that? Is it not a Christian principle? It is a very central one if it is. And it deserves inculcation by the most impressive means we have.

Now there is no means that we have so impressive as this act of Baptism solemnly performed. It has the ritual impressiveness visible to the eye; it has the imaginative impressiveness of unbroken antiquity and universal use in the Church; and, above all, it has the spiritual impressiveness of coming from Christ Himself, and not only uttering Him but conveying Him to His people. Is it right, if we hold earnestly so great a truth, to let go such a powerful and effectual expression of it? If we do let it go, does that not really imply that we have let go the truth it so finely, simply, and solemnly enshrines? It signifies regeneration, but it does not mean that the rite regenerates the child. It does not even mean that the blessing to the child is at the same time as the rite. That blessing may come years after, as the Cross comes home to our experience—the Cross which blessed us before our very forefathers were born.

But, though its first bearing is not on its subject but on the Church, yet even for the child it means much. It does mean that the stamp of being God's property has been put on the child in a public way, that the child is not only publicly offered to God, but (much more) is openly claimed by God for a destiny of salvation, that he is born to be born again, that he is declared by right a citizen of the heavenly kingdom, that he is earmarked for faith and bespoken for Christ, that his Christian education is promised by the Church of his parents, and that he will be false to his best antecedents and his social committal if he do not become regenerated in the Holy Ghost. It is the sacrament of his future. It plants Christ with a claim and a boon on the threshold of his earliest past. If it have no effect on him, that is the fault of his Christian parents and teachers, who should often remind him of this spiritual adoption and explain it. It is meant to work in upon his Christian faith as it grows up in the Church, and to solemnise him with the thought that he is much more to God than just what he feels he is; he is for God all that he was claimed to be when Christ by His minister took him as an infant in His arms. The Duke of Buccleuch, at the unveiling of the Scott monument at Westminster many years ago, said he had spoken with Scott (perhaps been fondled by him), but it was before he could remember, and yet it was one of the great *memories* of his life. Baptism should not be less to any than that.

§

There are some to whom this may come whose early associations and sympathies are with adult Baptism. Now, to these, as a modern pædobaptist, I would make two great concessions. (The question of immersion matters nothing.) First, *there is no infant Baptism in the New Testament.* I mean in the *practice* of the New Testament. It is within the principle of the Gospel, but not in the New Testament use. It is so in every mission. And Christianity began as a mission. The New Testament Church *practice*, here as elsewhere, is that of a missionary Church. But its *principles* are those of a universal, settled, and triumphant Church. And when, early in its history, the practice of the Church changed to infant Baptism, it was not departing from New Testament principles. It was applying them in a changed way to changed conditions—especially such a principle as the sanctity of the children of the children of the saved (1 Cor. vii. 14).

I think we have the advantage of the Baptists in this respect. We can recognise that their Baptism is right in certain circumstances, and to express certain aspects of Christian truth. But they cannot, at least they do not, recognise that ours is right as the consequence and expression of certain other Christian principles no less true. I think either may be justified, and has its right in the Church. But it is much gained when we agree to recognise that the *practice* of the first Church is one thing, and the *principle* of that Church is another. And the question must be settled by the meaning of Baptism in Christian principle, by the theology of Baptism, not by ritual precedent, not by the canonised usage of the Church at any time, which is not sacrosanct. If it were, there would be no divine form of the Church but the New Testament polity. And, if it were, also, perhaps, we ought to make a real meal of the Communion, and recline to it. (Reclining in the one case is what immersion is in the other.) A Baptism *unto* the confession of the Church faith may be as true to the Gospel Grace as a Baptism *upon* it, and less individualist.

The second concession I make to the Baptists is that *every infant Baptism should also be sympathetically an adult Baptism.* The Baptism of every infant should be a renewed Baptism for every adult present. Every baptized adult should feel it a Christian duty and happiness to be present —certainly every professed member of the Church. And it should be an occasion when they go back to the meaning of their own Baptism, and ask themselves whether it was an empty form or the hand of Christ laid on them by the long, long arm of the Church to claim them for a regenerate destiny. They should examine themselves how far they have kept the faith for which they were claimed, and have cleaved to the Cross by which they were bought. They were claimed and set apart as Christ's in Baptism by Christ's Church in His behalf. Have they continued Christ's? Has the Baptism gone in on them? Have they changed the Baptism of water for the Baptism of the Holy Ghost? Has the innocence of their infancy passed into the moral purity of the mature? Has the water turned spirit and fire? It is a time when the Baptism once performed is renewed in spirit, when the committal act is repeated in detail. In the Baptism of the infant the sympathetic Church confesses its regenerative faith, and is rebaptized in soul. Baptism does not mainly concern the child or parents, I repeat. It is an act principally for the Church. The whole Church in faith and spirit enters the cleansing stream. It revives by faith its sense of the new and eternal life of forgiveness. It measures its own faithfulness to its regenerative redemption. It makes profession by Baptism of its faith in the New Creation. It utters its repentance. And it resolves anew, prays anew, to be faithful to the end, to keep and renew its Baptism till death.

In this high, true, practical sense the whole Church of the baptized undergo adult Baptism at each infant Baptism. They go through consciously what they were put through unconsciously at the first. They are not *spectators* of a Baptism—they *assist*. And they do not only assist, they *participate* in the Baptism. They are baptized anew of the Holy Ghost. They undergo the true Baptism without hands which the outward signifies. They *take up* their own Baptism, as you might take up actually a citizenship, or a freedom, long yours by right.

§

Can it be doubted that the true Christian idea of Baptism is what I say? It is a truth beneath even the errors of the baptismal regenerationists that it is an act of the Church, and of the Spirit through the Church, that it is an act which is at least shared by others than the child and the parents. Well, if it be an act of the Church, must not the Church be there to perform it? Ought the Church to depute and leave not only the agency but the whole act to the minister? Somebody of course must be deputed to conduct the proceedings, and perform the visible deed. But the spiritual act—is that to be turned over completely to the minister? If that is done, the minister is no more a minister. He is a priest. He not only acts on behalf of the Church, but he acts instead of the Church. This is done in home Baptism, where, except the minister, only relatives are present, and no Church members as such. He is supposed to perform the act and administer the Sacrament just as effectively when the Church is not there as when it is there. The Church then voluntarily gives up its own prerogative to a deputy, and the Sacrament ceases to be a Sacrament at all. You object to the priest turning his back to the people in the Mass. Why not object equally to the people turning their back to the minister in Baptism by leaving the service? Is it not parallel? You say, when you see the priest going through all the ritual of the Mass with his back to the people, that this is an insult to the Church, a robbery of the Church in its rights. You say bluntly (whether rightly or not) that the Church which tolerates that has lost its Christian self-respect, its duty to itself as the trustee of Christ's Grace. It ought to assert itself against such proxies and monopolies. It is not the priest but the Church that is the trustee of the Word and of the Sacraments. It is the Church, not its minister, that performs that. Well, that is a mote; what about the beam?

If you think this (rightly or wrongly) about the Church which allows the priest to turn his back upon it in the Sacrament, what ought you to say about the Church which turns its back upon the minister when he faces them with its own Sacraments? In the Mass the faithful are at least required to be there a certain number of times. And the priest might plead that they were all facing one way, all engaged in some way in the same act of worship, and that his back meant no more than the back of the person in the pew in front of you, or the back of the officer turned to the troops he leads. But what would be said of the Church that turned from the priest at the altar, and occupied itself with the tracery of the west window? What would further be said of the Church which, when the minister faced them with the Word of God in his trust in its sacrament form, turned round and left the building? I am not speaking of manners but of something far more serious, not of the disrespectful treatment by the Church of its minister, but of the treatment by the Church of the Word of God for which Church and minister stand. Might it not be said that it was a Church that had lost faith in God's Word of Gospel, lost its self-respect, lost its sense of duty to hear and profit by the Word, its duty to be critical and see that it was the true, pure Word that was preached? It is the Church's duty, in our belief, to see that its ministers deal truly and faithfully with God's Word of Grace. And that is a Word which is as really in the Sacraments as in the sermons. And, so far as the Church is concerned, it is, in a way, more in the Sacraments than in the sermons, because the audible preaching is largely the minister's act, especially in its form, and it reflects his idiosyncrasy (which may dim the truth as well as wing it); but the Sacrament, the declaring the Word in that visible shape, is chiefly the venerable and unchanging act of the Church, in a form mainly prescribed, massive, and historic. It is "the utterance of the community, to which the minister does but lend his voice." The minister's personality goes for little in such a rite. He need make no address. He simply acts for the Church gathered round him. He is its hand and voice. But he cannot feel that he is that if the Church be mainly absent. The hand is severed from the body. The voice is a thin, disembodied voice, a mere ventriloquism. Baptism is the Church's act, and, if the Church is not there, the act falls to the ground as a Sacrament.

Well, as I say, you think it serious enough when the priest in the Sacrament is allowed to turn his back on the Church. But at least the presence of the people behind him shows that the Church has enough sense of its own calling left to believe in the Sacrament, however wrongly conceived. But, when the Church turns its back on the act altogether, on its own act, that is much more serious. It shows that the idea of a Sacrament has been abandoned by the Church, that its Sacraments are on the way to becoming a priestly monopoly, or else a mere rite, that the Church surrenders its trust from Christ to guard the purity and reality of His Word spoken or seen. It is a more faithful thing to Christ to maintain a form of Sacrament which is wrong than to let His cause go and His command fail by renouncing Sacraments altogether. And, when a Church does that, has it any right to the name of a Church? At any rate, a Church may survive with power errors about its Sacraments as tremendous as those of Rome, but neglect, starvation, and renunciation of Sacraments the Church cannot survive. It cools, dwindles, fumbles, and dies. "It is not the omission but the contempt of the Sacraments that kills," the Reformers said. In our principle the minister has really no right to administer Baptism except as the organ and agent of the Church. But, if the Church leave him, and a deacon or two, and a few women and children whose chief interest is the baby, to do it, how can he be said to be the Church's agent, except in the sense in which the priest is the agent of a Church whose Sacraments he performs equally well whether the people are present or not? It is the negligent Church that forces ministers to be priests far more than ambitious ministers that force the Church to make them priests.

If a Church should agree to reduce the Sacraments from two to one, if it consented to cease regarding Baptism as a Sacrament, if it treated it as a mere domestic dedication by parents, and not as a visible declaration of the Word and Gospel of Christ's regeneration by a Church—then it would have taken a very grave step, and one that cuts it off from the concert of the Catholic Evangelical Church. But at least it would know what it was doing, and be acting from a conviction, however mistaken. But to regard Baptism as a Sacrament, as a visible preaching of the historic Word of regeneration, as a prime part, therefore, of a Church's existence and work, and yet to retire almost wholly when Baptism is administered—is a far more grave and compromising step. The other might be a heresy, but this runs some risk of becoming a hypocrisy.

§

I would make most of the Sacraments because of their *right* within the Church as Christ's will, and, at their centre, Christ's act—the act of the Church's indwelling Christ. But I would also make much of them because of their *value* to the Church. I do not mean because of their value in themselves. They have no magical value—they are not fetish—but because of their value for the reality of Church life and its Gospel Word. I would do a great deal if I could to carry home the reality of Church life. I would make it as real in its place as our family life. I would have a house chosen not for its garden but for its proximity to a real Church and pulpit. I welcome anything that gives the Church definite rallying-points, points of attachment, practical expression, union in distinct and common acts. You often hear it said that to unite a Church it should be active, it should do something, it should multiply its agencies, its forms of well-doing. Well, these are very useful. How could we live without them? How much does the Church not owe to its workers? Every minister leans on them. But we have been perhaps expecting more from these things in this way than we can get. A multitude of agencies and societies tends sometimes to dissipate a Church's unity.

How often has a Church been rent because of differences with or between some of its working sections, which have drawn away sympathy from the Church? The editor of the *Missionary Record of the United Free Church of Scotland*, in an article a few years ago entitled "An Overworked Ministry," said:—"Among thoughtful laymen there is a growing conviction that the ministry of the Church occupies a false position; that it has gone too far in the direction of becoming a universal cure-all agency, and that we shall have to come back to a simpler and higher conception of the office. The ministry is not meant to be a social and philanthropic institution, to organise and run all kinds of movements and campaigns for the external reform of mankind. It is intended to be the soul of the world, not its arms and feet; an inspirer, a teacher, a healer, not an engineer. What one desires to see is the ministry relieved of the wrong work, and switched on to its proper work. It would find enough, and more than enough, to occupy its highest activities in this direction."

At present, according to this critic, its real and distinctive duties (like missions) are being inadequately performed, with the result that the Church is, on its own showing, on the downgrade. And it was complained, in one address from the Chair of the Congregational Union, that work has become feverish and distracting in its spiritual result by being overdriven, and by being trusted for spiritual effects it cannot give. Do not most of the perils to Church unity, most of the misunderstandings, arise out of what is secondary in the Church, its work, and not out of what is primary, its faith and worship? Does that not mean that the Church has come to treat the secondary thing as primary, and to lose faith, love, and worship in work? We have come to think religious work a spiritual act, which it often is not. And we have treated the chief act of the Church as otiose. Is he not a dangerous person in a Church's real life who has abounding energy but no quiet joy in worship, no repose of faith, no belief, because no experience, that a man's most taxing and fruitful energy is prayer?

The focus of a Church's unity, the outward focus, I mean, is truly enough some action in which the Church unites. But I desire to recall attention to the fact that the rallying acts of a Church are its worship, and especially its Sacraments, that these active centres have been provided by God as the supreme common acts of the Church. We do something in them. They are active centres of union in which all may and must partake, whereas all cannot do Church work. They are not sectional, they are not simply for those in the Church who may be disposed that way. They are the acts of the whole Church; they are organic with the great work of Redemption which made the Church. And they are the condensed, compendious, and practical confession of the vast principles, powers, and truths on which the Church lives and rests. There is no other symbol, for instance, which so expresses, like the act of Baptism, the unity of the whole Church in the regenerated life of its Head. Churches so far from us as the Roman Catholic yet recognise the validity of Protestant Baptism.

§

Baptism, as a Sacrament of the Church, is an act of the Church. I am pressing that now from this point of view. Those who do remain seem at times to regard themselves as spectators more that partakers of what is done. They stand by, but they do not assist. But how are they to assist? By making it an act of worship. By using the time in the way I have said, by renewing the sense of their own Baptism, by submitting themselves anew to the washing of the Spirit, by accepting anew the cleansing of forgiveness, by passing the time in an inward, spiritual, silent energy following the form of worship used.

Do not treat yourselves as spectators. Do not behave as if curiosity were uppermost in you. Do not make it evident that your chief desire is to see what goes on, to watch the behaviour of minister, mother, or child. Make it an act of worship. View what is done with the quiet sense that it is done also by you, that it is *your* minister, *your* agent, *your* representative who is doing this in your name, on your behalf, giving outward effect to what is really your corporate act. Tell yourself plainly that it is nobody's fault but your own if the occasion is empty of spiritual meaning, seriousness, and blessing to you. Take up your own Baptism by a spiritual assimilation. Do not by levity repudiate it. Own that it was the hand of God's love that was laid on you before you knew, and drew you into His Kingdom. Confess your citizenship of that Kingdom. Praise God that it is yours, that it once came to you individually, and made an inextinguishable claim to your individual soul. Confess how you have neglected it. Beg God to renew in you the Holy Ghost, to wash you in His cleansing grace, to unite you with the family in Heaven and on Earth. If you spend the time in that way, it is time redeemed.

CHAPTER X

NEW TESTAMENT BAPTISM

Faith's prime answer to the Gospel in a Church is worship, which is an act, a corporate act, which culminates in Sacraments. Each Sacrament confesses the whole Gospel and not an aspect of it. Faith in Christ *in the same act* commits us to a community into which the Sacraments articulate us. Baptism more than mere reception, as birth is more than a new unit added to the census. The moral nature of baptismal grace. Serious lack of theological adjustment when Baptism (originally adult only) was transferred to children. Baptism shows that the Sacraments flowed from the nature of the Gospel working in a Church more than from formal institution. But if the Word mean everything, why Sacraments at all? The Sacraments are specific functions of the Word, but not generically different. The psychology of the New Testament Baptism, and the facilities it gave for a theosophic interpretation. Baptism is a function of the Church more than of the recipient. It is done by the Church, it happens to the man. The gift in Word and Sacrament is the same. Does Baptism regenerate in any sense? It is more than a *That-predigt*. Sacraments necessary for the life of the Church but not for individual salvation. Baptism the Sacrament of the new birth and new life.

THE prime response of a Church to the Word of grace which creates it is worship. Free grace means free worship, rich grace full worship. But, as grace is God's eternal Act, and not merely His standing disposition nor an exhibition of it, so worship is an act even more that a word or a mood. The worshipping Church is not a group of people bringing to God a common temper, or developing a common frame of pious mind. In its nature it is action. The greatest thing man can *do* is to worship. It is responsive action. To confess to God a living Faith in His grace is man's greatest possible work: and, above all else that He desires, the Father seeketh such to worship Him. Hence the Church's faith meets the gift of grace by certain acts of worship congenial to it, and, within these, by certain more special acts, called Sacraments. These also are thought of as God's gift, because they are stirred or created by *the* gift of grace. For the Church's due cohesion as an active body it needs its Sacraments. They belong to it as they do not to the individual. They consummate its action towards God, and they consecrate and inspire its action towards man. They are not individual acts, valuable only as they do us sensible good. They are acts of the Church; nay, more, they are acts of Christ in His Church. They are functions of His Act of the Cross taken as a real Act no less than a supreme. And by a real Act I mean one supremely effective on God, the last Reality. Their place in other worship corresponds to the place of the Cross in the entire action of Christ.

All I am about to say is not only quite obscure but it falls to pieces if the Cross be but the last chapter in Christ's teaching, if it be but the great object-lesson of love, or the classic case of sacrifice or martyrdom. It is meaningless if the work of Christ culminating on the Cross be but affecting. If it is but a piece of religious impressionism, acting but on us, as the misnamed "moral" view of the Atonement says, then a sacrament like the Lord's Supper can be no more than a memorial of the like impressive kind, and need not be different from a good prayer meeting. There is no real meaning in Baptism, however impressive Christ may be, if He be not regenerative, if it means that we are to be but moved by the Spirit, and not born again.

We should remember all this specially in connection with Baptism, where the subjectivity and humanism of the day tempt us to think more of the child, or of the family, than of the Church as the centre of Christian action and interest. The natural affections take precedence of the gracious, and we found on sympathy rather than on penitence or rebirth. But the Baptism that Christ met and took from John made the divine call a call to repentance and regeneration; it was no mere consecration either of childhood, or family affection, or patriotism. And the message was not a cry only but also an act; and an act must answer it. Those who obeyed in kind God's act in this call were united not by a vague spirit of obedience, nor by a wave of sympathy, nor even by a mere feeling of repentance, but by a deed, by something ethical and not æsthetic, something imperative and not optional. The sinful state was abandoned by what was an act, and not a mood, nor a ceremony. Sin is action, and action is its cure. Jesus saw in John's Baptism both the divine judgment on sin and the divine forgiveness—each equally in its nature an act—both indeed one Act, as the Cross was to show. The decision John called for was more explicit, more positive than the response of a mere inward frame of mind is apt to be. And when Baptism became Christian it kept all that active and positive significance, and added to it. But it was an act now not of hope but of faith, not of a kingdom coming but of a kingdom come, not of an ideal expected but of a reality given, and now to be used. It attached the soul to Christ by a real and final committal. By its act it placed the believer in the organic fellowship of Christ's Act, and the enjoyment of Christ's corporate work and boon. From a disciple he became a member. Not only was Christ in him, but he was in Christ.

§

One meaning of this is that Baptism, like the Lord's Supper, declared and enacted the whole Gospel, and not merely an initiatory stage of it. It was not a single grace that was given in it, the grace suitable for beginners, but the whole grace of God as regenerative. It opened to the soul the whole treasury of Christ; therefore it did not need to be repeated. The rest of life was but living it out. After the morning bath we need during the day but the detail of it in a wash (John xii. 10). Baptism conveyed all that Christ brought by His Cross in its regenerative aspect. It sealed a man to be not an apostle, teacher, ruler, or the like, but that new creature—a Christian. He had part and lot in Christ's death, Resurrection, and Eternal life. The Church baptized into Christ's death, into a critical repentance due to that crucial Act, into a whole regeneration, into the life of the Spirit. When the new birth ceases to be part of our Christian experience and speech, this Sacrament at least must disappear—along with positive faith. And it cannot be denied that such is the tendency.

With the disappearance from religious speech of a term like regeneration there coincides the decay of Baptism except as a family occasion, which is no Sacrament at all. It was into the Cross, observe, that the Church baptized, into Christ's death; it was not (in the Gospel records) into some participation, by the subliminal soul, of Christ's glorified and celestial body in a superphysical way. It was *holy* Baptism, *i.e.* a Baptism affecting the soul and conscience of a moral being, by God's moral action in Christ, and applied by a society made entirely by that mystically moral bond. Therefore it was not a single grace but a central that was conveyed. It was not a baptismal grace alongside other gifts. The Spirit was not one gift among many. It was the power of the whole Gospel for the whole man, nay, of the whole God, as it is in the name of Father, Son, and Holy Ghost. Its bearing, therefore, is not on certain sins, not on past or "original" sin by nature's entail, but upon all that soils the soul and severs us from God, or may so sever us. It does not simply wash away; it floods with new life. It is not negative for the cleansing of the soul but positive for the gift of the Holy Ghost, and union with Christ in His life as well as in His death. It stirs not repentance only but living faith, and makes of these one act, as a Baptism into the One Cross must. It carries in its full forgiveness an eternal life. It regards the whole soul in its whole destiny—in its past, present, and future. It does not need, as I say, to be repeated; and there could be no talk of any succedaneum if the sacramental grace were lost.

In New Testament Baptism this whole Gospel, this whole Saviour given to the Church, is detailed by it, as His trustee, to each soul. There is a personal assignment of it, and a conscious appropriation. The act does not simply extend the Church roll by one, but it so grafts the one into the organism of the society that he is reared in that home to a true, new, and social person. The faith that unites us with Christ *in the same act* commits us to His community. It does something not only altruistic but social. It has therefore moral effect. It is not an empty rite of the Church, but a real act; for it is Christ's act even more than the Church's. The grace, the gift is to a Church. The boon given is collective; it is individualised to each soul by the Spirit. It is the solidary boon to all; and it becomes ours only as we unite with all. So that what arises from such faith and its action is not an ecclesiastical institution but a living society; it is certainly not a clerical compound. It is a society whose life is in the new life of all its members in the Holy Spirit.

To treat Baptism as a mere ceremony of reception into the Church and of addition to its roll does what its treatment as a mere dedication of an infant also does—it destroys it as a Sacrament. In the New Testament it was a personal matter—as individual as birth must be. And therefore it is a matter of conscience, and conscience before God, Who takes the real initiative. It involves the whole issue of guilt and its consequences, forgiveness and its conditions, the Spirit and His creative renewals. It raised such issues, according to the New Testament, and it answered them; bringing, by the grace of it, an overwhelming sense of personal repentance, breach with sin, and committal to Christ—all we most deeply mean by personal faith. It is realising this that really places a man in the true Church, which is the living company and organism of all such believers created anew; it is not a mere institution well officered and well found.

The perversions of Baptism have been said to take two main directions. On the one hand it drops to mere symbolism, on the other to mere magic. (We leave out of account its treatment as a bare memorial.) As a symbol it is but the parable of an idea. Its use is as a lesson, a piece of Christian instruction. As magic, on the other hand, it is but a rite, where attention is fixed on sensible elements and potent words on which an occult process entirely depends. Both views are not only inadequate but wrong. They are false to the genius of Christianity. It was not with Christian truth that Christ met the sin of the world, but with a saving Deed of mercy. It was not with doctrine He came, but with power. He did not preach about sin; He forgave. Nor did He glorify liberty. He redeemed. And His act is met by ours in kind. "The baptized does not exhibit repentance; he repents. Nor does he devise a symbol of God's acceptance of him; he trusts it. He does not reflect on God's call; he obeys it; and he finds the great call in the message of grace." Baptism is not a small miracle-play for didactic effect, but a real act, an act of will; an act of preaching and conveyance on the one side, of worship and confession on the other.

So also in regard to the magical tendency. We have no concern with a corporeal substratum involved in the act, the substratum of either the water or of the soul. There is nothing theurgic, nothing conjured. "Jesus did not mean us to believe in the water, but in Himself. The act of washing was not the Act of reconciliation, it only belonged to it." And Schlatter points out effectively that when attention goes to the element there is a disintegration both of the soul and of the gift of Grace. "Baptism then goes not to us but to some 'nature' in us where the regenerative germ is deposited, some soul-substance which is sublimated in the act—all being foreign categories, foreign to the Gospel, to the whole nature of Father, Son, and Holy Ghost, and their personal relation in the fulness of Grace." The whole living man lays hold of the whole living God. It is not a manipulation of our "nature,"[1] but a regeneration of *us* by hope and faith.

§

I shall have to enlarge later on the fact that we have originally, in the New Testament, only adult and believers' Baptism. It became infant Baptism at a later stage. And the huge mistake made was this—that things moral, things possible and true only for the adult experience, were transferred to the unconscious child, and thus became magic. The error was hurried on by the tendency which had grown up in the interval to treat the sacramental gift as something in the nature of an infused substance or stream or virtue. This meant the materialising of grace. The water absorbed and conveyed to the soul heavenly powers. Nature was renovated by a finer nature. And we have then not the supernatural but only the supernal, the preternatural. To treat the gift in a Sacrament as a commodity is to reproduce in that region the same fallacy which is costing us so much in economics, the fallacy of treating labour as a commodity which can be detached from the personal relations of employer and employed and from the moral nature of their co-operation.

[1] Nature is not a scriptural word, nor even a religious. And it is a point of philosophic discussion whether a personality has a "nature".

It was the essence of the Reformation to discard this pagan idea of grace. Grace was not an infusion of vital substance or supernal influence, but it was a relation of active persons. It was a moral thing and not a physical. It was mercy and not magic. It was not virtue going into us; it was the gracious will of the God of love acting on the soul, and (as He is the *holy* God) centrally on the moral soul, acting, through the Church's faith, as a felt forgiveness and a power for goodness. But the child could not experience grace as a conscious man could. He could not have faith. So baptismal grace in any moral sense was impossible. In Lutheranism, as in Anglicanism, there remained a survival of Catholicism, and Baptism became spiritual inoculation, a transfusion, and not a regeneration by the Spirit. There was postulated some refined physical action of God's rare Spirit on the soul. Even the old Protestant theologians spoke of a "heavenly material" in Baptism joined with water in "sacramental union," and effective in, with, and under the element. It was the same idea as in the consubstantiation of the other Sacrament. The desire was to bring both under one sacramental idea. Children were supposed to secure in Baptism the seed of the Spirit, as in the Eucharist the adult received a spiritual food or an elixir of immortality. But, as this seed could strike and fructify only by faith, a subconscious faith was postulated in the child, to obviate the idea of a mere *opus operatum*. An inchoate faith was supposed to be created by Baptism in the child. The thing was, of course, inconceivable, but it was believed in as a theological necessity. Besides, it ought to be there in advance, to make the Sacrament effectual on Protestant principles. Even to-day Lutheranism (like some Anglicans) talks so. Even Frank does. And the tendency was aided by the romantic, mystic theosophy of Schelling.

The fallacy was that, as in the New Testament Baptism meant the adult's regeneration (in a sense I shall describe later), it did so also when transferred to the child. And indeed, if in the New Testament the sacramental effect was magical and unconscious (as the Catholic interpretation is) and the moral man was passive, then it might act on the child as on the man. Regeneration would then mean providing the soul with latent possibility instead of bringing it into a new personal relation. The power, the seed, might slumber in the soul till maturity; or it might come to nothing, like many seeds. If a subconscious faith was too much, it was thought that without that postulate, and by the germ theory, the immediate value of Baptism for the child might be saved.

Our clue in traversing such an obscure region is this. It is the simplifying principle that the spiritual virtue of a Sacrament is not drawn from the ethereal action of the Word made flesh for us, but from the moral action of the Word made sin for us, and unto us righteousness, and from the social action of the Word made Church. That is the only body of Christ that concerns us much now, and that rests on the moral miracle of all miracles—the Son made sin for us, that we might be made righteousness in Him. The miracle of the Incarnation is not the Word made flesh but the Holy made sin for us. The whole Logos theology has done much to injure a true doctrine of the Spirit, to remove the centre of Christ's concern from a moral act to a spiritual process, and to interpret the spiritual as mind supremely reasonable or (as in the Sacraments) matter supremely rarefied. This has kept the Atonement as a moral power out of the hegemony of Christian doctrine in the Catholic tradition, and therefore the moral out of control of Christian life.

§

There is a considerable modification of the Catholic and magical view in the minds of many, and of some who think they hold the true Catholic position. They say that the Sacraments open the door for the life of Christ to flow into us. The "life" here they do not care to define. It means just the supernatural personality of Christ. The idea is that personality is the highest possible category, to which action is a subordinate thing. Religion is repose in a person, or reception of Him, rather than active union in kind with the mystic but moral Act in which He exists. The language used seems to hold that the death of Christ was but the closing experience of His personality, and not the act in which its whole life, power, and purpose was gathered up. Whereas the evangelical position is the latter. Redemption is a higher category than personality, since it gives personality its effect. Christ came to redeem, which He could only do by His Incarnation; He did not come to be incarnate, and incidentally to redeem.

The Roman or the Chalcedonian type of doctrine begins with the Incarnation, beyond experience but believed on authority, and then it descends on the Atonement; instead of beginning with the Atonement, in a moral departure, and going on from that experience to the Incarnation, since God only could atone. But between this and the evangelical position there is sought a *via media* which claims to be both evangelical and catholic. A *via media* is good tactics, but it is a bad foundation. Yet a *via media* is the ground taken by those who are engrossed with the Person of Christ as the Son of God in Whom we mystically live, but who do not give a first and crucial place to the New Creation in the Cross as the source of our life and the sum and crown and key of all the Person was. Christ is our food rather than our new Creator.

This removes the energetic, crucial, and tragic note from faith. It removes from it the moral dynamic. And when applied to the Sacraments it takes their special value away; for the mystic life of Christ (if that is all) can flow in at any opening of prayer, and any devout address. It reduces them to psychic or mystic experiences rather than moral acts, and to experiences individual rather than collective. There is nothing then to differentiate the Sacraments from other acts of worship. And the end is that of Quakerism; whose abolition of Sacraments is not unconnected with its purely mystic relation to Christ, and its shyness (to say the least) of any objective and crucial value in the Atonement for a faith which is not only rapt or solemn but above all holy.

§

It is a wrong method to start from a foregone idea of a Sacrament and make each conform. Perhaps the two Sacraments will not fall under one idea. It is said sometimes that a Sacrament has two conditions: first, it was instituted by Christ; and second, it uses a sensible sign for a spiritual meaning. But as to Baptism, the former condition is not nearly so clear as with the other sacraments.[1] And as to the second, the preaching of the Word does the same—only substituting the ear for the eye.

Let us begin rather from the work of Christ, which is the effective thing both in Him and in His Sacraments, the point where all begins and all takes order. Let us begin with the New Covenant, with which Christ was more concerned than with either Church or Sacrament. It is forgiveness to the conscience of the race, and the gift therein of a new and eternal life for the race, which, by its foundation in forgiveness, must be ethical in its nature, however mystic in its movement. As man Christ offers obedience to God on the scale of the race, atones for man, and is the ground of forgiveness; as God He acts creatively and royally in man, forgiving and creating life, and faith, and love. The two sides to the New Covenant are in a moral relation. The Atonement which founded it is the greatest moral act known, or possible, in the world.

The work of Christ produced a Church in kind, to work out in history His finality in principle, and to complete His creative perfection, as He Himself grew in the perfection which was always His. And this the Church did chiefly by the moral method of preaching the collective Gospel, the world Gospel, especially to individuals. The individualising Spirit in the Church details to our souls the double gift complete in Christ—forgiveness and regeneration. These

[1]Unless we take Matthew xxviii. 19 as its institution by the risen Christ (and a participial clause seems a very small apex on which to balance such a pyramid), Baptism was instituted by the ascended Christ through the Apostles as His will for the Church. It was not, like the Supper, expressly set up by the earthly Jesus. But He let His disciples do it. And if He instituted it through the very first Church, it was still His institution, especially as it must have attached to words or acts of His earthly life. They could not have given it the place they did without good footing in His wishes while He moved among them. Mark xvi. 16 is not genuine. Paul and the Acts know only of Baptism into the name of Christ, not of the Trinity. It will much clear our way if we recognise that *the Sacraments are valid not chiefly because they were instituted by the command of Christ, but because they arise from the nature of His Gospel in the Church.* And there is nothing in that Gospel that prescribes but two, or fetters the discretion of the Church in the matter.

are taken home by faith. But not by way of private bargain—which ignores the corporate nature of the gift. And not in a time succession—as if there were first a formal faith, which then was rewarded and filled with the new life. That is not the connection. Real forgiving is in the same act quickening and regenerating. Faith *is* Salvation; it is not rewarded with Salvation. To be forgiven much is to love much, which is to live much and live anew. The new life is the faith which constantly takes home forgiveness, regeneration, reconciliation, and all they imply for the heart. We may distinguish an outer side and an inner, God's act and the effect in us. And the inner side, the experience, is either regeneration or conversion, according as we think, theologically, of the action of God, or, psychologically, of the experience of men.

§

But now, if the same complete and double gift of forgiveness and eternal life was given both by the Word and by the Sacrament, what was the difference? Why Baptism?

The difference is not material but formal. It is not that there is a material entity conveyed by Baptism and lacking to the Word. The power in the Word and the Sacrament is the same. Yet the one does not just take the place of the other. For the New Testament the effect of Baptism (being only adult) presupposes the action of the Gospel and the Spirit; it comes at a certain stage of that action and its experience, and it works on it. The Sacrament does not produce saving grace, since it is effective only for the faith which that grace alone can produce. The soul is prepared by the Word for Baptism, but Baptism opens up the understanding of the Word in a never-to-be-forgotten experience. The effect is psychological.

In what sense then can we say that Baptism conveys the Gospel gift? Why not avoid the magical dangers by using the Word of the Gospel alone? Well, what was done in the first Church? The catechumens were taught about Christ, and the Gospel, and its blessings. These were the rudiments (Hebrews vi. 12). Do not think that the rule was for Baptism immediately to follow conversion. At the very first, and with a mass enthusiasm, that was so, perhaps, till the real nature of Baptism found its feet—as the "gift of tongues" also settled down. Then an intervening instruction was given. The Gospels may have been drawn up for such a purpose. And the Epistles presuppose such preparation. It did not mean mere instruction, but also impression, and the elementary culture of the Christian type of experience, schooling the sense of God, guilt, grace, forgiveness, and consecration. But there was need of a specific act which sealed and clinched all this in a personal way, by a formal and overt committal of the catechumen to membership of the new people of God.

There was need of an act of naturalisation into the Kingdom of God. Such was Baptism. It was a public act of a very solemn kind for one whose new experience had already keyed him to a high spiritual pitch. It was a public life-committal and confession of the yoke of Christ, amid circumstances of solemn excitement which crystallised all the prior discipline in a soul's life-bond. It clinched the relation. The engaged to Christ should be married. The previous instruction, the personal dealings of the older Christians, and the gracious movements of the neophyte soul—all worked up to a definite public act. They were gathered to a burning point of open decision on a high-wrought occasion, in an age when such a confession meant no small courage, and peril. There was final committal. The soul entered into life possession of what it had before but known or felt. The smouldering tinder burst into flame. The effect of such an individual act, in a sympathetic society, on a solemn occasion, was great, decisive, fundamental. But it was not magical. It did not depend on learning, owning, or hearing certain forms of words. It was psychological. It was a crucial experience in the spirit. It was the moral crisis, in a loving and spiritual society, of a psychological preparation maturing at a solemn moment which settled all the rest of life. It was the work of the Spirit. And it was led up to by all that had gone before, and sealed in great effect by the imposition of hands kind and holy, and by prayer, in the visitation of the Spirit, for the permanent gift of the Holy Ghost.

It is not hard to realise how elated, momentous, and final such an occasion must have been, how it released and how it braced the soul, and not the soul of the recipient alone, but of the Church more active still. Yet it was not a case of being hypnotised by suggestion; that would not be the result of preparation by Christian truth with its moral genius and effect. Keep thinking of the huge effect on a catechumen so severed from the world of a solemn act on him by the whole Church at the hands of an apostle or other representative of the community. There was (if one might so say) a settlement of the new order into the soul with a click, which at once steadied all and started all running free. The mixture set. Or, if we change the figure again, the bud burst with the public confession. Or, if we use another figure still, the truth he had learned glowed with the current and was fused up into a constituent of his soul. The Christian man slipped out of his youth. Maturity took the place of homage. He was among the full-grown, the initiate, the τέλειοι. He not only felt Christ in him; he felt "in Christ" as never before. Christ's blessings were "sealed, or made over to him.

There is nothing magical, or hypnotic, or auto-suggestive, say. All is in a spiritual psychology, all is but the terminus, the summit and goal in action, of a moral and spiritual process. The preparation may have been long or short. The crisis might be more deeply and swiftly realised by some than by others. But with many such differences the nature of the thing remains—a social climactic of the soul in the Spirit. It was a crisis of faith, not an act of magic. It flowed from a Word creative and not conjuring for the soul.

§

But we lose the real meaning of Baptism if we are more interested in the recipient than in the Church that administers it. The outward act of Baptism is something that *happens* to the votary, but it is *done* by the Church. In the one the experience is uppermost, in the other the act. It is given to the soul at the hands of the Church. It is an experience of the concurring subject, but it is chiefly an act of the

Church, within which act Christ stands the actor in chief. It is something the Church brings to the soul's door.[1] Even if he believed before, his faith takes a new and memorable development for his whole future life when it is confessed in a solemn and corporate act of a Church indwelt by Christ, of which act he is the immediate and co-operant occasion. This, and not actual rejuvenation by an inserted vitality, is the moral and psychological explanation of Paul's profound and decisive way of speaking of Baptism, as in Romans vi, and Colossians ii.

What Baptism represents and effects (in the sense of carrying it home) is the release from the guilt and bond of sin. It opens prison doors from that slavery. It flushes the whole life as it covers the whole body. And, with the threefold name, it means that the real author of the change is the triune God, the whole God acting on the whole man, and becoming eternal surety for his whole life. If the man pledges faith, the Church guarantees care. It is a great moment in our experience when Baptism carries home to us, in the corporate doing of it, our position as reconciled and redeemed into Christ's kingdom. In doing this it mediates grace under Christ's unique mediation. It is a living, acting channel for the indwelling of the Redeemer.

The form was that of a bath. When grace is so represented, it means that it covers the whole man, and cleanses him in an ideal but final committal. The whole man begins mightily to share the new power and reconciled experience of Christ which underlies Word, Church, and Sacrament. We have thus, first, a counterpoise to the tempting power of the flesh which is so close and urgent. *Noblesse oblige.* Second, we have a corrective to the distracting influences acting from the world (and even from the Church) on the unity of our personal life. We have a focus for potent memory, a vow which not only binds but rallies us. And we have, third, a pledge of the final consummation and transfiguration of the life that now is ours by the possession of

[1] Unless, of course, we are so individualist and so lost to the Church idea as to say that it is chiefly the individual's act of confession made before a Christian audience. It is then not an act of the Church, it is not a Sacrament. Indeed, there is then no Church, but only a soluble group.

the Holy Ghost. This comes home to us through the rite, which inserts and builds us concretely into the New Humanity of the ascending Church. To this end Christ has given the Church special and sanctifying power through the means of applying the Gospel in word and deed. The act of Baptism is indeed an act of personal confession. The adults each time renew their vows. But so, and still more, does the Church. Even in the case of infant Baptism, it is an act which pledges the members of the Church anew to each other as the Church performs the incorporation of the baptized not, indeed, into Christ, but into the body of Christ.

§

So the gifts of Word and Sacrament are the same—forgiveness and regeneration, newness of life and desire. The difference is not in matter but in form. It is psychological rather than ontological. New Testament Baptism was a relative goal, a crisis, a committal crowning the preparation by the Word. It was the recognition of spiritual adultness. And it was also a point of departure for the new life, an era to date from, an occasion central and fontal for the life in Christ and His community. It was a case of grafting the soul into the living Church rather than creating the new life—grafting it into the living stem and system of the Church. It ended the way to Christ, and began the life *in* Christ. But of course it was not a one-sided act of either the man or the Church, but the indwelling Christ was the chief Actor behind all, in what might be called a creative reciprocity. It was in each case a function of His Eternal Act.

Baptism, then, was for the subject an act once for all. But it was an act of the Church even more than of the individual, and of God, of the Spirit, most of all. These features, onceness and corporateness, together with the psychological preparations in the Gospel, distinguish it from the preached Word. Add to this that (as the immersion signified) it was corporeal and not merely sensible, *i.e.* it involved the whole man, and not only one of the senses, like hearing. He belongs to the enveloping spirit and society. *He* belongs and not merely certain interests or aspects of his. It was a thing most valuable to the Christian in the circumstances of that day to have a great public experience like this to fall back on amid the soul's doubts and persecutions. There was no written word, and the Christian society with its apostles went for so much the more. The believer's baptism into it was a great help against subjective variations of experience. The personal experience, integrated so decisively into that of the whole Church, caused an immense access of certainty, which did not cease to act through life. It is like having a historic Christ in the flux of history and the struggle of creeds.

§

Let us interpret rather than attack. So we may say that Baptism *regenerates* (remember we are dealing with adult Baptism); but it did so really in no other sense than the moral sense in which the Word of the Gospel does, though in another application. It acted by the way of a social psychology, and not merely an individual as was the case in conversion. We may compare with it the impressive solemnity of the coronation of the king, as something beyond his mere succession or proclamation. By the ceremony both king and people realise the change as never before; and it cannot be repeated. The gift in Baptism is the same as in preaching, the difference is the way of conveying it, and the consequent mode and effect of its experience. Each is a Sacrament—Word and Baptism. Each Sacrament is an act of conveyance of the Gospel—the Word by repetition and to individuals, Baptism by one social crisis. The difference is not objective and substantial, but subjective and psychological. It is well to bear the psychology of the matter in mind, and especially its social psychology, when modern scholarship seems to find magical regeneration in the New Testament.

The Sacrament, truly, not only declares, nor only conveys, but it effects, it does something; but it does it in a psychological and not an ontological way, in a way moral and not magical, as if the communication of God's essence were a greater thing than the gift of His grace. There is no immediate effect without the intelligent and significant Word, the Word appropriated by the Sacrament after it in a Church of the Spirit. In both we have the real presence of the saving Word, and in both it *acts*. If the Word regenerate, Baptism does, whose power is in the Word alone. The Word begins the process which Baptism seals and sets, as at a certain age a boy becomes a youth with all that implies in social sensibility and new relations.

When therefore we ask, What is the connection between the inner experience and the outward act? is there any truth in baptismal regeneration? how far does the change from the old man to the new coincide with the reception of the Sacrament? we must always start with the principle that the special thing in the Sacraments is not the conveyance of a spiritual commodity foreign in kind to the distinctive action or moral psychology of the personal life. The death of Christ was the crowning work of His personality; there at last He found His whole self, finished the work it was in Him to do, and began His Resurrection. So the Sacraments of His work bring our personality to its own. The gift conveyed in Baptism, therefore, in so far as it is a matter of personality, cannot be the infusion of an impersonal substance or influence. Such ideas are outside the New Testament atmosphere and quite alien to the mentality of Christ. And the gift is met by the recipient in a personal act, and not a mere exposure to action from without. As a holy person God respects personal action above all else. With such an axiom to protect us from magic, we have something to learn from the doctrine of Baptismal Regeneration. (I am still speaking of adult baptism.)

§

Sacraments are necessary for the health of the Church. They give an outlet not otherwise given for elements of the Gospel which would become either inflamed or stifled if they were repressed. Baptism is necessary for the weal of the Church, whose act it chiefly is. Therefore it is necessary for the world the Church has to convert. But is not necessary to individual salvation; whereas the preaching of the Word is. That is why we cannot think of Christ's prime legacy as the Sacraments, which bless Christianity but do not create it, do not make Christians. Baptism, therefore, is the corporate symbol (or rather action[1]) of the New Covenant, of the new relation between God and Humanity in Christ. It marks off the people of the New Covenant from the world in virtue of their corporate union with its Creator in a higher creation. It is the Sacrament of destination. We are earmarked for a life regenerate in a new creation.

The emergence from the water partly signified, partly promoted the rising from sin's death in a new birth, from egoism to a family life. The new life is, in its destination for moral personality, as much above the life of natural individuality as that is above mere vitality. It is as much above that of the decent man in the street as his is above that of the animal. Yet its value does not lie in the gift of some spiritual commodity—a view which would simply belie the moral foundations of the natural life; rather it brings these to their own. The rite certainly marked off individuals as Christians. But it did not "christen," or make them Christian. The boy ripens because he is a man; if we say he becomes a man when he ripens, we are using words in another and secondary sense. The converts were Christian before Baptism. They became Christian by an act of their native personality responding to God's mercy in Christ. Before Baptism they were Christ's. Therefore they were baptized. After it they were openly in the body of Christ. Therefore they received the Sacrament of His body. But as a Church's act Baptism does stamp the Church as distinct from the world. And it does say that the soul can never come to its true Christian self and take home the baptismal gift except in the Christian society. We cannot think of regeneration apart from a Church. By this visible incorporation of the individual into the community (and so far into Christ) it makes a practical declaration of a new birth as the foundation of the New Humanity. It declares for Humanity that it is in the mercy of our God that all our hopes begin.

[1] I point out later that a symbol does something and not merely shows it

§

It has been said that we may exaggerate and we may depreciate the value of the rite at each extreme—the sacramentarian or the Quaker. And it has been put thus:

1. Suppose we say the personal contribution of the subject by his faith is nil. We may still make either too little of the Sacrament or too much. On the one hand, we depreciate the Sacrament by saying that its action has no bearing whatever on personal relation to sin. The action is at any rate the Church's witness to the need of the new birth from sin everywhere. While, on the other hand, we exaggerate the value of the rite by saying that the action of the Church in the Sacrament is to produce the grand regenerative change in him, faith or none.

2. But suppose we say, with the Baptists, that the personal faith of the subject has everything to do with his regeneration, we can make too little or too much of the Sacrament there. We then depreciate the Sacrament (with a lack of spiritual subtlety or insight) by saying that it only confirms his experience. While we exaggerate its value by saying that Baptism is useless, and the Church's faith in connection with it vain, unless its effect coincide in time with the act.

§

Think of it this way. Think of what is involved.

1. Baptism is something that *happens to* the man at the Church's hand, much as it owes to his own act of faith. The baptismal act in which he enters the Church, like the birth whereby he enters the world, is something done rather on him than by him. Here Baptism differs from the other Sacrament. Even when the submission to Baptism is the believer's own act, this is so. Even if we say its chief value comes from the man's own faith, the Baptism is an act administered to him, in which he is but indirectly active. He is enveloped by the social body of grace (as by the water). It is the medium of faith and love in which Grace

is to have its way with him. Here Baptism differs also from conversion, in which the man is a more active subject as he is more alone with God. And it differs from conversion farther in that conversion is only in exceptional cases a sudden, memorable thing, occupying a point of time.

2. Consider also, and it is more important, what a Sacrament is. Next to its connection with the Word, it gets its meaning from the Church. I have already said that we are on the wrong tack, we ask the wrong question, when we seek an effect on the soul outside the psychological effect, the moral action, of the grace of the Gospel Word. But we are also wrong when we stake everything on its value to the subject of it. That debases its currency. Its first value as a Sacrament is not for the individual but for the Church and its Gospel. We are not to measure the worth of any Sacrament by the way we feel after it. For the individual alone we might say it has no value distinct from its effect as a proclamation and function of the Word, as a *That-predigt*, an enacted sermon.

An undue subjectivity, by way of sectarian individualism, is the worst depreciation of Baptism. It depreciates the significance of a communal and social life for the development of faith. That life is a thing whose moral value can hardly be exaggerated. What Baptism first means is the incorporation of the baptized into the Church, to which the evangelical promise is chiefly made and the Spirit given. He is entered of the Church especially as it is the social body of Christ, as the spiritual organism of history, as the soul's moral home and nursery, where Christ Himself moves as the unseen Providence and shaping power of His own salvation. It is not reception into the Church as a mere kindly community, a mere variant of other sympathetic associations; nor into the Church as a mere institution for the canalising of grace. It is Christ that receives you, not a friendly society. If you were brought up in a religious community of merely humane and helpful people, who took you by the hand, and comforted, cheered, or forwarded you in life, that would still not be the Church (though it is what a multitude of people think to be the Church's whole duty with its young). Such would not be the Church action on you which Baptism represents. All that might be done, yet nothing done with such distinctively Christian experiences as forgiveness in Christ's Cross, Reconciliation with God, or Regeneration by the Spirit. It might all be done without bringing the Christ of the Redemption to bear on you, or making you even begin to realise that you were reborn into the New Humanity with all its obligations. You might get nothing really which would be a counterpoise to the solid stream and pressure of the world, the flesh, and the natural man.

Baptism is really the Sacrament of the new birth, and so far it corresponds to the old circumcision on the threshold of the natural or racial life. It is the Sacrament of Regeneration; which, however, it does not produce, but richly conveys by our personal adoption into its home. Atmosphere is the most potent element in the education of a new life. To belong really to a real community does matter much. It makes a vital change to pass upon our native egoism, nay, on the religious egoism which may be acting even in the form of our conversion. The converted are not really regenerate except as they become real members of a real Church. They easily relapse unless they yield to the unique moral powers and influences of the community of the Spirit. Of course if these are not there it is not a true Church. It is easy now to denounce Baptismal Regeneration; but do our Churches exert a regenerating influence on the religious egoism of their baptized members? Is it the gift of the Church that becomes the determining power on their character? I have certainly known cases where but for that influence the man would have been a bully or a rowdy. On the other hand, there are cases where men have bullied or grieved the Spirit out of the Church. Against the Sacramentarians we ask, Is it we, or only something in us we know nothing about, that responds to the action of the Spirit? And of their opponents we ask, Is the sacramental gift in the Church the chief power that is making us what we are growing to be? Is our membership of a Church a matter of mere education, or is it a constant regeneration, which makes us not only wise to compass our moral desires but quite different in the things we come to desire? Do we grow in sonship or only in religious culture? The Church is only our true mother as it gives us to the Father. Our rebirth is not merely a hope ripening, but a process of creation. What acts upon us is not an imaginative ideal but a shaping power.

All the baptized are not regenerated. Some regenerates have not been baptized. Our regeneration is not in the Sacraments but in the Christ Who gave the Sacrament to the creature He had not merely influenced but remade. The Reformers said it was not the disuse of the Sacraments that damned, but the contempt of them; but we cannot say that of Christ, His Cross, and His Word of Gospel for which the Sacraments exist. His grace called into being both Salvation and Sacraments; but not Salvation through Sacraments, which are for the saved but not to save. The great legacy is that which saves, and Sacraments do not save. You cannot evangelise the world with a Gospel of Sacraments, but only with Sacraments of the Gospel, and of its Word-in-chief. We do not refer our new life to Baptism, but to God's grace which put Baptism there. It is baptismal grace, but it is not a grace that depends on Baptism. The main thing is not when and how we were reborn, but the fact that we are, that we have the reconciled regenerate life in Christ, that we have the life which new birth but began. It is no true faith that has its ground only in the past. It is the Spirit which makes the past present, it is the Spirit that quickens. The true nature of the regeneration at the beginning of the Christian life must be discerned by the true nature of its course.

CHAPTER XI

INFANT BAPTISM

Entire absence of infant Baptism in the New Testament. The difficulty created by its introduction became acute as the Reformation recovered the New Testament view of faith. Efforts at exit often led to extravagant theories. Each form of Baptism should be equally recognised. Each represents one aspect of the Church and its Gospel, the corporate and the individual. No ground for ecclesiastical severance between Congregationalists and Baptists, the perpetuation of which is therefore sectarianism. Baptism not repeated—covers all life, as grace does. Confirmation, or taking up membership, useful, but not a Sacrament. Baptism as a Sacrament is pre-eminently the act neither of the individual nor of the Church, but of God in Christ. Summary in eight heads.

MOST that I have said about the regenerative effect of Baptism applies directly only to adult Baptism. We have no other in the New Testament, as in other mission stages of the Church. In due course the practice was transferred to infants; and the moral psychology of the adult experience then appeared as a subconscious magic effect. And I will not say that there was no infection at this later stage from the pagan mysteries. But I will add that it was a noble and merciful magic compared with the conjurations to which religion can descend.

The point of origin for infant Baptism is obscure. It is not in the New Testament. 1 Corinthians vii. 14 even excludes it. Perhaps the growing influence of the heathen mysteries helped, since children were initiated there. Irenæus (A.D. 180) knew of infant Baptism. But Tertullian (200) was protesting against its adoption. "Why hurry the age of innocence to confession of sin?" Then it became popular, and its spread was rapid. A generation after it was the rule in Africa. Only in the third century, however, did it become quite universal, and especially as the Church became identified with a nation or a whole people.

The transfer of adult conditions to the child (may I repeat?) led to all kinds of theosophic speculations about the implanting of a germ of the new life to be long latent in the soul. Theories teemed, handling the darkest region of natural mysticism or psychological obscurity. Attempts were made to explain that the proceedings in Baptism come to effect in much the same way as the Hebrew recitations of the professor in his study came out in his servant's psychic disorder long after! Such hypotheses were the products of people who were hard up for an explanation how an unconscious and incapable child could receive what an adult had received in such a crucial experience. Psychology became ontology. The rite became unmoralised, and then demoralised, as if it made a soul Christian at some subliminal depth.

The Reformation raised the question of infant Baptism to an acute stage, and it seems as vivid in many quarters now as ever. The reasons then were various. The pre-Reformation mysticism had made religion so individual and inward that it seemed proper to many devout people that the Sacraments should only witness, in a tense form, the lone soul's personal and conscious state. Or, when a total breach with Rome became inevitable, this was urged: Should we not give up the baptismal practice which made people Christian without any personal faith at all, or, if with any, then with faith only in a Church? And, indeed, if New Testament Baptism could only be understood as regenerating the infants in the Roman sense, there would be nothing for it but to discard infant Baptism, with probably the other Sacraments also, and to make the real antithesis to Popery a Church gathered about personal faith alone and the Sacrament of the Word. Again, the more that recourse was had to the Bible with the historic sense yet undeveloped, and the more the Bible took the place of the Church and was treated as final pattern instead of final norm, the more were people bound to press the indubitable Bible usage. So adult Baptism had a strong case, with the then view of the Bible. Men forgot that we have there but the practice of a missionary Church. People came in out of Paganism, and could do so only on the principle of adult faith and confession. This the child of the Church does not. Again, it was objected, Christianity certainly was for Luther faith.

No faith, no Church, and no Baptism. But (it was replied) there is nothing to tie us down to the individual's faith as the one decisive thing in what was really a corporate act, in an act which, being a Sacrament, was the act of the society of faith more than that of the individual. Again, it was upon a Sacrament that the protest was raised against the old Church. If the perversion of the Mass was renounced, said the then Baptists, why not the other perversion, infant Baptism? Both had departed from the New Testament practice and principle. So, as the Reformers themselves split about the second Sacrament, the larger Reformation split also about the first, and we have the co-Reformation, the Anabaptists. And altogether we have a great clamour of contending voices.

Certainly in the New Testament Baptism takes place upon the confession of personal faith. And the Reformation could never give up that principle. The only question was as to the position and value of the Church's faith relative to that of the baptized. Luther found the effective faith to be in the Church, in the parents and sponsors. They placed the child within the sphere and influence of that faith, *i.e.* under the social action of grace. But has such vicarious faith any value? Yes, surely; we recognize its value in the most intimate exercise of faith—in prayer, in intercessory prayer. If our faith is self-engrossed, it dies. The grace that it answers is as much others' as ours. We are not saved by private bargain. The same act of grace saved all. But still faith can never be vicarious in such a way as to leave the beneficiary always passive; only so as to pledge and encourage him to a personal appropriation in due course. But then it was promptly asked, Why should not Baptism be deferred till the prayers and nurture of the Church and of the home resulted in this personal step?

This drove Luther to postulate some kind of subconscious faith in the child. We now see that such a thing can hardly be discussed even by the subliminal psychologists. We know nothing of the region. But theologically such a notion of faith is fatal to the evangelical idea. It is one of its chief depressants and demoralisers. It leads (we saw) to all kinds of theosophic theories about an implanted germ affecting unconsciously the child's human nature. It transfers the religious interest to the nature from the conscience. And the notion discourages conversion and personal religion. Faith loses intelligence and will.

No doubt one motive in introducing and maintaining infant Baptism was fear—lest the child should be lost in Hell. But, if that had been the chief motive, the Church would not have allowed it. There were wise men then also, jealous for Christian principle. It should not be taken for granted that infant Baptism only came because of the growth of the magic conception of Baptism, and the desire to hurry children into its safety. There were other and higher causes at work. Baptism should not rest on fear, which is faithless. "The ground of faith is not the water, but Christ. There can therefore be no fear of unbaptized children being lost. Christ does not fail them even if water do, or if the priest do not arrive in time."

§

Clearly the two Baptisms, infant and adult, are psychologically different, though they have in common the main thing —the connection with the Word and its blessings in a faithful Church. In one case the experience precedes the act, in the other it follows (or does not). The one flows from experience, the other seals and commits to it. In adult Baptism regard is had to the subject's past experience of the Word; in infant Baptism to a future experience expected and provided for within the Church. Apart from this provision, infant Baptism is a mere beautiful and suggestive ceremony, or, if effective, is so as magic. In adult Baptism the instruction precedes, in infant Baptism it must follow. In adult Baptism we are baptized *on* faith, in infant Baptism *unto* faith; but both are justified by faith only. And faith's influence and nurture should be secured always.

It would be well to accept the historic situation by at least making the question an open one in the same Church, with either practice at choice. Would Christianity really be reformed by abolishing infant Baptism? Can that now be hoped for? Is that the only way to keep magic out? Would it not be burning the house to roast the pig? Would it not reduce the Church to the permanent condition of a missionary Church only, amid a quite pagan society? And so long as this point keeps apart two communions identical in faith and polity, it can never be said that theological, or even ritual, differences have ceased to divide the Free Churches. The destruction of this gulf is the first step to their union.

The spread of infant Baptism was largely the result of the swift conversion of whole nations. But it was not due only to such identification of a Church and a people. It was due also to the nature of the Church itself under whose influence both adult and infant passed. With the believer Baptism was a voluntary entrance into this circle of the Word's work, with all its social atmosphere. But the infant of believing parents also entered this circle and its nurture at birth; and he grew up receiving, at the plastic time, and by subtle environment, the training that the adult convert got, but got too late to make his Christianity as ingrained as it was for the Christian child, youth, and man. If the adult was beginning his debt to the saving Church, the child had already begun it.

We may recall here the two aspects of the Church: first, as a voluntary association of individuals; and, second, as a spiritual body, the *prius* of the individual, creating his will to combine. It is empirically a society of consent; but, also, spiritually and really, it is not of man nor the will of man. Now each of these is a true and complementary aspect of the Church—the one actual and local, the other ideal and Catholic. And each corresponds to one of the two views of Baptism, before consent and after. But, if so, are not these complementary? Is not each form of Baptism equally justified? Let us accept the historical situation, as in the case of Episcopacy. Let us own each form to have an equal right according to circumstances and preference. Each (Episcopacy and infant Baptism) grew up out of something else. We do not now claim monopoly for Episcopacy or for Congregationalism; let us claim none for either form of Baptism. Each has its right, each is suggestive, none has monopoly, both are within the principle of the Gospel. By birth in the Christian family the child was placed by

God where the adult was placed also by his faith—under the moral benefits and formative influences of the Christian community; why keep from the child the religious blessings of Baptism? *The* religious thing in the New Testament after all is not the subjectivity of the baptized but the Church's magnifying of Christ's saving act. Christ, the object of faith, was in the worshipping rite more than man, its subject. The Church's confession of Christ was much more than man's confession of his experience. Even as experience, it was collective and not atomic. The parents, with the whole Church, confessed a God active in His Word and Spirit; they believed that God had chosen this child for that action by the fact of his Christian birth; and they purposed to submit the growth of the child to these regenerative influences with a view to his confession of them in due course, and to rear him as a real member of the Church and not a mere spectator. He has the blessings, why not the sign? It must of course be taken up by the child when he comes to riper years. And here we have made a great mistake in dropping confirmation, or in not treating the entry on membership in a like solemn way. It is a mistake aggravating that which was made in transferring to the infant the change that took place in the experience of the adult. Of course the child, as he grew up, could refuse the blessings offered him. But so could the adult. The one could fail to reach as the other could fall away. If it be said that the chances are in favour of the adult since he made a personal choice, that is balanced by the fact that the child, being in the Church, and having the sense that he was of it, was protected from the pagan education which misformed the man's plastic youth. And the child has all the parental and similar influences to the good.

§

What makes Baptism real is God's changeless will of salvation in Christ and the Church. It testifies chiefly to that, and not to a subjective attainment of confession, which might change. Sacraments are modes of the Gospel (not of our experience), and that is what the Gospel reveals.

And this reality may come home to A at once, and to B only gradually. It is sent home to A by his critical experience in his reception into the Church, and to B by his slow experience after reception. How the sense arrives is not the main thing, which is the fact that it comes. Modes are not worth quarrels. The witness of the rite to a real and necessary regeneration is not impaired by the manner of it. Only, when we say that it is the act and confession of the Church more than of the individual, we add that the Church's act must not end with the rite. It must make a reality of its care of the baptized child. And that we have failed to do—parents leaving it to the Church, and the Church to the parents.

To say that infant Baptism, as a witness to the Gospel and its faith by an act of the Church directed on the individual, is not scriptural because it is late, would be also to say that no existing form of Church government is scriptural, since none reproduces exactly the conditions of the first century. Or it would be to say that the spirit had no power in the Church to modify practice so as to give effect to faith's principle in new circumstances, but that the praxis of the first century is binding for ever. It would mean, for instance, that the Supper should be a real meal or follow it, and should be weekly, and taken reclining, or that we should restore for the sick extreme unction. The full scope of Baptism, or any other institution or doctrine, could not be reached in the practice of the first century. Let us correct any magic by a scriptural principle to which both Protestant forms bear witness. Both can express the evangelical conception of faith. And in both Baptism acts on the subject psychologically and not subliminally, in the one case by a crisis, and in the other by a nurture. In the one case it embodies a new and fontal experience, in the other it begins a regenerative education, or what would now be called a creative evolution.

Let us avoid canonising the subjectivism and individualism which here so easily beset us, as if the chief witness borne were to the state of the particular subject and not to the Gospel meant for him; as if the occasion were mainly confession of individual faith instead of the Church's on an individual occasion; as if it were, in chief, even the confession of the Church's faith rather than of God's grace; as if the inseparable connection of the Sacrament with faith were only *upon* faith, and not also *into* it. Too much attention to the individual is apt to cosset him into an impracticable egoist, dogmatist, and crank (as at the other and Catholic end the regenerate becomes an indifferent). Faith is more than individual—if it be the moral act which it has so often ceased to be. It is communal, solidary; it can be even vicarious. That there is such a thing as vicarious faith the healing of the centurion's servant shows. We get the benefit of the faith of our parents and of our Church, as we do of their prayers. (I am sure, if I am still able to believe in spite of my own thought and in spite of what is going on round us, it is due in no small measure to the faith and prayer of my parents.) Spiritual blessings come to belong to us in two stages: first, as they are made possible to us by God's grace, as they surround us, and they are sealed to us; second, as they are actual, as we appropriate them, as we are sealed to them. The baptized child represents the first stage, the confirmed youth the second. The child is *adopted* into the home and atmosphere of these gifts, the man takes them up as duties. In infant Baptism the grace is impropriated; in believer's Baptism it is appropriated. But there is no regeneration except as the man becomes spiritually active for himself, and the appropriation takes place. Till then it is only a destiny. Till when? There is no fixed rule or time. When the child can understand the Gospel enough to have real faith, and love, and dealings with God—not simply on the exhibition of religious interest. But the interval does not essentially matter. The connection between the Sacrament and the Word is not destroyed by waiting. The child is being reared under the Word to which he has been given, and transmuted by the Spirit which makes the Church.

The child needs salvation, and under due influence grows every day more amenable to it. And, as Baptism is the sign and gage of regeneration, why should it be postponed indefinitely? In an age already too subjective and individual, why should the rite be sacrificed entirely to its subjective side, to the individual confession at the cost of the Church's?

We must not even sacrifice to the Church's confession Christ's act and proffer within it, Christ's confession and claim of us there. We may not lose in our confessional side the Spirit's objective, exhibitory, and conveying side of it. If we do regard the individual in chief, at what point should the rite come? Is confession, is even conversion, necessarily regenerative? Is individual conversion or confession always sound or permanent? Allowing that we must be born again, is it not at least as easy to attain Christian personality, and be reared to a sound confession, inside the Church as out? Besides, all the great acts of our Redemption "prevent" us. They anticipate. They commit us before we have a voice. We were saved, so far as God is concerned (just as we are named), before we could be consulted—God calling things that are not as though they were. They commit us before we can choose. In Christ we are foredoomed to faith. Why not so commit the child in Baptism, and cast God's mantle of grace over him?

There can (as I have said) be no talk of an implanted germ of the new life or an unconscious faith. There must be, for due regeneration, an experience impossible to the child. He has no organ of the soul to receive saving action, in the absence of either thought or will. And, if there be no moral or spiritual receptivity, and yet an effective act, it is magic. A mere passivity could not receive even in germ such action as we associate with the Holy Spirit. We can only think of a personal regeneration. But, if the infant cannot experience or confess such regeneration, the Church does in the act of Baptism. It conveys to the child, in God's name, not only a claim but a reality, a membership in the Church; it conveys a right to all its blessings as the soul grows in power to receive them; and in the end it imposes the duty to take up personal responsibility and confession. Baptized children are members *in petto*, in reserve.

So the Baptism of the child is not its regeneration except in title, but it is a real act of the Church and of Christ in the Church. It is the Church's praise and promise round the child. The Church thanks God for its own regeneration and promises in respect of the child's. It is the objective, and practical, and promissory assurance of it, the committal of

16

the child to it as his Christian destiny. It does not effect the regeneration but intends it. We repudiate a Baptism which effects regeneration whether in child or adult. There remains but the Baptism which confesses it and the Baptism which intends and pursues it. We would accept each of these as complementary aspects of it, represented by complementary groups which respect each other in the same Church and administer at choice. The difference is not worth severance any more.

§

Fix your minds on the fundamental relation between grace and faith which the Sacraments express. They are not there chiefly to testify anything so subjective as individual religion. Their standing witness is the priority of grace, the free, nutritive, creative nature of God's grace, and the most worshipful wonder of it. They do not testify the priority of faith, as if it were a meritorious and qualifying work of ours that determines a Christian Sacrament, and makes the matter worth dividing upon. When we were without strength, Christ died for the ungodly. First grace, then faith. Grace is the cause, faith the effect. The grace is there for us and acting on us long before we believe it; it lies about us in our infancy, when as yet we have no faith. The Baptist position could be so used so as to make faith the condition of grace. That is bad theology. It is too legalist. As if we must first believe, and then we receive grace if we believe duly. As if grace were not ours, and not acting on us, till we have power to grasp it, till we qualify by faith. Yet it is only grace that can create the power, and faith itself is the gift of God's grace. Nothing can create the response of faith but grace. No individualist theory, for all its value, must tempt us to trust our faith and its correctness, or its intensity, more than God. And, again, if we wait for personal faith and confession, we must keep asking when there is enough faith of the right kind to justify Baptism, and who is to decide. It is an unanswerable question. We are to be much more sure of God's grace in our faith than of our faith in God's grace. Faith is not getting up a certain degree of receptivity and so inviting, facilitating, or even deserving God's grace. It is answering grace's prevenience. And there is no statutory interval between the grace and the faith, between the gift and the response. It may be twenty, thirty, sixty years. Infant Baptism is a means of exhibiting to the whole Church and world this right relation of grace and faith, that grace precedes and is the condition of faith, that it is not its reward, and that the element of time between grace and faith does not wither nor change the grace and its power.

It is not fatal to infant Baptism to say that individual faith was absent in the Baptism; but it would be if we said that individual grace was absent—that Christ did not expressly in His Church's act claim and commit the child. In the Gospel every child belongs to Christ, and the Church claims every child in the name of Him Who reconciled the whole world. So the children are baptized not really to place them in God's grace, but because by Christ's work they are meant to be there.

§

If Baptism be an expression of the Gospel of regenerating grace it covers the whole of life, I have said. For which reason it is not repeated. The second birth is sole like the first. It cannot therefore be confined to the erasure of inherited and original sin. It concerns all that man needs and God gives. If it dealt only with original sin, it would be reduced to be but one means of grace among others, and we should come to think of the other Sacrament as making good what was lacking in Baptism—whereas the two are not supplementary, but two centres in the orbit of the New World. Or else we should never be sure we had gone far enough in the grace thus conveyed to secure our being in grace for good and all, and to read our title clear to any Sacrament.

It is an easy error to compress the virtue of this Sacrament into a single act, instead of spreading it over the whole of life. As if Baptism were the one startling act of God's really gracious treatment of us; whereas His grace is His one act and attitude of will to all human souls; so that Baptism need not be repeated, even if there is a long and faithless interval. Truly the grace of Baptism is not in conscious possession then; but it is not therefore unreal. It does not cease to bear on us even while we ignore or resist. We kick against its pricks; but there comes a time when the memory of the Father's house we were brought up in comes back and comes home, and a truth, a text, or a hymn, stamped on the mind when it was soft, stands out in the soul's very hardening, and restores the prodigal to the circle of grace where he began. Our faith is the appropriation of the Baptism in which God hastened to exercise openly His grace on us. He precaptured us. He was not like those wild individualists who refuse to teach their children religion or Bible lest it should deflect their minds and impair their freedom before they turned freely to such things when they were fit to choose. Perhaps it was the same respect for freedom that led them not to chain up the world, the flesh, and the devil from exploiting the unique opportunity thus given.

§

Infant Baptism has also been regarded as the successor of circumcision, and therefore it was held to be for all children. It was the Christian form of the Jewish legacy. But this was chiefly urged by those who would make the Church identical with the nation, as in Judaism. So that entrance into the Church should not be separate from entrance into the nation. But the Baptist plea was a strong one, that the new thing, the very thing that made the Church, was not the natural birth or people, but the supernatural, the free turning of the man to God. Christ did not come to perpetuate theistic nationalism in a new form, they said. Baptism must remain what Christ's Gospel made it—not particularist but the sacrament of the New Humanity; it must not be adjusted to some other idea, or justified by some other consideration not distinctively Christian. Baptism must be justified by faith as the new and startling thing. There the Baptists were right. They were less right in another point drawn from the case of Israel. I have already said that the fear of Hell for the children was not the only reason leading to infant Baptism. There was also the sense and desire of family unity, the desire to convey to the children, as God had to Israel, the propædeutic blessing of grace, and to enrich the Kingdom of God with them. It were a poor Kingdom with no children in it.

Baptism is wrong, not when applied to children, but when separated from the other means of grace, from the nurture of the Church, and especially from the Word of the Gospel, whose vehicle it is. It should not be given where there is no prospect of Christian nurture. We may not give Baptism unless we also bring the Gospel, and promise to keep bringing it, to the young life till it can assume responsibility in confirmation or in taking up membership.

Whatever is meant by an occasion so valuable as confirmation, it is not a second Baptism, a second Sacrament, nor is it even an extension of Baptism. It gives no divine gift that Baptism did not give. But it realises the gift, the grace that was assigned there. It does transfer most of the responsibility to the soul, and it forms a fresh step in the action of the Spirit which individualises Salvation. It causes the man to take up the gift and its duties as his personal own. Be it remembered that real and full membership is not privilege but responsibility. It is individual confession. The soul becomes less dependent on the Church; and it is in more direct contact with Christ, as in the Communion.

Baptism, as it must be coupled closely with the Church, must also be kept clearly in the service of the Gospel. It is useless and superstitious as an institutional rite apart from the preaching (and *its own* preaching) of the Word of grace. We may have the Word without Baptism but not Baptism without the Word. That is why it should not be administered except where the circumstances permit a reasonable belief that the child will be reared in Christian nurture, and where the Church makes it a prime part of its business to see that it has it. The Church would not be justified in doing as is done in Germany, and baptizing, for civic reasons, the children of pronounced anti-Christians. That is making Baptism a State test—a debasement which in this country we have long outgrown.

§

The truth is, I repeat, that the Church should provide each form of Baptism at choice, as it does on the mission-field. Each signifies one aspect without excluding the other. It is a question of emphasis or of occasion. Any criticism of adult Baptism here made is only against those who would make it sole. The two usages did coexist in the Church of the Roman Empire—as they do to-day, according as the Church is more or less in missionary conditions, even at home. Such a rite is of much use to help gross and hardened sinners who start to break away from the old life. And there is one point about adult Baptism which should be observed also in infant Baptism. There should be none but public Baptisms. Baptism on personal confession does secure this. And it ought to be the rule for infant Baptism, where of course the collective confession of the Church, whose Sacrament it is, is secure of the precedence. But in all cases public confession; not, however, chiefly of sin but of grace.

But even the Church's confession is not all, much as it transcends the individual's. Baptism, like the Supper, is more than a confession; it is a Sacrament. It is not simply the individual or the Church doing something, but God. It is not the Church doing something (confessing) through God, but God doing something (offering, giving Himself to us) through the Church. We have both. We have real, subjective appropriation answering a real objective bestowal. And we are Pædobaptists or Baptists according to which is prime. It is a matter of accent, not of monopoly. As the two Sacraments stand for a double attitude to one Salvation, so the two Baptisms stand for a double attitude to one Sacrament.

§

We may note therefore in summing up:

1. Baptism is an act and concern of the Church. It is a ritual witness of the New Birth, borne to the world by the Church in the case of the individual. But primarily it is an act of the Lord, the Spirit, whose indwelling makes the

Church. It is a function of His great Act, a detailing of His complete gift. It is not chiefly a witness to anything individual (like conversion), but to the grand universal of regeneration. The Baptist transfers so much stress to this individualism as to make it the ground of a separate community, throwing all the other Churches into error. As is so often the case, they are right where they affirm, wrong where they deny. We are both right. Baptism is always connected with faith; but we need not make it depend wholly on the *individual's* faith at a particular moment. Baptism *unto* faith has as good a right in the principle of the Gospel as Baptism *upon* faith. The service of the Baptists to personal faith and its liberty can never be fitly expressed. We invite them to a like acknowledgment of the value of pædobaptism to the Christian Church. The Gospel in the Sacraments has an equal power to individualise and to socialise.

2. As Baptism is an act and function primarily of the believing Church, the Church has power to apply it to infants or to confessors in its discretion in the Spirit, notwithstanding New Testament praxis, so long as due effect is given to the Word and principle it expresses of the new birth of the race in the reconciliation by Christ, its Redeemer.

3. So far as the subject of Baptism is concerned, he is affected much more by the acting Church than by the act of the hour, through its influence upon him as a social *milieu* and a body of Christ. He is affected as the Church opens to his soul, by its discipline, atmosphere, and means of grace, by the Kingdom of Heaven. Hence the Church may apply the act to infants, organising them into its sphere of influence, and into that special action of Christ which He associated inseparably with the Church and its domain of grace. Baptism is incorporation, not into Christ, but into the body of Christ, with its moral, spiritual, social influence on the soul. The child is not given the Spirit, but placed where the Spirit moves. It must make much difference to a young soul whether it is taught to believe it is a member of Christ's body, and takes its discipline as a child of the house, or whether it is taught to regard itself as an outsider, spectator, and by-product of the Church's grace.

4. Clearly then Baptism has not its effect on the child but on childhood, *i.e.*, on the Church's idea and treatment of childhood, its responsibility for it, and only therefore for the particular child.

5. As a Sacrament Baptism not only symbolises but conveys grace. It is not eloquent only but effective. It is a real act and not merely a picture. But the conveyance is much more to the worshipping Church than to the individual subject—except in so far as he is able to join the worship. Hence the effect on the infant at the moment is nil. It is prospective and psychological; it is not immediate and subliminal.

6. The conveyance is not through the element, but through the act; it is only in connection with the element.

7. The Church should not give Baptism where there is no prospect of Christian discipline and nurture in its own interior. Baptism, apart from that, easily becomes a mere salving rite, instead of a saving grace, indulging the superstition of the parents.

8. The great effect of Baptism in the New Testament is psychological, not magical, not actually regenerative. But it soon came to be thought of as regenerative. The "bath of regeneration" came to mean the bath which effects it rather than the one which preaches and conveys it. When infant Baptism came in the regenerative idea was retained after the psychological nature of it had gone; and the mischief was done. The fallacies were the perversion of a great experience to be a magical act, and the transfer of this effect to the unconscious child. The centre of gravity from moral became ontological, and the whole note of the conscience was tuned down. The remedy is not the Baptist one, for its Orthodoxy took over much of the ontological theology of Catholicism. But it is a revised, revived, and moralised conception of the nature of Faith, Church and Sacrament. That will clarify and enlarge our ideas of the baptismal witness. You cannot cure a social error by the protest of extreme individualism, whose virtue is but protest, and which is too little positive, and too passing. And Reformation is much other than repristination, whether in truth, rite, or ethic.

CHAPTER XII

COMMUNION

Origin of the Supper in the symbolic action of the prophets. The symbolism is not in the elements but in the act. It was much more than commemoration. True sense of *opus operatum.* It was a real act (the Cross) that had to be symbolised, therefore a real act symbolised it and conveyed it. The object not *doctrinaire.* The three actions in the rite integral to the entire act, which is Christ's consignment to the Church of the Cross He was offering to God. Bread broken, given, eaten. So wine. The consignment to us and assimilation by us of the great sacrifice—not the offering of it to God. Its repetition is its own reverberation. Christ renews His "finished work." He does not repeat the sacrifice, and certainly the Church cannot in humility do so. He presents His sacrifice to us more than we present it to God; we cannot in any sense effect it.

YOU will think it singular that the most solemn act of the Church's worship should be the arena of its greatest strife, that the centre of the Church's devotion should be the point on which great Churches divide and devour each other. But this, if it show nothing else, shows the cardinal importance of the ideas and powers involved. The opponents felt they were fighting for the Church's true life.

Let us look again into the matter. There is more fresh light than you might think.

The key of the New Testament is in the Old Testament. The Old Testament explains the New Testament, as the New Testament interprets the Old. We cannot understand the Old Testament without the New; and we cannot account for the New Testament without the Old, which it fulfils. The child may be father of the man, but it is only the man that understands the child. Our adult destiny is the key of our infant life. So the Old Testament "arrives" in the New. It is not just broadened, which often means but thinned; it is fulfilled, which means enriched, and especially deepened. If the germ of the *doctrines* and ideas of the Cross is in the priestly part of the Old Testament, in the Law, the precedents of the *act* of the Supper are in the other part of it—in the prophets.

Let us recall a method sometimes used by the prophets—the method of laden action instead of pregnant words, the method of acted symbol. The overburdened thought passes from speech into a practical symbol in a way which our late Western minds and our common hours think extravagant. It has been thought grotesque when Burke brought into the House of Commons a concealed dagger which, at a point in his speech, he threw dramatically on the floor. But in the East it was otherwise. To prophesy calamity and activity Jeremiah lays a yoke on his shoulder (Jeremiah xxvii. 2, xxviii. 10). Or Isaiah goes barefoot (Isaiah xx.). To express a victory a prophet puts on horns, the symbol of power (1 Kings xxii. 11). So, to express the rending of the kingdom, Ahijah rends his garment, and gives ten pieces to Jeroboam (1 Kings xi. 30, *cp.* Jeremiah xix.). So also the domestic history of the prophet is used. His life tragedy becomes symbolic, as with Hosea under his wife's infidelity. Or his life joy is sealed for historic significance, as with Isaiah in his children's birth (Isaiah vii, viii). So the two sticks parted and joined, as Judah and Israel (Ezekiel xxxvii. 15). And we have the like thing done by Christ shortly before the Supper, in the washing of the disciples' feet.

This act of the Supper was parallel to these in a deeper and loftier way. It was Christ's "last parable." It was more than that, but it was that. And it was a parable of action. It was enacted rather than spoken. Teaching was now inadequate. It had failed. He must teach by real action—as the monitions of a parent are often fruitless till a deathbed fix and hallow them. It would have saved the Church and the world endless strife if this principle of interpretation had been recognised earlier.

§

Let us at least get rid of the idea which has impoverished worship beyond measure, that the act is mainly commemoration. No Church can live on that. How can we have a mere memorial of one who is still alive, still our life, still present with us and acting in us? Symbol is a better word than memorial. Only that the modern sense of the word symbol differs from the ancient, and differs for the poorer and not the richer. The modern symbol is but æsthetic and not energetic. It shows us, it does not act on us. The ring does not marry, it only means marriage. The symbol does not convey the thing signified. It just depicts it or suggests it. It impresses, it does not change us. It is not associated with change. The modern symbol does not do justice to the significate, to the present reality of God's action as the cause within our act. It is for eye or ear. It is not action but only expression. It is emblem. And we do not mind emblem, but we are too afraid of ritual.

A Sacrament is as much more than a symbol as a symbol is more than a memorial. It is quite inadequate to speak of the Sacrament as an object-lesson—as if its purpose were to convey new truth instead of the living Redeemer. It is not an hour of instruction but of communion. It is an act, not a lesson; and it is not a spectacle nor a ceremony. It does something. It is an *opus operatum*. More, it is an act of the Church more than of the individual. Further still, it is an act created by the eternal Act of Christ which made and makes the Church. At the last it is the act of Christ present in the Church, which does not so much live as Christ lives in it. It is Christ's act offering Himself to men rather than the act of the Church offering Christ to God. Now, as at the first, it is Christ giving over to men the sacrifice He was making once for all to God. So that we may say this. The elements are symbolic only in the modern sense of the word symbol—only as signs. They convey nothing. They point to the significate but do not include it. But the action (of the Church and chiefly of Christ in the Church) is symbolic in the greater and older sense in which the symbol contains and conveys the significate, and is a really sacramental thing. Christ offers anew to us, as He did at the Supper, the finished offering which on the Cross He gave to God once for all.

But the phrase *opus operatum* has perhaps put someone on the alert. For the fundamental objection we take to the Roman doctrine of the Sacraments is that they are supposed to be effectual in just being done by the Church, apart from the personal faith either of the priest or of the people. They are *opera operata*, spiritual operations performed on the patient over his head. The technical way of putting the Roman view is to say they are effectual *ex opere operato* and not *ex opere operantis*, by the deed and not the doer, by their statutory performance and not by the personal response, the spiritual life and experience, of the parties concerned. That is a sound protest we make. But there is a sense in which the Roman phrase is true. The fundamental value of the Sacrament lies in a supreme and final Act. It lies in an Act accomplished already, and here delivered to our address. The reservoir, always full in heavenly hills, is laid on to our door. The value lies in something done to our hand, in a finished work of Christ before and outside of our faith, before our faith was there—indeed, it puts our faith there, it creates it. For faith is a gift of God, not vaguely and supplementarily to enable us to believe on the Cross, but through the gift of the Cross and its native action on us. It is our moral response to the Cross, and not our qualification. The Sacraments get their whole meaning from an *opus operatum* never to be repeated. It is wrong to say they are but memorials; but it is equally wrong at the other end to say they are valuable and effective as conjurations, with their power acting in them in a magical way, as if the formula employed had a coercing effect on the spiritual world when done by a duly canonical person recognised there, as if they acted on the elements and not on the people. They are not magic, nor machinery.

But it is not wrong to say that they act only in virtue of the foregone and complete Act of God's will in Christ's Cross which gave them their existence. They rest on an *opus operatum* there of the God whose grace so appointed them that the conduit is as much of grace as the stream. Only, God's *opus operatum* is not an act quite over our head, like baptismal regeneration, without action on the moral soul. As a moral act it creates moral action in response. Its nature is intelligible. Its effects cannot remain outside the conscious soul—though, as its scope is the whole world, the vast part of its range is beyond our conscious grasp or experience. This grace fills the Sacraments always with the same power that gave them being. And they are useless without the reverberation of that foregone and incessant Act of Christ, which is the Act of grace, and, as the Act of the Holy, is a moral Act, and not one of mere power and fiat. So there is a certain place for the idea of an *opus operatum* in the Sacraments.

And there is, on the other hand, a certain drawback if we stand too stiffly on the other idea. When you say that the Sacraments have their value entirely *ex opere operantis*, that is, from the faith of the acting party, and especially of the minister, as a believing man, you are in the main right. But, if you are not careful, you will be wrong. If you stood on that only, thinking but of the faith and not of the object of it, you would have people asking, "Why then Sacraments at all? If the Sacraments are a confession by us, or an offering to us of the grace of God just as the immediate parties feel it, do we not find more of that element in the preaching of the Word, where you have far more scope for the spiritual character of the preacher, its idiosyncrasy, its subjective variety and mobility? The Gospel can be presented more richly by the audible Word of a faithful temperament than by the visible Sacraments, more effectually through a person than through an act." That is what is said. How are we to deal with it?

Why, thus. In certain respects, the preacher's personality may obscure the very message it wings, just as a magical Sacrament may in another way. There may easily be too much of his sermon and too little of Christ's Gospel, too much of his temperament and too little of his message. The Gospel may suffer from too many sermons and too little preaching. We have our active side ministered to at the cost of our receptive. We do not feed our souls in a wise passiveness. The preacher is strained in preaching, and we in following. We may feel contributors as much as receivers. We do not receive the word or its organ with due reverence. We may lose the sense of the givenness, of the simple, silent massiveness of God's grace, and its independence of human energy. Many Churches have come to idolise the gifts of the preacher more than the gift of grace. And they frequent and pamper the man of temperament till he may come to be more full of his egoism and his quality than of the message he has to give, which indeed may wear quite thin. Now it is here that the Sacrament may come as a corrective.

Our idolatry of the popular preacher needs to be balanced by more stress on the Sacraments. There the common gift comes out, the administrant fades away. His idiosyncrasy is silent, and God's Act speaks in the act of the Church, of which He is but the organ. The personality as endowed with ability becomes for the moment indifferent compared with the personality as commissioned by grace; and the deed of God comes home through a living soul indeed but chiefly in its own wealth and power, the same yesterday, to-day, and for ever. It is realised in the act of the silent but worshipful Church as it is not perhaps with all the comment of the pulpit. The thing done lives in our still but potent deed. We do not act, but God acts in us. Such is the massive effect of the brief, grave, and still Sacrament by contrast with the prolonged and vivid Word. The statutory element brings out the changeless note. The individual variation retires, and the eternal and universal arrives. If we would take the spiritual pains to realise this, and make the realisation common property, there would be less than there is to lament in connection with the reverence and the profit of such an act of worship.

§

The Sacrament is an act of obedience, but an obedience to Christ, not to a precept of His, nor to an institution of mere homage. Yet it is not obedience to Christ's person alone, ideal or saintly, but to His person put wholly into His office, His saving task; it is to the eternal Act of Redemption and Gospel in which His person took final effect. Our act is created by the Gospel active in the Church more than continued as a compliance with prescription, even Christ's. Its value, therefore, as an act of the soul's obedience and surrender is not in the feelings that go with it, either before or after. It was not Christ's feelings that made the value of the

Cross, but His complete obedience, and willing confession of God's holy love, in the face of what might well have seemed God's ill-treatment of Him, and in the exhaustion of all feeling. The value of the rite is in the holy obedience, and in its obedience not to Christ's command chiefly but to His inspiration. It is the reverberation of Christ's Gospel; to His coming, His grace, His work, His gift, His cross, His atoning sacrifice—the obedience and response we call faith. The nature of His obedience is shown to be thankful or eucharistic when we recall that in the Supper the cup was the cup of thanksgiving. We do not meet an injunction, nor even thrill to a person as good, noble, or glorious; but we answer in kind God's act of grace in Christ's whole person as crucified Redeemer. We obey, in faith and love, the one compendious thing He did in the Eternal Spirit whose source and spring is there—that act as the key of what He said in exposition. Had Christ not said "Do this," the Church would still have been impelled to some act of worship which returned the special note of Christ's one grand Act of death and salvation.

If the elements are and remain material the act which uses them is spiritual. Therefore it is real. Whatever is symbolical, the action is real. In so far as our action is symbolical, it is symbolical of Christ's Act, not of His essence. But it is symbolical in the ancient sense of the word symbol. It does not simply point to the thing signified, nor suggest it, but conveys it, has it within it, brings it with it, gives it, does something, is really sacramental. We do not enact a small "mystery" or tableau of Christ's sacrifice; but Christ, the Redeemer, in His Church's Act gives Himself and His saving Act to us anew (to us, not to God); and we give ourselves anew to Him in responsive faith. When you reflect after Communion, "What have I done to-day?" say to yourself, "I have done more than on any busiest day of the week. I have yielded myself to take part with the Church in Christ's finished Act of Redemption which is greater than the making of the world." To view it in this light (let me repeat) should suppress much of the irreverent bustle that often goes with the rite. And it should discourage those large occasions like "United Communions," where the size of the company and the nature of the day's proceedings make silence, reverence, and collectedness of any depth almost impossible.

There is an illustration, old, but used by Dr. Dale on this subject of the reality of the symbolism.[1]

If the commander of a conquered town presents the keys to the general of the enemy, that is more than a symbol. It is real. The symbolic act carries in it the act of surrender.

But, if the besieging soldiers in a long leaguer have a ceremony in which they present keys to their own general, that is an expression of their trust in him, it is symbolic of the real surrender which they are sure of, but which may yet never arrive.

§

The exact point is that *such symbolism did not lie in the elements but in the action*, the entire action—word and deed.[2] It lay in action first on Christ's part, then on the part of the Church.

It was the *action* that was symbolical, the breaking rather than the bread, the outpouring rather than the wine. "This" is not this object but this act. Remove the comma after "body." "This is my body broken." "This thing I now do means the breaking of my body soon, which means the surrender of my person." So with the cup. It is the action, the outpouring of the cup, that is meant, more than its contents. "This is my blood shed." Else how could it be called a covenant, which is a mutual *act*? "This my outpouring, and your partaking, of the cup (of my life) is God's new covenant with you." And here is the point where the description of the Supper as a parable is defective. There was not simply an exposition of Christian ideas, but the conveyance of the Act of Christian grace. Something was *done* with His impending deed. What was symbolised was

[1] *Essays and Addresses* 1899, p. 394 f.

[2] To fail to realise this is the defect of the patristic, the Chalcedonian mind. It is the lame foot of Anglicanism (be it said with respect), and it endangers the whole evangelical element so deep within it. The reformation most needed by such Churches, however, is not the discarding but the moralising of Chalcedonism, the conversion of its metaphysic (*i.e.* its mental habit) from thinking of underlying substance to think of energy and ethic. It is a change parallel to that effected in recent physics as to the nature of the atom.

in the symbol also given and made over. In the Supper we have not something pictured or shown, but something done with the great coming deed. We have something not merely represented but conveyed. We have not merely Christ, or the principle of sacrifice in Him, shown forth, but His Act of atonement made over in advance. It concerned not the love of God but His grace, not a disposition but a deed. So with Baptism. The essence of it does not lie in the element (which is Romanism), nor in the subject (which is Baptist Protestantism), but in the significance of the Church's act in close and organic connection with Christ's historic Act and Gift. This is the line to pursue to adjust the baptismal controversy.

§

I will go on to make my point more clear to your patience.

1. *It was an action that was to be symbolised*, i.e. *conveyed.* It was the work Christ had begun to do in His passion, the act of our Redemption, that He was now making over in advance to His own by a minor act in the same kind within it. The Eternal Christ, Who is an everlasting Now, anticipates by a few hours His finished work. He preludes. In cognate symbol He says it is done, and that His whole person comes to a head in His office. It comes to a head and comes home. It is yours, He says. I shall die soon unto God. This rite means that that death is yours, I die for you. In that exalted moment (far greater than the Transfiguration) He knew and felt it was so. The great Redemption was now being completed, and could be conveyed. The value of His actual flesh and blood as substances was by comparison little at such a moment. Only metaphysical theories and patristic survivals have made of them so much. The precious thing was His person, His will, its perfect obedience, His final achievement, and its communicability. It was His person in supreme and final action. There lies personality—in the action of holy will, as supreme though not sole, supreme amid affection and intelligence.

2. It was an action that was to be symbolised; *therefore it was an act which symbolised it, and conveyed it*, not the elements.

"*Do* this." It was not a contemplative religion He was setting up, nor a *doctrinaire*. He was not teaching certain ideas pictorially. He has not a class of pupils before Him. An act is a spiritual thing, as being the supreme effectuation of the spirit, the living person; therefore its true symbol is another act. The crowning Act of the Cross is symbolised in a prior act which is yet within it. The elements are not the symbols; they are only materials to enable the symbolic act to be carried out, like the letters in a word or the sounds in speech. And do not feel uneasy surprise. It is a question of the kind of symbol that does most justice to the Gospel to be conveyed, to the divine gift, which was more energetic than material, more moral than physical, more active for life than æsthetic for contemplation, or substantial for absorption.

We may thus illustrate. Think of three things—the spoken word, its letters (or its tone), and the meaning it conveys. A spoken word is the symbol or vehicle of a thought it conveys; but it is also the thought itself in action. The visible letters of the word only enable us to handle it. So think of these other things—the bread and wine, the act of the Supper, and the Act of the Cross. What the letters are to the word, that are the bread and wine to the act in the Supper. And what the word actively spoken is to the active thought which moves it, that is Christ's symbolic act here to His real final Act of the Cross. The Supper was an under-agent of the Cross—not the great Act to God but the transfer of it to believers. The word is repeated often; but the thought is there once for all. In music we repeat the performance often by means of the score (the elements); but the composer's finished work stands there ideally, eternally, functioning in many generations. So Christ's redeeming Act functioned in the Supper, conveying itself to its beneficiaries, and it goes on doing so in the Church. We repeat the ordinance often, and Christ acts as often in our midst, conveying *to us* His Act in chief. The work of Christ it symbolises is done to God once and for ever, it cannot be repeated, but only given to us anew.

§

This puts an end to the worship of the elements, or the monopoly of the priest. The essence of the Sacrament in the Church is the common *act*, the act of the community inhabited by the "common person" of Christ, therefore Christ's act detailed by Him. That is where its connection with the Cross resided—in Christ's act of donation. But in that act as real action and not pictorial. It was a real assignment, and not an exhibition. It was a symbol which not only showed or commemorated, but *did* something, effected something, conveyed something. It made over Christ's death to His own. The symbol act is one function in the greater significate Act already begun, it does not simply point to it. Therefore it is more than a symbol. It is a real sacrament. Even as an act it is not an image, an exhibition; it is a real transaction, a real deed, a real donation.

If the element were the symbolic thing, then the door would be open for all kinds of theosophic transubstantiations. And Christ's thought never moved to a theosophy of matter, but to a theology of conscience and its action, to the meaning of a deed, and a gift. But when the symbol lies in the Church's act, using the elements but as sacred tools, it is that act and not the element that contains Christ and appropriates His Act. His indwelling as Redeemer creates all His Church's most sacred action. And the Sacrament is an act which conveys the sacrificial Christ in one way, as the act of preaching the Gospel does in another.

Hence we must interpret "This is my body broken for you" in some such way as thus. First, "This broken bread *represents* my body as broken, not as substantial; not in the substance, but in the act of being broken for you." So, second, the essential thing was not His body but His will's act of devoting it to be broken. We interpret, therefore, "This visible breaking which I now do represents the spiritual breaking and passion which I always inwardly suffer, now begin outwardly to do, and shortly shall complete. This act of breaking and dispensing bread shows outwardly what I now inly begin to finish with God; and I here consign that and its value to you as your very own salvation. This present deed is to give and assign to you the great deed now in process and shortly to be finished. I here give to you for your salvation what I have begun to give to God as your atonement. This giving to you makes yours my sacrifice to God. My spiritual, redeeming act of giving my broken heart in atonement to a holy God, of giving to Him my soul poured out unto death, is for you. This breaking of bread represents the breaking of my body and will. This my act of giving to you, and giving it round, represents, nay carries home to you, all and sundry, the large inclusive Act of giving myself to God for you which is now coming to a head. Now I give it expressly to you in advance; shortly I shall give it expressly to God with little thought of you. Your act of eating represents the way you must assimilate and live on Me crucified and given to God. This bread, broken and eaten, represents the giving and the partaking of My person, which comes acutely, passionately, tragically to a head in the pouring of My blood, that I may be in you as the active life and kindling Redeemer." There is no suggestion of a higher gift than grace, of God's essence all-divine, being infused into the soul. But there is far more than a memorial of an event, or a mere symbol of an idea.

§

Here we may perhaps take occasion to distinguish between prayer and sacrament. Prayer is a gift and sacrifice that we make; sacrament is a gift and sacrifice that God makes. One error of the Mass is that the priest offers God. But no man can offer God; God offers Himself. He makes the sacrifice. He did in Christ, and He always does. In prayer we go to God, in Sacrament He comes to us. The Sacrament is not an occasion of offering even ourselves to God, nor chiefly of our presenting Christ's offering; but it is an occasion of God in Christ offering, giving Himself anew to us in His Church. In this respect you may perceive that the Sacrament is really more akin to preaching than to prayer; it is God offering Himself more than it is we inviting Him, or approaching Him. Only, the spoken Word is more mobile, and carries more of the preacher's idiosyncrasy for good or ill, while the rite is more statutory, venerable, massive, as of the whole historic Church. But *idem effectus verbi et ritus*. The Word and the rite do the same thing. Which is another reason why the minister should not turn his back on the people in the Sacrament. He is not uniting with them in prayer or sacrifice so much as giving them the Gospel from God in action. Such considerations will answer the question sometimes raised whether a warm and intimate prayer-meeting does not do all that the Sacrament does. The meeting is not done by Christ through the Church; it is done by the Church through Christ; it is not Christ proffering, but man offering.

§

In the entire action there were three acts, if I may gather up with some fulness.

1. The bread was broken. It *must* be broken. The loaf cannot be eaten whole. So it was a spiritual necessity, a necessity in God, that Christ should die. He could have escaped if He had not felt that He obeyed a divine law which even He could not change, because He could not wish to change it. It was a law of His soul, of His heaven. It was a requirement of His God, felt the more, and honoured the more, the nearer He drew to His Father. Just as truly as food must be destroyed before it can be of use to us, so *He* had to be destroyed before *He* could savingly serve us. *We must be broken ere we deeply bless*. Self-will, self-seeking, self-love must be broken (by whatever judgments) in a divine love, else every other contribution we may offer, even for the purposes of Christ, is rejected by God. We try to escape this, to compound, to evade, to give *things* while withholding self. But all the courses of Heaven move against such a man. As Christ broke His bread, so He gave His body to be broken. As His body was broken, so was His heart. As His heart was broken, so was His self-will. Without this breaking there is no redemption, no share in redemption. So also (and pointing the tragedy and inwardness of the rite rather than adding a second half—since the blood is part

of the body) without shedding of blood there is no remission of sins. The tragic is nature's law, which cannot be evaded by an immanent God. But He bears it in an Act of holy love which makes all end in divinest comedy. Without the thoroughness of tragedy, without that offering up not of a decease but of a whole life in crisis, the supreme purification does not come. There is, indeed, no intrinsic sanctity, whatever eloquence, in the bread or wine. The elements are suggestive instruments, but the real effect is in the act. The sanctity is in the act of breaking, of pouring out; the real sanctity was in the deed of broken heart and will, that outpouring of the central soul, of which such procedure was but the outward sign. The sanctity of the elements is but the reverence of association with the intrinsic holiness of His act. We reverence them because we worship Him. And we worship Him in His Act rather than in His essence.

2. The bread was given to the disciples. The occasion is an act of consignment, making over, by a symbol in kind, His great impending act. His person is made over, and not in its mere mystic being but in the moral achievement which consummated it. In that signified Act the body, the heart of Christ was to be broken for their salvation, to be given chiefly *to God*, but also *for them*. And here, in this prelusive act, it is made over as for them, as not only obedience to God, but blessing to them. He is there not as static for their admiration, nor just reciprocal for their fellowship, but energetic for their redemption. His person is not their spiritual superlative, but their divine Saviour. It was not broken, and He did not suffer, for a purpose of God irrelevant to them, nor independent of its effect on them and over their heads. That is the bad old severance of justification from sanctification, of Christ's official work from His indwelling person and Spirit. Nor was it for an egoist purpose of His own. Truly He died for Himself in one sense, as Ritschl urged. It was His soul's vocation, and to have shirked it would have lost His soul. If He had not died, He would have been false to Himself and His mission, His call, His conscience. By dying He saved Himself in that sense. He made His calling and election as the first-born sure. He was called and sent to die. He was born to die. It was in

His blood. If He had not died, He would have lived an untrue and a lost life. He would have thrown His life away —*His* life, earmarked as it was for divine death. He only gained His true soul by losing life. He who is called to die can never gain life by living. But yet He was not there to indulge a *penchant* for sacrifice, to find His ideal self in it, to make it contribute to His complete personality. The mere completion of our personality is no Christian object. He was called to be Redeemer, not to be a personality, not to think of His duty to His own soul, His own dignity, His own moral welfare, His own spiritual culture, as we now say—not even to think of His duty, but of His God. His work, His "genius," His mission was from God; and it was to be the Lover, Seeker, Saviour for God of others, not of Himself. He gave Himself. His life no man took from Him. He gave Himself even in thought and habit. That is the hard thing both with weak people and strong. Weak people cling to self with a desperate tenacity they show in nothing else. None are so obstinate as the weak playing at being firm. Strong people cling to self by the very natural force of their powerful and hopeful personality, its masterfulness, its ambitions, its achievements. But He *gave* Himself. Doing, giving was not simply His generous instinct but the habitual, natural bent and movement of His moral mind. He not only loved people, He loved giving. So He gave to all, not to a family few. But He did not spend Himself in an indiscriminate charity, nor for sacrifice *per se*. To live for sacrifice *per se* is immoral. We must live as He did for God. It was done in the service of His vocation from God, in the execution of God's purpose. When He was broken, it was not as many men are calamitously broken down in the pursuit of a fortune, an idea, a private good, a public passion; but His breaking was the great consummation of a lifetime of moral obedience, of such self-surrender first to God in worship and thereby to the world of His disciples. And in the Supper we have not merely a symbol of His sacrifice to God but the actual consignment of it to them, as being *for them* and not simply for some (say cosmic) purpose of God to which they could contribute but which they could never share.

3. They were invited to eat the bread. So they were invited to assimilate Christ, not as ideal but as crucified, not as hopeful but as final. As life is action it feeds on the divinest Act. He is broken in vain if He be not, as crucified, eaten and commingled fully with our life and soul. He is not *for* us effectually till He is *in* us, He does not fully bless till He occupy us. What He is in His mysterious nature is of little moment compared with what He makes our moral need realise Him to be. He is meant by God for our experience, as food is. He is not simply for our contemplation or our thought. "This is to know Christ," says Melanchthon in a passage now familiar, "not to contemplate or believe the two natures in one person, nor the modes of incarnation, but to realise the *benefits* of His death in our souls' experience." Hold to the old phrase about the *benefits of His death*.

But, farther, as He is not only *for* us but *in* us, so, as He is in us, we are in Him. No phrase due to Paul was more original or powerful than that. But if we are in Him we are, as He was, chiefly, wholly for God. That is how it was with Him at His grand consummation. God's will was His one concern. He died for men so fully because He died completely for God when in His death He was perfected. His death was indeed anthropocentric (as theology puts it); it was for us, in our interest, for our benefit. But only because it was more, because it was supremely theocentric, because it was given, not chiefly to man's need, but to God's will. He is "for us," to make us "for God." The more we are "in Christ," therefore, the more we are "unto God." Now the Cross was the complete gift and offering of Himself and His obedience to God; the Supper was the gift to us of that gift of Himself to God. The Supper was the act, the gift, as anthropocentric, the Cross was the same act and gift as theocentric. And in the latter the former was implicit.

The solemnity of the Communion is this, that it is a symbolic act on our part which is created by the indwelling presence of Christ, the eternal action of His act; therefore it is also a real act, mystic and wonderful as His was. We are under-agents of His great action on that evening, when the Cross began by His consigning to man its final value to God.

In the Sacrament a present Christ continues that gift for our response in a Church's faith. We perpetuate it antiphonally, so to say. We live not, but His death lives, resounds, acts itself out in us. We help to make it one long act, like one great note on many instruments, with endless reverberation, or like one body acting in many cells. Or rather He does this, He acts in us. He renews His sacrificial gift in our receptive act—our worship. It is not we who die to the world, but He that keeps dying to the world in us and living unto God (for the blood is the life).

As in all our great and true oblations of life, so in the greatest of them, in our worship, the tremors of His greatest act by His own gift of it move and thrill through us. His death returns upon itself, through us, bringing our inmost souls with it. We fill in the fulness and finality of Christ. We are perfected in His perfection. We are filled with the fulness of God and His redeeming love. It is not that the finished sacrifice is offered to God afresh, even by Christ (far less by a priest), but the sacrifice made once for all functions afresh. We are not quiescent. We do not *listen* as a congregation; we take part and *do* as a Church in a receptivity which is action in response. A mere religious association cannot do this act, however it go through the rite. It can be done only by the society which He created by His act, which lives in the faith of it, and to which He gives, through His Spirit's indwelling, a personal yet corporate unity—by the one society, the group-personality, of the Church of His Spirit.

We show forth His death on an occasion, as He Himself did in the upper room. But the real fellowship of His death is in our total habit of soul, bent of will, and course of life, in the standing act of our personal self-disposal. To show forth His death in an act of real worship is only an aspect of realising it inwardly. But in turn it helps us to realise it afresh for life, so that in the strength of that food we go nights and days till we come to the next mount of God.

§

Sacraments, and not socialities, make the centre of our Church life and social unity—Sacraments, and not even social beneficence. Make much of them. Clothe them with great seemliness, great earnestness, great reverence, great, but not formidable, solemnity. For it is more than the consecration of our sorrow, it is the forgiveness of our sin and our life eternal that is here held out to us and taken. And for a Church this is the thing most important of all. A Church rests not on sacred sorrow but on a holy Redemption. Christianity is not the worship of sorrow (which may be but poetic and æsthetic) but of grace. The great thing, however, is not to be sure that something was done, but to have part and lot in doing it, to have it done in our soul, to be doing it with Christ, with Him to die and with Him continually to rise.

CHAPTER XIII

COMMUNION—*continued*

The repetition of the rite. The variety but substantial truth of the records. A continuation of the prophets' habit of symbolic action. It is an act of Christ in real presence consigning to the Church the great Act of His death. Not borrowed from the mysteries even if coloured by them. The meaning really depends on our Christology. The Church's fatal passage from sacrament to sacrifice. The value of corporeal contact for society. Sacrament, sacrifice, and sentiment. Is a rite or an apostle the greater gift?

I

IN the record of the Supper let us allow that we cannot get at our Lord's precise words with stenographic accuracy. There are several differences in the reports. Are we to believe that from the very first Christ's act and speech here were hopelessly perverted and beclouded?

Suppose we reduced everything to "This is my body. This is my blood," would that not also reduce the act to something which must have been unintelligible to the disciples? We could not conjecture how the Christian ordinance should have risen out of it immediately on Christ's death. With the suggestion of an infection from the pagan mysteries we shall deal later. That might colour, it could not create, the rite. But the work of true criticism is not done by simple subtraction, nor is the mind most to be trusted that has acquired the habit of discounting every mystery by the elision of the difficult. Jesus must have said enough to His disciples to convey some idea of the meaning of the death He was making over to them. And not only so, but enough to make a very great and quite indelible impression on them. Both here and in the ransom passage can we doubt a reference, made explicit in Matthew and Mark, to Isaiah liii., "for many"? The synoptics, like Paul, treat the reference as being to Christ's death, and take Christ's view of His death to be sacrificial and atoning.

Paul treats the rite as meant to be recurrent; and while the synoptics do not do so expressly, they do not forbid it. We cannot think that the repetition just grew up spontaneously in the Church, that it settled in owing to an inner need, and that Paul or another added the injunction. Surely the synoptics (as Feine says) are giving an account of the foundation of the *rite of their time*, of the rite as repeated. They say nothing to show that they had ever heard it questioned, or that they had any other idea than that it was meant to be repeated. For Paul ("I have received of the Lord") it was part of the young tradition. The observance came in at once after Christ's death (Acts ii. 42 and 46). From 1 Corinthians xi. 20 and 23 it was associated with every common meal. Is the simplest explanation not to suppose Christ's instruction to repeat?

Amid all differences we may believe that substantially that took place in the upper room which the historic tradition embodies. Paul says he had it from the rest (1 Corinthians xi. 23) in the same solemn way as he had from the disciples the story of the Resurrection (1 Corinthians xv. 3). He did not have it by rapt revelation (which would be παρά or ὑπὸ κυρίου, not ἀπό). And, besides, it was not the way of Jesus to give supernatural information about things that could be reached by the ordinary historical way. Paul went to the sources, and got the best information. And he says he transmitted it as he got it.

Possibly he got his information on his visit to Peter three years after his conversion (Galatians i. 18). So the tradition would go back to about six years after Christ's death. This gives very little time for foreign and gnostic influences to creep in from the mysteries in a formative way, *i.e.* so far as the origin of the rite was concerned, and apart from its interpretation. These influences may have given Paul a certain calculus of ideas, or thought-forms for putting aspects of it, of which he found Christ to be the reality (ideas connected, for instance, with dying and rising with Christ, or ideas of corporeal transmission, or communion by food), but they could not have given him the historic institution itself. No such influence can be proved in that respect. It is not only unprovable but it is improbable. It is a mere dogmatic (or anti-dogmatic) postulate. And we may remember how in Acts vi. the first community resented Hellenic ideas, and influence of a gnostic kind. Both the first Church and Paul were against such a borrowing.

I have said that what we have is a symbolic act, in the manner of the old prophets. I gave cases, and there are others. Take for instance Jeremiah xix., where the breaking of a vessel in the valley of Hinnom meant to the magnates the destruction of Jerusalem. Still more close is Ezra v., where the prophet takes a portion of hair, and makes of it three parts; of which one was burned, one was surrounded with sword slashes, and one was scattered to the wind. "This is Jerusalem," he says in verse 5. Or again Genesis xli. 26: "The seven kine are seven years." So Christ says "This is my body,"—though His body stood before them. He puts His death into a symbolic form of bread and wine—a double symbol, corresponding to the duplication of His parables.

Apparently He took bread, broke, and gave to them, saying, "This is my body," and probably added some words more, indicating His life as given to God for them in His impending death. He took the cup of red wine, uttered the prayer of thanksgiving, and passed it round. "This is my covenant blood" (Exodus xxiv. 8) "shed for many" (Isaiah liii). Jesus has both passages in His mind. He indicates that with His death a new covenant was entered with God. He made over to His own the value of this covenant for man. Then followed an injunction to repeat the observance as carrying home the climax of His death to the Church and to the world, as pledging His indwelling presence, and offering to men His offering to God.

The essential thing, we must repeat, is the *bestowal*. Christ was not here doing His great work. He was presenting to man that offering to God. It is the *consignment* of a blessing. What was the blessing? With the words "shed for many" we have indicated the sacrificial, the atoning idea uppermost in His death. It was to be a sacrifice to God for His people. It was not an accident cutting short His career. And it is here made over to them by Himself proleptically, through an enacted symbol. He is not dying for them, but giving them His death as a sin offering, which should ransom the world from the condemnation of guilt to eternal life.

We then blend the covenant idea, the sacrificial idea, and the paschal or redemptive.

§

The act can hardly have been extemporised at this moment, but, like the parables, was prepared for the purpose I have named. And not only so, but it was a sacrificial meal renewing communion with God. Was this a pagan idea? No, it was Jewish also. 1 Corinthians x. 14-22 shows that it was a current idea, well understood, and going without the proof that a novelty would need. The act was more than a symbol or parable. It was more than emblematic. It was donative. It was *symbolic* in the great sense, and really sacramental. It does more than *mean*, it *conveys* what it means. "I make over to you my death in blood, which is *covenant* blood and *atoning* (for many)."

In the rite there are three centres of interest—the elements, His act, their act. But the ruling thing is not the elements but the act. And it is His act, not theirs, that is in the foreground. He did something, gave; they did something, and took. He did not just symbolise and they perceive. What He gave was the coming Atonement; what they took was its new and eternal life.

§

The great meaning of the passage and of the rite depends on our personal and present relation to Christ and on our conception of Him. It belongs to Christology really. We should bring to the question, as a real element of criticism, our experience of His salvation—just as to the evidence of the Resurrection we bring the experience of dealings with the Risen.

If we only see in Christ a supreme case of human religion, or if we see in the Cross but a manifestation of love and not its grand crucial action of judgment grace, we cannot see in the Supper the meaning the Church has found in it; and we may be anxious to dismiss that meaning as gratuitous theology. But if the Church has found Him as Redeemer, taking away the sin of the world, we cannot keep that idea out of His last great hours, when He was at the summit of His Messianic vocation, and not lamenting its arrest and failure. Let us keep the rite in the great context, first, of His whole life and vocation; and, second, of the total New Testament Christ as expounded by the men kindled to be its authoritative expositors. Let us not examine it as an isolated episode (as some critics do each miracle), nor as a martyrdom. Jesus knew that God had sent salvation in Himself. Pre-eminently did He know it now. And the disciples so came to understand it. When the Resurrection, when Pentecost, raised them from their lapse, they realised the Cross as theirs by this deed of gift which so profoundly impressed them, even while it bewildered them (as on the Mount of Transfiguration), after their great and damnable treason. They felt as never before that the gift of His death conveyed by the Supper was not vision but life. It was not like any former gift, for never before had they betrayed Him at His height and sinned unto death. The gift was not the daily forgiveness, but the Atonement and Redemption that forgave the world for good and all. It was the forgiveness which all other forgiveness but detailed. It was the forgiveness which gave a new Eternal Life for life forfeit. There came not a new impulse, but a new creation. The gift opened out, as it did in Paul, and most in John, to be the provision of more than a spiritual food—of an Eternal Life continually creating them and rooted in remission of the fatal past. The repeated rite became the stated and pointed expression of what life must now be for them—the appropriation of Christ's heavenly, and eternal, and regenerating personality in a new creation. Life but brought out the sacramentality of faith's experience to the new soul, the riches of the unspeakable gift in Christ's act and word.

II

Let us go farther into this.

Both Baptism and the Lord's Supper were historically

attached to Jewish usages—Baptism to the baptism of proselytes, and the Lord's Supper to the paschal feast. It was parallel to the transfer, conversion, and transfiguration of old ideas like the Kingdom of God, Repentance, Faith, or the Last Judgment.

Considerable variation we have seen to exist in the accounts. As we are not dealing with anything statutory, this matters less. The documents in the matter are not charters or protocols. Paul's account in 1 Corinthians xi. is the oldest. The sequence was the bread, the meal, the cup (corresponding to the third cup in the paschal meal). Central to the paschal meal was the eating of the paschal lamb. But Jesus, though keeping that order, removes that accent, and lays it on the bread and the wine before and after the substantial repast. First He lays stress on the bread as the essence of the matter. He does not lay it on the flesh in the meal—as if He would avert a connection with His mere *flesh*, and fix it on His *body* or person. Then He fixes on wine, as representing the real sacrificial element drawn off from the flesh—the blood, the life. The main things in His use of the occasion were before they had supped and after. Hence the subsequent separation of the rite from the love-feast with flesh food—a refinement partly due to the disorders that crept in therewith—disorders so typical of the dreadful conflicts resulting in the history of the Church from the concentration of interest on the elements more than the act.

It is important, when we discuss the influence of the pagan mysteries on the Eucharist, to notice a certain distinction. The Greek had no difficulty in thinking of food consecrated by certain magic words so as to be the vehicle of a god, and the means of communion with him. But that is not the New Testament idea. Christ's words mean that, besides the material food, there was a spiritual and heavenly food, which the material food but conveyed. This heavenly food it was which was enjoyed, not the material. So that the act was not a meal, but an adjunct to a meal. It was Christ's body that was taken, not His flesh. And it was connected with a historical event as the Greek mysteries were not.

§

But it is the meaning that chiefly concerns us, and not the archæology of the matter. We have the main features. And the additions in Matthew or Luke only show how the briefer words were understood by those who have the best right to be their expositors.

They did understand (we have seen) a permanent memorial and repetition, but also an act and a promise making it more than a memorial. The Church has not tremendously misunderstood Christ in carrying it on, nor in making it a real Sacrament. It was not merely for momentary impression, a sentimental occasion of hopeful melancholy. And it was not a mere parable or enacted exposition of Christian *truth*. We here receive a life gift; we do not learn a valuable truth. It was an institution, a promise, and a gift.

There are two features in the situation.[1] First, He is united with them and they with Him; second, farther off, beyond Time, they will be united again in the glory of the consummation. What lay between? The Church's repetition of the meal in His refinement of it. But He will not be there. "Yes," He says, "I will. Be this My presence. When you break bread together (always, not at paschaltide with its flesh), let the bread you daily live on symbolise Me and My real personal atoning, creative presence among you and in you." The bread should stand for the missing visibility, His personal presence, once mediated by His body. It would not replace His absence, but it would signify His presence.

§

Body meant then more than it does now. It meant the whole *person* in visible form, and not the mere organism. It meant neither His earthly body (which stood before them) nor some glorified mystic body. The presence of His body meant, in symbolic language, the presence of His person. The breaking of the body was the consummation of the

[1] Seeberg.

whole unity of that person in a sacrificial act. That presence could only be in persons, not on a table, not in a piece of matter. The sacramental unity was a personal one. Christ did not say, "I give myself to you in two half parts," in two instalments, as it were—life and death. The gift of Himself was completely symbolised in the broken food. The wine does not add something new, but points the real inner meaning of the bread, as the Cross does the person. The body means the entire person and presence of Christ. He will, symbolised by the bread, be there in person breaking the bread of life. The institution of the Supper was complete in principle with the distribution and appropriation of the bread, representing the body which mediated the person. But union with Christ's person is not the whole of the Christian life—which, when we go in and come to close quarters, is union with the Redeemer, with the Christ of the Cross. So the rest of the rite is not an extension of it but an exposition, a nearer definition. It is not an addition but an elucidation; for the blood is part of the body, and is already included in the gift of it. The wine "opens up" the bread, the blood defines the meaning, the achievement, the concentration of the person, and especially its supreme function and achievement in death. And, note farther, the bread and wine do not follow closely. We have not two co-ordinate factors of one act, two hemispheres of it; but the second is a closer specification of the first. It unveils within the gift of the person the tragic note so lacking to many mystic or pietist phases of faith. There was a relative finish with the bread. This is shown in explaining the cup as the *function* (not a *part*) of the person. "This is the new covenant." Luke's account makes the institution complete with the bread. The covenant cup, therefore, details and points the whole gift already given. It does not add to it. The oldest name for the Supper was the "breaking of bread."

What then is the closer definition in the wine? The bread assured His vital presence, the wine the nature and object of it. It added, as I say, the dramatic, the tragic note to the mystic. "The new covenant in my blood." "*In*" means "through" or "by." The really new and precious thing was what came not merely kindling or calming by Christ's presence as Lord and Master, but poignant and creative by His work as Redeemer, which is the real ground of His Mastership, and in which all His person took effect. The value of His presence was more than impressive or edifying or sheltering, as He came over wave and storm; it was His presence as atoning Saviour; and it involved not His body merely but His benefit. It is an imperfect Christianity when Christ is chiefly but Master or King by personal dignity or excellence. It is but a youth's Christ (leading to greater things) when He is but Hero, Leader, and Friend. He really masters and rules, not by the impression of a solemn and spacious presence, loving and beloved, however mystical, but by humiliation, agony, sacrifice, death, forgiveness, and regeneration—by specific action, by all that is meant most keenly and creatively by the Cross. The new order of things turns on that, on that action of Christ's person (not only noble but tragic, nor with blessing only but with a deadly sting and a last trump) which is represented by the wine and the blood. The bread means the person in presence; the wine the person in action, showing what He was present for—not in endearment but in redemption, not as theosophic food but as theological salvation.[1]

In the Supper Christ is present not to bless a religious coterie, but as having suffered and conquered in history for a sinful people, to whom His Passion brings the saving gift of forgiveness and regeneration. The new covenant or order is not merely the sense of an invisible, sublime, uplifting, and consoling presence (which is not covenant, only

[1] There is a whole type of piety represented by the Fourth Gospel, which detaches the Eucharist from the atoning death of Christ and connects it with the spiritual appropriation of His person, regarding Him as food rather than Redeemer. It is the high mystic way of such souls as Catharine of Genoa, who were enraptured or fortified by the mystic participation in Christ's person without reference to moral redemption. A real atonement goes out of their spiritual purview, and if not denied is at least inert, so far as their spiritual habit goes. We cannot call this Catholic off-hand, for it is not the view at the central point of Catholicism—the Mass, with its Agnus Dei. But it would seem to be both Anglican and Quaker, and it provides the affinity between these which draws many across the line. Quakers often become High Church and never Low. In the theology of both (which determines their religion) a real atonement is not the key to the person, nor is it the marrow of the Cross. Their Key to the incarnation is not Christ's work but His birth or excellence.

communion), but of a new moral order of things, a new creation of a new Israel by forgiveness, atonement, redemption, and the indwelling of the Spirit (Jeremiah xxxi. 31). Something not only stands by us and is over us, but it acts and locks, so to say. The phrase "for the remission of sins" is thus a true gloss on the institutions. There is a crisis, reflecting the crisis of the whole moral world in the Cross. It is not a case of a divine visitation by Christ, nor of friendly communion, nor of Christ as our constant spiritual co-efficient, but of a decisive Act of His offered to us by Him anew and decisively answered by ours, by our taking home the work, benefit, and result of Christ's historic deed. The blood points the body, the wine the bread; it does not extend it. It concentrates, it does not enlarge; it deepens, but does not add. It reveals the vital core of the person to be the Cross. If you discard the atoning, redeeming function of the Cross, there is no reason why you should not stop with the bread—if you can then believe Christ really present at all, which the Church could not continue to do. But the wine is the interpretation of His personal presence as the thrill and tragedy of redeeming grace, of a Redemption once for all, whose once-for-all-ness means a dramatic thing, a new creation.

§

So the rite does not reflect the melancholy of a great soul going to his martyr death and failure, but it promises, nay it gives, the presence and action of a great and solemn Victor over death and evil for ever. It reflects not a Master only, but a Saviour who regenerates men into His own crucial life, and does not merely hold communion with them. It reflects Him as essentially Saviour, and not incidentally so. It is a fellowship, but more—a redeeming royalty, that we experience. It is the Kingdom. It is the Lordship of the Priest, it is Christ as Redeemer, and not only as friend, benefactor, or ideal. And the Lord's Supper is the actual and constant gift to us by Him of this moral relation and this vital work.

The supreme thing in the rite is Christ's renewed act of

gift. Remove that, and the whole event loses its perpetual meaning. "This do in remembrance not only of Me but of My timeless passion and action, in recognition of it, in the energy of it, in the response it creates." So it was for the first circle (as now) an act of His, and only thus a communion with Him. We have more here than an emblem. For Christ was not simply using a practical parable to put His disciples at the right point of view for His death, which they had either deprecated or misconstrued. He would then be an ideologue incorrigible to the end. He was making over to them all the moral, mystic, and eternal value He knew to be in it *with the Father*. They were regarding His death as a calamity quashing all their hopes; it took Him from them. He presents it to them in a way words could not, by an act of symbol which was also the reality, for the gift at the table was a part and a moment of the gift on the Cross. It was anything but a diremption, it was a closer donation. It was less a farewell than His great arrival. As if He should say, "My death I give you with its eternal life and grace. My death I leave to you for ever. Not as the world giveth give I unto you. The death you dread is not a disaster either to you or to Me. It is the one gift I came from God to give Him. And as such I give it to you here. This is not yet the Atonement, but the gift of it to you. I am not making the sacrifice, but making it yours. And in my giving it it is given you by God, as the institution of sacrifice in our old religion was, as the old covenant sealed by sacrifice was."

The great Act was sacrificial. It was in the nature of a gift, and the gift of Himself. But the prime aspect of His self-giving was for Him its gift toward God. His grand concern, which in the end swallowed up every other, was His offering of Himself to God, His sacrifice as made to God, the atoning side of His sacrifice. He was thinking, at the very last, not of His disciples but of His Father and of what Israel had done to its King—the sin not to be forgiven it. He was absorbed in the obedience He presented to God for men rather than in the blessing He gave to men. He felt that this offering of the Cross to God, this hallowing of His desecrated name, this effectuation of an absolute holiness in His own universal person, this proleptic achievement of the

Kingdom in Himself, was the one thing He came into the world to do. It was God's chief behest on Him. He was born thus to die. God set Him forth as an expiation, to use the words in which Paul so truly grasped His life's purpose and end. His supreme work was the gift of His obedience and honour to God when everything had gone from Him but the power to obey and praise. At its depth and height he was too engrossed with this tremendous oblation to be occupied with the aspect of His gift towards man. Had He been free to dwell on the full and far result of His work on man, He could have suffered but little for joy of a new world born to God. Yet the supreme act of His self-oblation to God was also His supreme gift to man. And the deed of gift was the Supper. If the Son's death for us was God's sacrifice due to His *holy* love, the giving of that death to us was the boon of His holy *love*. When then did He make the gift to man if on the Cross He was giving to God? That was done beforehand in the Supper. Was it that He might be free to give His whole heart and soul and strength and mind to His Father on the Cross? Soon His thought would be so absorbed with God that He would have none to spare for man. Yet this offering of Himself to God was the one great thing He should do for man and leave to him. Already, as I say, He was in act to die. The gift to man was integral to the gift to God. For He was all of one. Already the Passion had begun. And before it came to the pitch that took away the thought of man, He consigned to men in a subsidiary act what He gave to God in the great compendious Act of the Cross. The same Act moved in two directions at once, and the Supper was the donation of its salvation manward, as the Cross was its oblation to God.

III

Here, then, we have not a memorial of an ancient Christ, nor the symbol of a Christ remote, but the self-gift of a present and living Redeemer in His vocation as such. Thus He is present in the Church's act rather than in the elements. The bread and wine remain such—points of attachment, vehicles, occasions, agents, not the essence of Christ nor its envelope. The elements are made sacramental by promise, and by use; they are not transmuted in substance. Their value is theological and not theosophic, moral and not substantial. They are charged with Christ but not converted into Christ—as the spoken words are charged with the Gospel, but are not themselves the Gospel, and the blessing hangs on no single formula. Matter is not spirit, but it is sacramental for spirit. The passing is sacramental for the eternal—as time and space are, as the body is for the personality that leaves it, as the whole history of the Church is; which does not prolong the Incarnation, but confess and convey it, as the bread and wine do not continue it but only mediate it. The bread was not His literal body (which they saw before them) nor His glorified. Everything is against this. The word "is" is not there, which seems odd if so much turn on it. If it were there, it would be interpreted as in Luke viii. 11, "The seed is the word." Consider that the disciples could not have understood anything else. And this was no moment for metaphysical riddles; they were all too deeply moved. Was it then a parable? "As bread is broken, my body will be; as wine is poured, so will my blood be for your good." That, I have said, would make it but teaching—an announcement and interpretation of His death. Christ would be saying something but doing nothing. It also overlooks the fact that the bread and wine were not simply texts but food—*meant to be consumed.* They all ate and drank of the same loaf and cup. The symbol was in the eating. Something was not shown but done with productive effect. A close intimacy was set up with Him and with each other.

For much that is valuable here (I have said) we must go back to Semitic ideas, to the common meal of the tribe as a sacred act, denoting and effecting the closest communion with the god. Eating the same food was renewing the blood from the same source; it was therefore the same blood. But here, as the food was spiritual, the disciples understood Christ to set up closer communion among them, uniting them in a new covenant or moral order of things (I Corinthians x. 16). And the new thing was not the fraternity, but its cohesion in His ever-present lordship through the Cross, with its forgiveness, its ransom, and its regeneration to eternal life. Hence the Church is different from a mere brotherhood. Christ gives Himself as their food and future, the blood and bond of a new created life. "Your unity depends on your possessing and assimilating Me, on your living on Me, Me Who abolish by death (and do not merely submerge in My person) the one thing that destroys unity, Me Who reconcile sinners with God." Central to all was the atoning element, reconciling with a holy God and creating a holy Kingdom. This is the valuable feature, in which the Levitical system outgrew, under moral pressure, the early Semitic and social idea of the consumed flesh as the uniting substance, and developed that of the offered blood of life as the common grace.

In the attempts made to parallelise the Lord's Supper with similar phenomena in the history of religion, and even so to account for it, we should note that these set up the communion, while in our Sacraments we but nourish it. Also, the initiative there was on the human side, not on the god's. It was the worshippers who acted. Whereas in Christianity all lay in the response of faith to the creative and historic Act of Christ. His Act created the faith that took congenial shape in an act. Again, in those rites there was no refined substitute like our elements. They did not present wine for blood, nor bread for flesh. They had a harshness and coarseness absent from the Lord's Supper. But we avoid such tasteless materialism. And we avoid at the other end a mere spirituality. For Christ does not speak as if the occasion were a parting of affectionate hearts, but in a reciprocal and moral act of giving and taking His body in some more searching and personal sense. Christ's institution is as unique in its delicacy as in its significance—in its significance as a real act and gift, and not merely in its suggestion as a lively symbol.

§

In the apostolic Church the full meal, instead of being inserted between the bread and wine as at the first, preceded them, and these were joined up as now we do. Hence abuses arose. Some were drunk, some stupid before coming to the rite. Cliques were formed, the well-to-do sitting and dining together, and the poor hungry. It seems strange to us, this combination of fraternal exaltation with such behaviour. And the danger was great. We have another form of the same danger to-day. The social, not to say convivial, element is getting the upper hand of the sacramental. The tea meeting is much more welcome to many Christians than the Communion, more remembered, more felt as a Church bond. The Christmas food, festivities, and charities hide from us the child Who was born to die, and thus give us the gospel according to Dickens. Churches complain of lack of sociality more than the lack of spirituality. And social work comes to count for more than the work of worship.

The early abuses drew from Paul a rebuke and an alteration. The meal was to be taken at home. Thus, first, he accentuated the element of worship in the rite more than that of social union; the fraternal meal especially is thrown to the rear of the sacramental rite. Second, he gave the occasion the character of a proclamation, a local outcrop, reception, and confession in act of Christ's universal and final death. Third, he demanded moral conditions in the way of preparation. Such was his genius. The spirits of the prophets must be subject to the prophets. With all his exaltation and revelation he took oversight and control of all disorder and excess. The Spirit was not an exciting thing like a nature force. It was attached to the Word of the Gospel, to conscience and its control. But the idea of Christ's redeeming presence and gift was always there. The unworthy partakers were not those who were short of moral or spiritual perfection, but those who treated the elements as mere food or the act as mere ritual, to whom they were not really sacramental of Christ's person, and work, and presence. The judgment they incurred Paul found, rightly or wrongly, in sickness in the Church. Only he did not find in it *the* judgment, which is damnation. Their judgment is a chastisement, *lest* they be judged with the world at last (1 Corinthians xi. 31, 32). It was not damnation but discipline. But the rite, in thus becoming an isolated act of worship, fell to the other extreme. It was stripped of the social and intimate character of a communion of saints, and came to be administered to individuals by the clergy. It came to be a medicine for the cure of souls. Evangelical communion ceased. The Agape then became a high-class supper, as it might be a sociality in a Church parlour; or it turned to the feeding of the poor.

The Lord's Supper is the most complete and plenary of all the cultic ways of confessing the work of reconciliation, where the sin of humanity is conquered by the grace of God in a holy Kingdom. It is *therefore the real centre of the Church's common and social life.* This should not be sought in social reunions, or ecclesiastical monarchy, or philanthropic cohesion, but in the spiritual region, in the worship, and the theology moulding it. For here we are summoned to what is our vital centre deep within all the individual wills that wish to unite, to what is the centre of the faith that makes the new Humanity, and to the goal which rounds all. And that cannot be expressed except as a theological statement.

§

The act thus isolated was less a symbol than a sacrament. The bread and wine were symbolic in the sense of being emblems, but there was more than that. The rite was symbolic in the richer sense of being effective and productive. For, first, Christ founded a fraternity of His unseen but real presence. Second, He gave Himself to them as really, though not so deeply, as He was giving Himself to God for them. He gave them part and lot and right in the living power of His death always. Third, they experienced the gift in the consuming of the symbols, which were eaten and not merely adored. Especially with Paul the rite did not only set forth Christ crucified; it was the local outbreak, through their spiritual act, of the Lord's creative and universal act in them, just as the great Church looked out in each local Church, or as Christ rose in every case of faith in His Resurrection. And it effected communion ever anew. Indeed, for antiquity generally all symbols were not only pregnant but potent. They suggested but also *effected,* in a mystical (but not necessarily magical) way. Even the heathen meal was held to effect communion with demons (so the Christians reckoned the heathen gods), as the Christian meal effected it with Christ.

As the Christian Churches had their parallels (I do not say origins) in the many religious guilds of the day, and as these guilds made much of the common meal (especially memorial meals and funeral baked meats for the dead), so the Supper became affected for the worse, as it had been also by the full meal of the paschal feast. (Compare the effect of the Christmas dinner.) Most Christians were previously members of some guild or lodge. We have relics of that in Corinth, and it was signs of that old abuse which Paul had to weed out. So a phrase like "table of the Lord" is paralleled by "table of the Lord Serapis" in the papyri, which represent the worshippers of the guild as boon companions of the deity, who probably was no ascetic. The "mysteries" of Mithras and Attis are especially to be named as examples of the belief in the communication of the divine power by eating and drinking in this way. But to trace the invention of the Lord's Supper to such sources is comparative religion run wild. As well say that meals are a product of banquets. Rather such usages were but presentiments, and they received in the Lord's Supper a true fulfilment, conversion, and refinement. They were mere natural religion if separated from the personal and spiritual religion of Christ, which rose out of their wreck to fulfil their dark prophecy and glorify it. It is the existence of these mystery rites and the saturation of the religious atmosphere by them that explain the rapid capture of Christianity by such theosophic forms of the sacramental idea as led to the description of the Eucharist as the φάρμακον ἀθανασίας, the specific of immortality, as if sin were but a disease and not a guilt. But for these rites and their semiphysical notions of spiritual things it is hard to see how the magical interpretation of the Sacraments should have come in so swiftly as to capture even apostles, when it came to conceiving their *modus operandi*. There must have been some deflecting influence from without. If the evangelical idea gave to the mysteries the fulfilment for which they groped, on the other hand that idea did not come out unscathed from its conflict with them. It is well known that the whole conquest by the Church of the gnosticism collateral with the mysteries did not leave the Church's creed unaffected by gnostic ideas. And the like thing took place perhaps with the Church's rites.

In the Gospel what is given is power and not powers. It is grace or mercy through the acts of a moral and spiritual faith, it is not competencies through rites working by a finely material infusion. This is shown by the prominence of the covenant idea, which involves action, moral and reciprocal action, and which does not raise the question of substance. It is not a question of partaking of Christ's heavenly body just for renewed spiritual vitality. We need much more than recharging. And as for His corporeity, in the upper room it stood before them, not to be eaten, and not to be extended by a miraculous annexe, so far as we are told. The pagan residue in Romanism consists in making grace mean such emanative power or ethereal virtue going out like a fine force, rather than a personal relation and communion; the idea is *virtus* instead of *favor*. The pagan notion was such as we find in the very old form of sacrifice, where the animal was not offered to the deity as an oblation, but the deity was held to be incorporated in the animal, which was then eaten and its life absorbed. This is nothing so fine as transubstantiation, but it makes a point of attachment for that doctrine. It represents a notion or form which the Christian Gospel filled with sublimated meaning, though it was in constant danger of falling back and falling over into the pagan way. But since the main matter was being "in Christ"[1] (as even the pagan enthusiasts also spoke of being in their god), and since Christ was the *moral and spiritual* object of faith, and its creator (as the pagan god was not), the gulf between Christianity and a natural religion was really great. The communion was ethical, however mystic—as the justifying faith behind it was; it was not mystic in the natural sense of imaginative elation and individual absorption.

The gift of Christ in the Supper was something quite by

[1] Paul invented the phrase for Christianity; did he find among the pagan debris the jewel which he cut and set in his miraculous experience?

itself in its evangelical quality. The mysteries do not explain it, any more than does the paschal meal—because of the essential differences I have pointed out. These mysteries give but the notion of a fellowship—a κοινωνία of Christ, without the idea either of atonement or redemption, in which, however, the Supper comes to a head, and which is the root of all Christian reconciliation. What the eating of the bread means is pointed in the drinking of the wine; as in the Old Testament the animal is presented to God not in the flesh (which did not go to God) but only in the blood, *i.e.* as life. "In the blood is the life." It is the offering of the life in the victim that is the precious thing, not its death, its slaughter. It is the presentation of a life (which dwells in the blood and not in the flesh) that had passed through death by a crisis, and that could not die. The cup carries us far beyond and above the analogies of the other rites. We are beyond a heavenly food, we are in a heavenly atonement and redemption. We are in the region of creation and not sustenance merely. The idea is more tragic and more potent than the suggestions of feeding convey. We have not the assignment of a heavenly manna, of a celestial body, for our spiritual nutriment, but the self-assignment of Christ in His Act of atoning sacrifice.

What elevates the Supper from the mysteries is the eternal nature of Christ's moral act of sacrifice. It is the unique idea of atonement that makes the difference, God's atonement of Himself in Christ. It is that which effects a communion so spiritual between God and His people, and between the people who live by it and in it. A revelation of Atonement is a revelation really synthetic, *i.e.* it sets up a new relation; it is not merely analytic, *i.e.* expounding a standing relation, and merely showing something deep instead of doing something new. The synthetic, the original, the creative thing is the act, and the moral nature of the act. It puts us together, the holy and the guilty, it does not show us how much closer we were than we thought. The evangelists say that the rite was the eating and drinking of Christ *through the agency* of bread and wine. These were the handled elements, what was enjoyed was Christ's person, but His person as centring in the wondrous Act of regenerating grace in His death. The physical matter of the elements, however rarefied, was still natural. Its sacramentality was that of a mere wire, conductive of the personality at each end, whose real union was in the reciprocal act set up by Christ. The Act of Christ which the rite met was not an incident in His person, it was its supreme function; in the rite of His death that person was supremely partaken and assimilated. It was theirs by no mere mystic and substantial union of transfusion, but by the Passion as an Eternal Act vibrating in their observance. It was theirs by a moral and atoning redemption in which Christ came all the way, with an absolute initiative and a capture of us, and not by a junction with our souls already some way on in this spiritual quest. It was by a creative redemption and not a benediction, not a large grant in aid.

§

Christ then was doing much more than symbolising in the Lord's Supper—whether it represented His death's moral act and purpose, or the relation with His mystic person expressed as eating and drinking Him who acted so. This latter is the Johannine point of view. The Supper is often connected with the close of John vi., but it contains much more than we have there. It is somewhat doubtful if that chapter is connected with the Sacrament. The eating and drinking of His flesh and blood there is but symbolic of participation in His person, however humiliated, as the soul's food and life. That is why the flesh is spoken of, not the body. Such a communion is conceivable without the Cross, or without the centrality of it; and indeed that conception of it has been common from the days of eating the god, or eating with him, downwards. The idea of sacrifice is not there, nor atonement, nor our reliance on His Cross as the vital point of His person. We have nourishment but not the New Creation. There is not even a symbolic act—only mystic union more or less theosophic. We have a symbol but not of atoning sacrifice, a symbol of personality and its communion, not of action and its reciprocity, of love, not of grace and faith. We have a symbol of the vitalising or reparatory influence of transfusion with Christ's celestial person instead of transfer into His death, a symbol of a substantive union of the spiritual soul with the glorified apart from redemption. We miss the regenerative effect of the act on the Cross as the act of a quite new creation, a moral transubstantiation.[1]

In each repetition of the Sacrament Christ gives Himself anew, or rather renews the gift to us of the Act done once for all to God. So the line of John vi. is in the Supper not only prolonged but raised to a far greater height. The eating and drinking in the Supper is a thing much more deep, high, and powerful, more tragic, searching and intimate than in the discourse. But there is no talk of the communication of higher life forces, nor of food celestial for the resurrection body. It is the gift anew of the moral redemption, forgiveness, and reconciliation created in the Cross. It is the communion not simply of Christ's personality but of *the Redeemer*. We are baptized into the Lord's death, and we assimilate it as a real death that took place, as a moral achievement of mystic majesty in historic flesh and blood. It is the real Christ, the historic and crucified person that enters, super-historic and timeless, and that by His triumphant redemption makes our eternal life. There can be no peace here without victory, no reconciliation without redemption. It is the same Lord Who as flesh and blood walked the earth, the same Lord Who came to a head on the conquering Cross. It is no docetic, ideal Christ. That is a great point. The Christ is Jesus.

Far be it from me to say that the idea of a heavenly food is foreign to the rite, but it is not the ruling idea. It has the note neither of the divine tragedy nor of the fellowship of believers. It prescribes the administration by a consecrating priest to individuals, and not the common act of a community. And it lends itself easily to the unpleasant demand for fasting communion, as if the contact of the consecrated bread with other food soiled the sanctity of

[1] John, of course, does not mean to stop theosophically at substantive union with Christ's person instead of going on theologically to moral re-creation by His death, since we know otherwise how central and crucial that was for Him.

Christ. The idea of partaking of a heavenly food, however, is too deep in the rite to be parted with, and too much in the line of some of Christ's own words. If only we can keep it subordinate to the more moral conception of a common act, with Christ as chief actor and giver in the midst. That is Paul's ruling conception, as is shown by his close connection of it with Christ's death, which John tends to dissolve. "Ye proclaim the Lord's death," says Paul,—meaning the Church in a collective act. "Drink ye *all* of it," —not each. The invitation is collective. And in the cases of unworthy communion, the nemesis of sickness and death to which Paul alludes fell on the Church—at least there is nothing to show that it fell on the culprits.

§

Our results so far might justify us in such statements as these:—

1. In the Sacraments we have much more than emblems, we have a real conveyance. The eternal Act of Christ functions afresh in the Church, and anew He gives Himself and His death and eternal life to us in our responsive act.

2. The gift is nothing material, however fine. We are in a region theological rather than theosophical. What concerns us is God's will and work and not His esssence. What is given to us is Christ Himself, His person in its supreme redeeming and regenerating Act given to God. It is a moral gift, with the mysticism of personality rather than substance, of magnetism and not magic. It is not certain that Paul did not conceive the Sacraments in a theosophic way; but if he did, that was only their secondary aspect; it concerned their conception more than their reality. Their primary aspect was the moral and redeeming action of Christ in righteousness for faith, the holy One in an act of new creation and not simply in the emission of vitality. "I live, and yet not I, but Christ liveth in me. The life that I now live I live by the faith of the Son of God [not by virtue of a sacramental infusion], Who loved me and gave Himself for me [not a theosophic gift but a moral, holy, and atoning]."

3. By John's time the gift (developing an element in Paul?) had become more corporealised. The flesh of Christ

replaces the body of Christ—a vivifying substance or food replaces a person in regenerating action on the moral soul.

John's form (like the isolation of the rite and its detachment from the meal) was a serious step. It was a new form (unless it had points of attachment in Paul), and it lent itself to pagan misunderstanding, especially when separated from the Passion. No doubt for John the flesh and blood meant the personality of Jesus; but it was easy to misconceive the word flesh, as if, not the personal Christ, but His material flesh and His material blood in some rarefied form were the gifts, instead of the mere agents or elements of the gift; as if these glorified "ingredients" entered men like a medicine to permeate and immortalise them, as if the "flesh profited" much if it were only fine and astral. At this point the sacrament began to stray from Christ's meaning, and the Church went on to be wasted on insoluble questions about transubstantiation, substance and accident, the ubiquity of Christ's body, and the like.

Both Paul and John have given us in the final *action* of the Gospel a moral power and principle which has the right to overrule and regulate even their mystical *theory* of the Sacraments. Their conceptions of the *modus operandi* need not be the soul of its secret. They may have been partly borrowed from their day, and might safely retire with the fashion thereof, Hellenic and patristic; while the practical realisation by such saints of the occasion meant a moral action in them and on them which grows in weight with the whole moral growth in history of personality and of faith. If we should have, in loyalty to truth scholarly and historic, to recognise the strong position that sacramentarianism has in the Bible, we have also to realise that for the Gospel, to which the Bible is plastic, theories of its sacramental action are secondary, or might be even otiose. This is what we had to do in the case of Infant Baptism. Faith in the Gospel justifies a view different from the practice or speculation of the New Testament. The principle of faith as active must be bolder than that of theory, and it is the principle of evangelical faith that rules the situation. So we take faith's bold course and say that the practical apprehension of the Sacrament is a matter of inspiration in a much more intimate and authoritative sense than the comprehension of it. The primary theology of faith in it is much more permanent than the secondary theology of thought about it. The former is of revelation and the latter is not.

Our real experience of a present Christ in His saving act for conscience and person (renewed in the Sacraments) is the great gift; and it gives us the principle for all else. But the theory of a subliminal and corporeal virtue more mystic than moral, or of transfusion by a personal essence less atoning and creative than tonic and antiseptic, is not an integral part of the gift. Nor is such belief a condition of the blessing. If it helps you to think in this way, so think, and give God thanks. But do not unchurch me if I construe the experience and the relation otherwise, more ethically—more dramatically, more evangelically, and less in the way of a re-charging process—more in the way of new creation and less in the way of heavenly manna. The great matter is to recognise the real Presence in holy and saving action; the minor matter is the rationale of His procedure. And the antiquation of Greek views of matter and substance, or the growth (with the long growth in Christian faith) of the moral ideas more congenial to personality, to its development, and to its mode of action—these things may and must affect our conception of sacramental action while not impairing its reality and value, nay, while perhaps energising them.

Is there any reason in the nature of the Gospel why the metaphysical conceptions should take the lead (not to say the monopoly) of the moral experiences, why mystical interpretations should look down upon moral psychology? Rather the other way. And the more so as religious thought moves from the categories of substance, or even of ideas, to those of a subject's moral energy. That is all in the direction of moralising both thought and religion, if the holy God is *Actus purus*, and His morality is the nature of things. At any rate it is in the way of subordinating substantial process to moral action, even in an apostle—unless we are still bound in the old net that revelation was a revelation of truths instead of grace, and of a theology more abstruse than elemental and massive. If one might become personal, it would not trouble me to know that Paul conceived in the Sacrament a substantial influx. It would not follow that that was what it really or solely effected, that that was the true *mode* of Christ's access to the soul. It is not that kind of union that can now be supposed to underlie the union of persons and their interpenetration. No entity called love unites lovers. Paul's concepts of modality were not necessarily revelation, which was not conceptual but dynamic, not theological except in so far as it was evangelical. His treasure was in earthen vessels, and the breaking of the pitcher may make much more of the lamp. Modern Christianity has done much—ever since the Reformation—to kindle and clear the true power of personality and its unique modes of action. And among other results it has helped to make the contact of Christ and the soul less directly dependent on either rite or substance, though quite independent of neither.

§

4. Loofs says, sadly and finely, that the history of the doctrine of the Supper has been itself a *Leidensgeschichte*. And the sources of its unhappy and fatal career have been three in chief. First, as I have said, was the detachment of the rite from the actual meal, a step which became necessary even in Paul's time, owing partly to the transfer of the whole occasion from the social manners of Israel, with its family purity and reverence, to the atmosphere of a place like Corinth. By A.D. 150 the detachment was nearly universal, and it greatly aided the change from a social edification to a cultic act and a tremendous mystery. The Supper is the point at which began the conversion of Christian worship from a function of the moral soul into a cult of mystery.

This led on to the second change, the detachment of interest from the act, and its concentration on the elements. By the second century this side of Paulinism had begun to submerge its dominant element, the moral and evangelical; and it was generally held that in some sense, not well defined, the bread and wine *were* the body and blood of Christ. And we have the completion of the Johannine parable of eating Christ's flesh and drinking His blood (John vi.) taken alone, and detached from what we otherwise know of John's view of Christ's death. It is a part of the whole tendency to become pre-occupied with Christianity as light and truth, and to become detached from action, moral, energetic, and special to the Cross. The symbol has not its force as an act, and therefore not as a sacrament (which John does not name), and there is more idea of the illuminating or *vitalising* influence of contact with Christ's celestial person than of the morally *regenerating effect* of His deed on the historic Cross. So also we mark the diversion of attention from the act to the elements, with all the theosophic mists that hang about that region to confuse the soul and de-ethicise the mystery, as if Christ were but a more or less inert person, and His glorified substance were enclosed in the bread and wine, which went through a preternatural chemistry, and became a higher "nature," a finer thing in things, both without us and within. This tendency engrossed and bewildered centuries of thought that should have gone in a more fertile way, to obviate the Reformation, and quicken Christian ethic. They should have realised Christ's person as reaching us in His Act of redeeming grace, and therefore working in the reciprocal act of a personal faith, with its moral mysticism and its conduct to correspond. The mystery of such a long wandering by the Church in a theosophic waste of moral decline is among those that will be solved only when, in the last theodicy, world wars have been adjusted to the rule and providence of an all-good and almighty God.

It is of great moment to note that the Apostles and Evangelists do not think primarily (though they may think) of the exalted Christ providing a heavenly food to eat or a transfigured blood to drink, but they thought of what Jesus did in self-donation on the Cross. They thought of the body which hung on the Cross and the blood there shed to His death. Paul says "We were baptized into Christ's death," not into His glorified and celestial body. The introduction of a heavenly substance into the account was due to a desire to make the experience more intelligible than moral, and more impressionist than regenerating to the soul. We have nowhere a distinction between the body eaten and the body slain to the prejudice of the latter. The believer's eye is turned on the Cross and the body there, not on Heaven and a celestial body there. They ate of that person *in His Act*, not in His substance; they ate of the body, not the flesh. Christ was *cæsus non esus*. So that even if the rite and not the Word had been Christ's great legacy which made the Church, it was not the sacrament as understood by those who now give it the first place.

Then, thirdly, we have the long deep error to which Loofs chiefly alludes—not only the association with the Eucharist of the idea of sacrifice, but the treating of it as a sacrifice (in a cult, which the "breaking of bread" was not). It is easy to see how the idea would creep in. We begin rightly enough by treating the occasion as a sacrifice of praise. The εὐχαριστία was an offering of thanksgiving. We have it so in the Didache. It was the fruit, the calves, of the lips. In the New Testament prayer is figuratively spoken of in this way. And well-doing and fellowship (Revelation xiii. 16) are sacrifices that delight God. The gifts of love brought at the Supper for the poor could easily be so described. But the transfer of the idea to the whole rite was of the most fatal import and consequence. There is no such description of it in the New Testament, though it came in soon after. It is proper enough in the Act to present before God the finished sacrifice of Christ as His gift to us, and therefore the best sacrifice we have to give. But when we re-enact the sacrifice of Christ, when we repeat the Cross instead of pleading it, we not only cause man to offer up a Christ Who alone could offer Himself (as Judas forced His hand), but we hide the ruling idea of Christ in the Church's midst, offering Himself and His finished work afresh to His own. The more the act was removed from the community to the official, so much the more deadly was its transfer to be a real sacrifice or a repetition of Christ's sacrifice, and the transfer of the administrator to be a priest. "As the sacrificial idea passed from its innocent use it took up seriously the priestly idea. And as the priestly idea emerged beyond its first and innocent form it drew to it a more serious sacrificial idea." The sacramental side was subordinated to the sacrificial. In the end it came to this, that, while the New Testament teaching is that Christ offered Himself, now the priest offered Him. "The priest imitates what Christ did" (Cyprian). It was an absolutely unscriptural change. When Cyprian described the priest as "imitating Christ's sacrifice, and offering a true and full sacrifice to God the Father," he was the chief culprit in effecting the change from a *sacrificium laudis* by the Church to a *sacrificium propitiatorium* by the priest.

As Baptism is not regenerative, so the Lord's Supper is not sacrificial. The import of it is certainly dependent on the sacrifice of Christ (as Baptism is connected with regeneration), but it is not in the nature of an atoning sacrifice which we offer anew—as is shown by the form in which it was founded. It is Christ, giving us anew His finished and full sacrifice. It is not we who offer Christ to God, but Christ in the midst giving Himself to us. It is not the bloodless sacrifice of the Mass. He does not offer Himself to God again. We do not thus interpret Pascal, "Christ is crucified to the world's end." The finished Act is certainly in its nature an Eternal Act, an eternal once-for-all; and the gift of it to us in the Supper may "function" still in the Church; but that is another thing from the Church, as the prolonged Incarnation, repeating Christ's sacrifice.

It was a sacrament that Christ made at the Lord's Supper, not a sacrifice. A sacrament is objective—an act by which God's love is witnessed to us and his gift conveyed; a sacrifice is subjective—an act by which we testify our love to God by our gift. It made all the difference to the religious history of the first Church that they observed a sacrament in the centre of their worship, and did not offer a sacrifice. The corruption of the sacrament began when that changed and it was treated as a sacrifice.

The grand giver always is thus not man but God. "For all things come of thee, and of thine own have we given thee." "Whatever you bring to offer as a sacrifice you are bringing as the property of God and not as your own" (Philo). Man but confesses God's gift by response to it. Matthew and Mark in their account do not even quote the words about repeating the rite, so wholly are they engrossed with what Jesus did and *gave*. So wholly was it a sacrament from Christ and not a sacrifice from the Church. Their act did nothing for God, but gave them fresh part and lot in what Christ did, and what He made theirs. The Lord's Supper was a deed of gift, and what was given was the Cross in which He offered Himself to God. Christ was not poetising or symbolising about His death for mere memory. He was making its fruits over to His own in a decisive way. He had given them forgiveness from the first. What He does now is to make over to them that Cross in which His right and power to forgive as God (so that it was God forgiving) was sealed, in which it had its full foundation, final revelation, and eternal action. True, it was a solemn and tender meal of parting love, but it was much more. The melancholy sentiment was there, but there was much else. The rite could not have survived as but the sentimental recalling of a sentiment. So viewed, we see it die even among ourselves.

§

Whatever be *not* meant by the words "This is my body, etc.," this *is* meant. His legacy is not words, doctrines, precepts, institutions, or powers. It is not even life in the sense of more life but of new life, a new creation, where the increate dwells in the create. It is nothing apart from Himself, nothing communicable, but Himself as sacrifice and Redeemer. Himself, offered to God for us on the Cross, is in the rite His own gift and legacy to us. He was Himself the donor, link, and channel for all the wealth of God and His Kingdom. He was, in this act, our new life, its food and its glow. The thought He had given them before. He now adds the deed of gift in this ceremony.

Besides, it is meant that for the cohesion of the members with their Head and with each other corporeal contact has (as in marriage) a permanent and sacramental value—as distinct from the platonic relation of a mystic and individual piety, detached from material contact, moral reality, and historic relations. And so the rite becomes not only a symbol but a pledge of the completion of the new humanity and its perpetuation through the perfecting of its second Head.

If we ask more particularly about the connection between *what* the Lord's Supper does for the Church and *how* it is done, we may note these points, similar to some we had to mark in Baptism. First, while it gets its value from faith, the *connection does not depend on the frame of mind of individual communicants*, nor on their number. It is primarily the Act of the Church, not of an individual. And the Church has done all that the Sacrament means to do even if there are several in the wrong frame of mind, so long as it is a living Church of the New Humanity, and observes the occasion in the faith and obedience of the Redeemer. The Lord's Supper is essentially a social and communal act—the worshipful centre of a social Christianity. Hence *we are not to seek its prime value in the special significance it may have for the individual's experience of Christ, as an individual.* We have here no contact of the individual with Christ different in nature from what constitutes the Church as a whole. This is shown by the express reference of the rite to the historical and collective reconciliation in the Cross (in which common salvation each is saved), and also to Christ's return. It is a great confessional act of the Church. Do not mistake the prime place in a Church's life of worship and of confession—not the confession of sin only or chiefly, nor, on the other hand, the confession of our faith, but most of all the confession of a Saviour and a salvation. To incorporate a confession of creed in our worship may be well. It is better than to have no public, intelligible, and impressive acknowledgment of the great salvation and reconciliation for which the Church exists. But the supreme confession is this act of worship. With such a content a sacrament is raised above a mere rite. To confess a Saviour and a salvation is not saying something, nor thinking, but doing. It is the Church rising with its Lord to the height of *action*—active reception of His gift who is acting in its midst with the utmost that God could do.

Secondly, *the spiritual blessing does not follow inevitably and at once on a mere sensible participation.* We are not to consider the observance fruitless if we go away feeling much as we came. The Spirit bloweth as it listeth. Our part is obedience; comfort is at God's good time. Still, do not go away with the idea that participation is indifferent, otiose. To think so is to lack the vital spirit of the New Covenant. It is to detach yourself from the Christian community in its chief collective function of worship. To grasp the New Covenant, and yet to renounce interest in its practical and eloquent confession in the region of worship, must entail as much loss as there is blessing in the observance. We have only to think of the state, tendency, or prospect of spiritual life in those communities which belittle Sacraments.

§

Baptism is not repeated, the Lord's Supper is. The difference lies in their nature. Baptism is the sacrament of the new birth, and birth begins life once for all. But the Lord's Supper is the sacrament of the new life continued, and this is by the repeated gift of grace. The life both of the individual and of the community must be sustained by constant recurrence to its source. In Baptism the Church gathers all together into one basal act, corresponding to the forgiveness and reconciliation of the world once for all in the Cross as the final creation of the New Humanity; but there is also the daily and particular forgiveness, and, correspondingly to that, the Church in the other sacrament acts in an exercise frequent and particular.

Is an apostle or a sacrament the greater means of grace? A great personality or a great act of the Church? Paul or Baptism? Francis, Bernhard, and Luther, or Baptism and the Eucharist? We remember that Paul said, "To some He gave apostles, etc.," where the Sacraments are not mentioned. Perhaps the question is insoluble because the antithesis is false, as if we asked whether the violin or the steam engine meant more for mankind. The act also is the act of persons who are at the same time both subjects and channels, disciples and apostles, of Christ's grace. It may be the difference between the act of a single great personality and that of the collective personality of the Church.

§

Résumé

The Sacraments—or let us use the wider term, the means of grace, which include the Word—draw all their meaning from their connection with Christ's vocation. They serve and convey not His person alone but His person as consummated in His saving work. The ruling note in them, therefore, is evangelical. That is the real catholic because the real apostolic note—the evangelical, the redemptive, the morally regenerative. The true apostolic succession is the evangelical. The means of grace are but secondarily food; primarily they are salvation. They are re-creation more than refreshment. They convey an act and not merely a nutriment, nor an influence. They are there for their effect on saving faith and not on spiritual life—when these two are distinguished. They serve the cohesion of the Church through common faith and not through influx of life. What we receive is increase of faith and not simply of vitality. It is nothing which *streams* in, in a way unconscious, but something that *works* in by our moral co-operation. Whatever else the part of the Spirit is, it is the prosecution of Christ's work rather than the communication of His being.

The means of grace correspond to the great interests or junctures of life actual, practical, and historic—to birth, conduct, and growth. To these correspond baptism, communion, and preaching. What they all convey is the Gospel's word unto newness of life. The Word preached is not the Bible, but the witness of the classic Christian soul to its Redeemer, which went on before there was a Bible, and which created both the Bible and the Church. As the redeeming God was present and active in the historic Christ, so He was present and powerful in the Church's historic and hearty witness of Christ and His work. The common life which flowed from what Christ did is a historic life; it is not a mystic life detached from history in the depths of individual souls that then fall into groups of affinity. The bond is not the affinity, but the common source and object of a moral faith. Therefore the means of securing and spreading that life are ethical and historic. They are on the line of tradition and not simply contagion. They use the past, they do not simply enthuse the present. They involve common acts of a community and not merely a simultaneous glow. They make one light of so many candle power, not a chandelier of so many separate flames. The Light of the World stands in the midst. The community covers 2000 years, and is made by the experience and confession of the saving authority of Christ; therefore the means of grace are there under His authority whether by express institution or not. The life thus born and bred flows from a source beyond the world; where we have the Sacraments we have the real presence and action of Christ, of God, upon those who receive.

These means of grace belong to the historic form of the Spirit's regime. Their object therefore is identical with the work and purpose of Christ. So they can have no end outside the soul's redemption. Physical effects therefore, however fine, are outside their intent. No germ is planted in Baptism. In the Communion there is no feeding of the resurrection body. The action of the Sacraments is that of the morally mystic and creative Word. Their purpose is that of preaching. Christ continues, in real presence, to present and preach to His Church the Cross He offered for it to God. The only difference is one of the mode of application or of the sense concerned—just as the divine revelation may have law or gospel more prominent, but is God's Word always. The object is the creation or increase of faith. The power in the Sacraments, therefore, is the power of the Word of redeeming grace, and their purpose is its confession and glory. Their gift is the kind of grace that produces faith, and not mere vitality, and not mere status.

The action on the soul by the means of grace is in the psychic region, and not in that of either physics or metaphysics. It is not like the action of two chemical substances, nor is it an infusion of divine essence. The action of person on person, the production of one act by another, belongs to the region of psychology yet unexplored. But the fact remains. Word and Sacraments produce on the soul certain impressions and ideas in a psychological way; then these impressions act sacramentally on a still more inward life, and carry home to our moral centre the real presence of God in His saving power. But just how, who can tell? How does impression become creative, become regeneration? There is much yet to be done for the psychology of revelation. Perhaps we shall never reach the heart of the process. The effect is more than that left by a messenger. For in this case the sender is not only virtually but really present. He acts directly and not far off, by a mediated immediacy, with the timeless simultaneity of Eternity. We have no means of conceiving just how the human medium is united with the divine presence and effect, how the impression made on our psychic nature is transmuted into the regenerative effect on the deeper soul. It is a unique thing, and more or less miraculous. It does not fit into any of the forms of psychic process. It is a new form, this *unio sacramentalis*. Seeberg points out that we may still apply the old formulary that the body of Christ is in, with, and under, the elements, but in this way. God's action on the heart proceeds "in" the human word and act; but as a second thing "with" or alongside that word or deed; yet so that it acts only "under" this procedure of speech or rite.

CHAPTER XIV

COMMUNION—THE MYSTIC NOTE

The lacuna in what I have said—lack of magic in the air—the magic of the spiritual imagination. But worship of the holy turns on moral faith, not on imagination, however fine and needful. Grace not the superlative of nature, nor holiness of beauty. The mysticism is that of action, not of substance; of conscience, not of being; of freedom, not process. It is the act of a living God, more than the atmosphere of a *grand être*. Transubstantiation and regeneration. Analyse the idea of transubstantiation and it is an empty term. No dynamic change in the elements. Only a person can be the conveying symbol of a person. Men are God's sacraments. No desire to use the word magical disrespectfully. Among several descriptive words theosophic may be best, though unfamiliar. The region of the moral imagination, though less impressive than the spiritual, is more effective, because more regenerative, more creative. Is grace medicine, food, vitality, or mercy?

I AM conscious that, in the interpretation of the Lord's Supper which I have offered, it will be felt by some that there is a lack. What is it? It is not the mystic element which some will promptly suggest. For still, to the mystic soul, the unseen Redeemer stands in the midst of every Communion, dispensing His atoning and creating life for the world. With mystic power He flows from heart to heart of those who are one with Him, and He is Himself the timeless bond that no mere tradition can ever be, and that no mere fraternity can ever realise. It might be more correct to describe the missing element as magical rather than mystical, as glamour rather than atmosphere—the element of spiritual imagination so absent from individualist religion. I do not wish to use the word magic here in an unpleasant sense, the sense of thaumaturgy or hocus-pocus. I would use it rather in the sense in which Matthew Arnold used it in speaking of the Celtic element in our literature, in the sense of an imaginative mysticism rather than a spiritual. I am not alluding to a theurgy in the transmutation of the elements, nor to anything in the nature of incantation, but rather to the poetic glamour or temperamental aura which appeals to the religious instincts so much more powerfully than a mysticism of the conscience does. I am speaking of the æsthetical rather than the ethical imagination. I do feel that some will miss that atmosphere which makes the Mass the loveliest of all errors, the most wonderful of all the forms of imaginative worship, and which floats like the incense round the elements at the centre. Now if worship were a function of the imagination this lack would be fatal. But worship is not such. It is not æsthetic. Worship is a function of faith, and of faith neither in a physical miracle nor in an imposing system either of ritual or creed. It is, therefore, a great moral act, with the mysticism that belongs to personality rather than temperament, an act gathering to the central and supreme moral Act of the Universe in the Cross of Christ.

The imaginative grandeur of this act is sublime, yet that is not the real greatness of its effect. The hush of the altar is that of holiness, and it is not parallel with the hush of the infinite sky, nor with the peace which is on the high snows or burning plains, nor with the calm of boundless seas, nor the lull of league-long moors, nor the silence which is in the lonely hills. It is a deeper peace upon a deeper victory than nature wins even at her most occult. It enfolds a death more effective than that of heroes, and a resurrection more rousing than the incessant recuperation of spring, or the irrepressible hope in disillusioned generations. It has something more impressive than these—the blessedness that glows in the whole moral conquest, rebirth, and recovery of the world. No doubt the spell of nature upon the imagination is divine and deep; and it grows as the research of science and the intuitions of poetry present us with nature as a living and speaking thing. To many a poetic mind nature is a sacramental thing. From its beauties messages reach us, and from its grandeurs a peace finds us, we know not how, ineffably exalting, touching, and subduing. When it comes to its height in Art, in Music especially, desire is lost in delight. For the hour we are full and complete. Nature becomes for many a whole sacramental system. And especially when it rises to human nature. If we are moved and silenced by the "sacrament of morning," how are we hushed and crushed by the sacrifice of our beloved, who perhaps pay for our life's comfort by the loss of their own, and in securing us a home fall too early into a tomb! Such things kindle or quiet us with a divine eloquence, and prepare us to find in the whole frame of nature a teeming significance which makes the vast order of nature one endless symbol of things, movements, and powers unseen It is not hard then for minds accustomed to regard Christianity as the grand consummation of Creation (instead of a New Creation) to treat the Christian Sacraments as pointed summits of the long ascending chain, or the focus of that divine meaning which creation pours forth to the attuned soul, and the site of the condensed solemnity of Nature's greatness or of human grief outgrown.

But the transfer is, after all, somewhat illicit. Grace is not the superlative of nature. The Cross is more than the epitome of human sorrow, or the acme of noble sacrifice. The meaning in nature is more æsthetic than moral, more general than personal; and she has no word for the guilty or remorseful soul. The eloquence of nature is rhetoric compared with the action of revelation. She has no balm for our self-accusation, and, wide as are her margins of impunity, she has no forgiveness when at last our sin finds us out. She is far more eloquent to our imagination than active for our conscience. Conscience she does more to crush than to restore. But the sacraments are channels of another message and another might. They do not consummate nature, walk in beauty like her night, nor speak with her daily voice. They give us a Gospel where nature gives but a process or an ideal; and the just live by their faith, and not by their imagination nor their sensibility. So that to invest the sacraments with a splendour or a sanctity condensing the imaginative symbolism of a nature which they do more to cross than to crown, is to clothe them with a reverence somewhat alien to their kind, and to adore a spell rather than a redemption.

This, however, is the element that some may find absent from such a version of the sacraments as I have offered, compared with much of the Catholic spell. But it is an element associated with them rather than issuing from them, an element of the preternatural rather than the supernatural.

It is the result of an inversion of the true process of our thought. It is revealing nature to herself rather than a new power and principle to nature. It is making nature 'arrive' from below, rather than arriving at nature from above. It is importing into the sacraments an imaginative value drawn from a symbolic interpretation of the world, instead of imparting to the world from the sacraments a meaning fashioned at last by the historic act of cosmic deliverance which put them there, and finding the purpose and burthen of creation in its destiny to be redeemed. For they were not part of a nature religion—not mystery plays of ideas, nor parables of the natural heart. They were the product of a historic Act of God, which did more to impose on nature a revolution than to deify its long process or condense its subtle magic. Those who miss from our discussion that element of imaginative glamour or temperamental religion have perhaps been still wandering in the plane of nature as poets when they thought they were pacing heaven as subjects of grace. The significance, the suggestion, of nature is one thing, the revelation, the certainty, of grace is another. And in the proper sense it is only in grace that we have certain revelation as distinct from suggestive symbol. The eloquence of creation is one thing, and the Act which redeems it in a new creation is another. And it is possible to invest the second with the atmosphere of the first in a way which confuses them rather than blends them, and which submerges the Word of God in the fecundity of His creature. And that because we do not take the regeneration with due seriousness as a new creation by the saving God of the moral soul in a historic society.

The sacramental idea, so great and fine, must have its due. Is that due denied it when the act of man becomes the sacrament of the Act of God? Is that not a diviner mysticism, because a holier, than belongs to any such miracle in a piece of matter as makes the care of the crumbs more than a decency? It surely gives more and not less scope to the action of a *holy* God, and therefore to the sacramental idea. And it protects it from those magical suggestions which have done so much to exploit it and degrade it. The theosophic idea of the sacraments, with its æsthetic profundity, is attractive to the imagination of an age when mystic has taken the control from ethic in religion, and an imagination, more active than conscience, beclouds the deep things of God. People try to find there an objectivity which they lost from history in an inner light. Hence so many who leave Quakerism plunge into a sacramental rather than an evangelical Christianity—the more so as they never learned the doctrine of grace in their early school.

§

There is a certain spell about the idea of transubstantiation, for instance, which gives it to many minds the attraction in which the magical always excels the moral to the natural man. I would not, indeed, have it thought that I am indifferent to the impressive nature of a spectacle in which a crumb of bread is under our eyes converted into the very body of Christ at the word of a man. If Christ worked by impression, it could go no farther than that, except by the vulgar way of increasing the size of the prodigy, deifying in like way the Church fabric which made a tabernacle for the host, and turning a handy house as it were into the house not made with hands. But Christianity does not work by impression, for then we should always be driven to increase the size at any cost of quality—as revivalists hanker for huger audiences and an atmosphere accordingly, or as the miracle of the altar expands through a pyx to a tabernacle, and from that to huge and splendid cathedrals with not only an unspeakable and romantic beauty but with a sacrosanctity as the temple of the incarnate Lord.

Christianity works by regeneration and not impression, and by regeneration moral and not magical. Let us hold fast to that. The temple of the Lord are *ye*. It is the flock that hallows the fold, not the fold the flock. And the flock is a community of living souls or persons with a corporate consciousness. What acts on the souls of a Church is the personal soul of the Church—the Holy Spirit of its redemption. It is the personal Christ in His Holy Spirit. And personal action is moral action, not substantial movement—it is the act of a will and not the mutation of a substance.

it is influence and not infusion. The real presence is moral redemptive, evangelical for heart and, especially, concience. It is person dealing with person. It is a personal act(and not only an official) flowing through our acts and making them pure—and especially through our greatest act, wor ship. It is not the infusion of a vital substance, it is the quickening action of a moral soul on moral souls, the congenial action of a *Holy* Spirit on spirits destined for holiness. And as we become more sanctified this is the sacramental action on us that we prize. We become increasingly regenerate. The new birth spreads out into the new life. The sacrament develops the constant regeneration by its own congenial moral method. Nothing but personal holiness can make another soul holy. It is the unction of the Holy One that gives us life, it is not a magic touch. That makes the essence of the sacrament which makes the essence of our regeneration. The essence of our regeneration is notinoculation with a celestial substance, like ichor in the veins, but it is the saving effect of a person in a person. Christ crucified lives in us from faith to faith. And the life of Christ is not substantial vitality but moral holiness, holy love, the sanctification which rears a personality into a person, not the subliminal substance which forms a hyperphysical basis of personality.

Transubstantiation is a mere and empty idea when we follow it up and track its suggestions to their inmost cell. Even granting that the thing conveyed were a finer substance, the lower matter of the bread is not transubstantiated into the higher; but, for the purposes of the inner man, it just falls away, and it is replaced by the finer substance which is unchangeable. The magic is a transplacement and not a real transmutation. It is of a mechanical rather than a chemical nature. You can see how the whole of this magical world leads downward into terms which seem almost tawdry, like the flowers on Roman altars. That warns us that we should leave the whole category of substance out of the question, and speak of personal action instead of essential infusion. If we feel that we lose in impressiveness by so doing, does that not mean that we are still at a stage when the material impresses us less than the moral that we are victims of sense more than freemen of the spirit, and denizens of the world while we thought we were citizens of heaven? We have not passed beyond reverence into that real worship in which all that makes us personal beings bows down to the truly holy and not the merely sacred. We are suffused with vitality rather than raised to newness of life or indwelt by the Spirit. We are more inspired mystically than remade morally. Our imagination of a spiritual world is more vivid than our faith in a world redeemed and a will reborn. We are thinking more about heaven than about Christ, about spirituality than about salvation, about miracles than about the Cross, about the miracles of power than about the miracle of grace. And we think about grace as a tincture rather than as mercy, as a Pelagian amalgam rather than a moral reconciliation. "The natural man is a born Catholic."

The elements are not the *body* of Christ, and cannot be, even on theosophic lines. To eat the finest and purest material cannot be to receive the person of Christ our Redeemer. Nor are they the *symbol* of Christ. For a material substance cannot symbolise a spiritual person, however it may suggest it by association. Only a person can really represent a person; his proxy is a person still. Only a person can enter a person, or really impress what is centrally personal in us. It is with the holy we have to do, and not with the merely spiritual. It is not with an unseen world but with a Holy Spirit, with a personal Holy Father and Saviour. The body of Christ is the person of Christ. If there is any meaning at all in "immaterial corporeality" it can only mean spirit "formed" as personality, and not vague as emanation—personality whose extension is not space but influence, and whose native movement is moral action. The grand and prime sacrament is the action of that person at its height in His holy Act. It is the Act and Word of Cross and Gospel. And the elements are but the vehicles of that person in His Eternal Act, the vehicles and carriers (not to say the tools), that disappear when they have done their duty, as a corpse does. They are not sections nor extensions but vehicles of Christ, and of Christ as moral saviour, and not simply as our spiritual atmosphere, or our mystic vitality. They bear upon our sin and not our weakness. And the poetry in them is moral tragedy and not only spiritual beauty. The action involved is creative, and is not adjutorial. The soul needs saving more than feeding (though it needs both). And it can feed on no kind of substance, but only on a bread which is itself soul, life, power, heart, will, and conscience. About the substance of such personality we know nothing, nor for faith do we need to know. But we do know that whatever is material is created, however fine; nor can it become increate and creator. And it is on no created thing that the soul can live. If there be a substance which is not material it can only be spiritual. And spiritual means for Christianity personal and holy. And these are moral categories, not substantial. Their connection with what we call substance is the mystery of creation; only we know creature cannot be converted into creator. The first creation is quite a mystery, except as we can explain it by the second and higher, which is the only one we can experience in consciousness, and which is a moral and eternal act of love's holy Power. The matter feeds and passes; the Spirit feeds and stays. Our Feeder is our food. Our Christian food is that which Christ eternally and centrally is; and that is an energy which is the inexhaustible creative centre of the moral, the holy, world. There He places our centre. From that centre He quickens us at ours, and from thence feeds us, undivided into substantial parts. He shines on us, and rouses all the buried potencies in us that meet the sun. The sun not only feeds everything but it calls these powers to birth; and yet it remains the same sun; it is not distributed by all its radiation.

§

In this discussion I have felt obliged to use the word magical several times, but I do it with some protest and some reserve. It certainly does help to express what I mean about the subliminal, not to say occult, action, without moral points of attachment, which is supposed to be that of the sacraments as working below the region of the conscious, personal, and moral in man. At the same time it carries associations which I do not wish to suggest, because they would be repudiated by the best of those who cherish the ideas I discard. I do not think it is quite fair to suggest that such people hold any view which would entitle us to describe their form of the rite as conjuring with the spiritual world. For the reference on the priest's part to the living Saviour as the real agent on the occasion puts his act on a different footing from that of the magician, whose power acts in direct control of the occult forces he uses. St. Paul contrasts the communion of Christ and that of devils; and the true antithesis to the action of Christ is not magic but *diablerie*, or the invocation to the evil power to set forces at work which no man can directly command. As nobody could suggest such a thing in connection with any form of the Christian religion, and as the idea of the priest's direct control of the occult world is also out of the question (through his faith in the mediation of Christ), there are risks of injustice in using such a word as magical except to express a contrast with the moral on the one hand and the natural on the other. The word mechanical has a laboured suggestion, which makes it also hardly the *mot juste*. While chemical is still worse—though it is tempting in view of fasting communion. Some would call it gnostic, and treat it as part of the infection which the Church brought back from its victory over gnosticism.

Underlying the forms of Catholicism which escape the grosser interpretations it will be found that there is a certain philosophy which is imported into Christ's words, or rather into the mentality of Christ in uttering the words. It would be more accurate indeed to say, instead of philosophy, theosophy, as distinct from theology, which arises out of God's Word or logos. The interpretations we reject really rest on certain theosophic views which were alien to the Hebrew mind, which we have no ground for supposing Christ knew, and which are thrust into His meaning rather than found there. One fine Roman writer, for instance, says this: "To understand the nature of a sacrament, as indeed of all worship and sacrifice, presupposes an insight of a special kind. It supposes that we realise how inseparable are theosophy and physiosophy. It supposes that we grasp the difference between the action of two natures or corporealities—a material and a non-material, a lower and a higher, a temporal and a material." That is to say, we must be more or less at home in dealing with natures human and divine. That is theosophy, or the explorations of God's intrinsic nature, as distinct from theology, or the understanding of the word of God as active and revealed. The one works with insight, or penetration, or vision, or discovery of a certain kind, the other with the faith of revelation, the self-committal to that, the response of person to person in an act which is moral and not "natural" (in any grade of nature, however fine). Speculations of this theosophic kind are thrust under the intention of Christ, having been imported from a Hellenic type of thought very early in the career of the Church (to say nothing of the Apostles), and developed, under a fascination it is not hard to feel, down to the later days of Behmen and Law, Hegel and Schelling. If the word theosophic were better understood (see note at the close of this chapter); if the general public did not hate it (and every new word), as making a call for effort, or as offering the possibility of anything so odious as an extension of their education; or if it had not been captured by the advance agents for an Oriental cult dealing in a mixture of Buddhism and banality—then that word would have been a more accurate name than either magical or mechanical for the physico-spiritual view of the sacraments which we disown, and which thrusts its own interpretation on precious words like "This is My body," or "I am the bread of life." Jacob Behmen, for instance, says this: "With the active or creative Word of Christ, 'This is My Body,' His eternal corporeality passes as a 'tincture' into the bread without being cut off from Him or dividing Him, as the light and warmth that change the face of the earth do not forsake or dispart the sun." Behmen, being much ahead of his time, took the term "tincture," like many others, from the most penetrating scientist of his day, Paracelsus, while as yet science was trailing nebulous frills from worlds not realised. And by it he meant something like what others understood by a "virtue." It was a middle something between spirit and matter, the intermediary by which the soul works on the body for instance, an *impenetrabile*, a *substantia intra substantiam*, "a mediating nature between spirit and corporeity, which works both physically and spiritually." Without it all is pallor and decay. "A poem, for instance," he says, "may be excellently and elaborately composed, but if it lack the tincture it produces no effect." It lacks the power, the life, the "lift," the quality, the *mirum quid*. The tincture is a very hypothetical entity, it will be seen; but it is one that can pass, as hypostatic, as a finer thing in things. It is an "immaterial corporeality"—a phrase to which it is now hard to give any meaning if we think of the deepest and most powerful action as the moral action of person on person, where the features are not contours of spatial line or form but spiritual character or idiosyncrasy.

It is with such ideas as that covered by the word tincture that we must work, ideas more or less spatial and not moral, theosophic and not theologic, if we are to discuss sacraments as many do to whom they stand as Christ's chief legacy to the world. But it is a region where discussion is very difficult, since the quantities are so slippery, and the speculative imagination so active. It was not in this region that Christ lived or the Gospel moved. It is a gnostic region. It claims to be the region where we find the *pleroma*, or plenitude, of the world; which, however, the New Testament declares to be not an occult wealth of being but the cosmic personality of Christ, with a moral universality and not a corporeal ubiquity. For Christian faith there is more wealth and fulness in personal contacts and their moral relations than in all the power and interplay of the material world. The grace of Christ as a moral power is richer than all the charm, wonder, or variety of the material world, however fine its corporeality may be. There is more wealth and marvel in the moral and personal world of social relations than in any degree of physicality, were it the most ethereal substance we could conceive. We are in another, a choicer, a disparate kind. If the world of forces is marvellous in its mystery, much more the mystic world of moral souls. To be morally and mystically in Christ by the sacrament of His word must be worlds more than to have Christ in us by eating a piece of matter so substantial (whatever its consecration) that it could be tainted by contact with the previous contents of the stomach.

My case is that the imaginative spell associated with such views of the sacrament as deal with the mysticism of things, rather than of action and person, is not a monopoly of these views. And we only feel it more impressive because we are still at a stage where the æsthetic imagination of nature is more active than the moral imagination of sanctity, and where mere spirituality is more prompt than conscience, and is more prized than holy love by the general mind. It is grace as mercy and not as "virtue" that is the rich grace of Christ. "He shut them all up in unbelief that He might have *mercy on* all. O the *depth* of the riches (not of the nature but) of the wisdom and knowledge of God (in such mercy); how unsearchable are His judgments (not His essence), and His ways (not His being) past finding out." "The unsearchable riches of Christ" is the riches of His grace, not of His nature. So utterly foreign is it to the Gospel when we sing, how grotesque it is when Protestants sing, the theosophy of the Mass.

> "And that a higher gift than Grace
> Should flesh and blood refine,
> God's presence, and His very self,
> And essence all-divine."

He is not more of Himself in His essence (which we know nothing about) than in His grace (which we know intimately). But if the Catholic is sure he has Christ in his way, and I am equally sure in mine, it is the same atoning Christ. I have the person He really means. And ought we to be on no speaking or visiting terms when we are nearest Him because our views part about essence, corporeality, substance, virtue, validity, and such like quiddities? He knew nothing of them; and what we seem to know is vanity, except for the scientists of matter rather than spirit, the students of force rather than power, and the searchers of the atom rather than of the individual. The division is less the nearer we come to the Atonement as the focus of faith. Where we part so hopelessly is on the Church, the ministry, and their authority. The Gospel unites, the ministration of it divides.

§

So on the other side I feel a certain moral lack as they may feel on mine the æsthetic—and I am using that word in a more broad and philosophic sense than the merely artistic. I feel their lack, which is so conspicuous for instance in the three creeds, of the idea of redemption as the essence of Christianity. I will not say it is not in these creeds, but it is not expressed, where such an essential should be. These creeds belong to an age (whose non-ethical mark they have stamped on the whole Catholic Church) when that central idea of moral redemption had not come to its own, when attention was wholly fixed on the person of Christ, and on a construction of it more metaphysical than either moral or religious. Therein they differ profoundly from the great confessions, where faith in Christ found its access to His person by His Cross rather than by His cradle, and by the New Testament rather than by the councils; and when piety meant moral reliance on an atoning Redeemer and not sacramental union with the essence of the Son. In Protestantism we have more confidence in what Christ morally did as the Holy One; in the Catholic type we still have the stress on what He mystically is as the celestial One. And something is lacking if we have a repose in Christ's person detached from a vital, central, and personal trust in His Act of the Cross. The Catholic tendency, especially in its Anglican form, seems as if it tended to ignore the Christ for us in comparison with the Christ in us—and above all sacramentally in us. The idea of communion obscures the idea of redemption; and the moral effect both of Church and Gospel for righteousness public and private comes short. The religion is more Christian than the ethic, which is Aristotelian—the best paganism, but pagan.

There is one good feature, I have said, about the Mass—it keeps the rite in the closest connection with the sacrifice of Christ and the virtue of His Cross. This is not always a mark of the type of faith which claims to be Catholic. The most devout forms of non-Roman Catholicism often seem to lose the poignancy of Christ's Cross, and its cruciality for the moral universe, in the participation of His person; or to lose it as anything beyond a great sacrifice, as anything like a moral atonement or a divine judgment. The effect of the Eucharist is then to convey the virtue of that person without what used to be called the benefits of His death. Sacrifice is detached from judgment, and loses the ethical quality of a moral redemption. This view produces a type of piety which is very deeply felt and very attractive; but it may also lose moral verve and evangelical passion in a subdued style more devotional sometimes than devout, more reverential than solemn, more aloof than potent, more fine than strong.

There is a form of this view which wins a certain attractiveness at this humanist day at an even greater cost to the crucial value of Christ's death. It is said that in the sacrament we take into ourselves, and "hold in us," in a special way, the humanity of Christ. Unless by humanity we mean historicity, this does not seem to fit the two truths, that the supreme act of worship should reflect the supreme feature of faith, and that the supreme thing in the Cross of our faith is not what was done by the divinest humanity but by the act of God in Christ. The precious thing is not that Christ redeemed, but that God was redeeming in Christ. Humanity is always a creature, and cannot wield or feed salvation. The body means the person. What was the person-making element in the Saviour? Was it not that resolve of the uncreated Son to empty Himself which was the foundation both of Incarnation and Atonement? It was no mere action of the historic and human Jesus when Incarnation had taken place. And that superhistoric element is what should dominate our chief act of worship. The idea of communion with Christ's person without a prime reference to atonement and regeneration in His Cross is one that takes the heart out of faith in the long run by robbing it of moral crisis and moral verve. And I am here alluding to the type of faith which marks a Church and its conscience; I am far from insisting on such a conscious crisis in the case of each individual, which would often be deforcing the soul instead of converting it.

If the chief thing in the sacrament is appropriating the

humanity of Christ, this does not seem to apply to both sacraments. And it is not clear how the Eucharist differs from other acts of intense worship. It is not clear how it is to be connected with the unique function of the Cross in the total act of Christ's person or the several acts of His life. It seems either to detach redemption from the central function of Christ and of His revelation, or to be detached from redemption in a way for which the fourth Gospel gives some colour. It is not in His humanity that Christ is Redeemer. If we are to keep up the old language of natures, the Humanity is rather the living element and moral medium in which the redemption takes place, while the real agent is the divinity, the gracious God, in Christ.

There are signs that this type of Catholicism begins to feel conscious of its evangelical defect and is making efforts to meet the need. It seems to be growing more clear to it that the great Pauline element is the main thing, and that it is Paul's ethical element; that the mystical is to be construed by the ethical; that conduct and character are not secured unless this is so; that we can have but the one moral centre in a religion for the whole man; which centre, if humanity is in a tragic crisis with a holy God, is in the Atonement; which atonement, therefore, becomes the centre, source, and norm from a God of holy love for an ethical religion and a moral redemption.

§

A religion of mystic communion is very well for a time of settled peace and its pieties, when a reference to blood becomes for some more tasteless than solemn. But a time of crisis calls for a faith more profound in its note, more tragic in its tone, and more redemptive in its effect. In all the history of religion, when order and civilisation are well settled the ordinary goods of life are secured, and therefore are less prayed for. But that is only for a time. Not only does crisis end peace, but desire itself becomes ill-satisfied by all that is supplied to it. The desire is met, but the desiring soul is not. All desire has deep within it the instinct of eternity, of making itself and its satisfaction perpetual. But in experience either the desire fades or the things fail that filled it. Then comes the note of pessimism; and therewith the passion for religion as redemption. In the East we are familiar with it as Buddhism. In the West it took other forms, some as recent as the type of redemption so finely represented by Eduard von Hartmann. But this may yield no more than a religion of æsthetic redemption, as I have before explained the word. It may mean but a rescue from ills that the natural man feels or a fulfilment of aspirations he cherishes—the benediction and refinement of human nature, the eudæmonist treatment of its egoism, however spiritual. Religion is then what satisfies the best desires, or gives us escape from life's poverty or its fears. It might be but the precautionary religion of the healthy, happy *Weltkind* who attends to his religious duties. In all such cases religion is æsthetic as distinct from ethical because it does not seek first rescue from guilt, and it wants even Christ as boon rather than grace. It gives spiritual good rather than moral change. In Christianity it seeks rest in Christ, peace in believing, but it knows no tragedy of conscience or of the Cross. Its faith is of the soothing, consoling, edifying kind. Its sacraments are mystical without being crucial, and all is quiet, happy, and supprest.

But as we pursue the history of religion we meet with another and deeper need, the need not for redemption only but for moral redemption. Besides the affections, aspirations, and purposes that are crossed, there is the will that thwarts the love and crosses the purpose of God. We become less egoist, and we turn to think of what was due to God rather than man. We are then in the region not of feeling personal or æsthetic, but of conscience; not of feeling towards the dear and desirable but of obedience towards the holy and imperative. The mysticism inseparable from deep religion grows moral because we are placed before the holy and not the solemn only. In this moral region the redemption must be more individual (as the sense of guilt is) and at the same time more universal and social than mysticism can be. It founds a new society, which enters active history to take command of the nations, and to surprise them with a missionary passion to which national religions are strange. And, another thing, the desire is for union with the god and not merely vision or contact. It is true the union may be still at a stage more æsthetic than ethical. The communion with the god is entered by rites, lustrations, feasts—eating of the god or of some supernatural food which he blesses or shares. The idea is not fully moralised. Escape is sought, not now indeed from ills, but from impurity rather than guilt. The devotion is wholly mystical; and the practices are ascetic and disciplinary rather than morally atoning. Subjective peace is the object rather than reparation to a wounded deity. The eye is still not on the object but on the self. The rite has its initiative in the man, not in the god; the idea of the god being self-atoned is unheard of. It is a gift to the god, not an obedience. It is not a response in kind to a divine act, an act of the holy, an act therefore of moral achievement, giving to man's act both truth and value.

The recurrent sense of sin is not to be stilled by any ascetic nor by any rite. And rites that depreciate that sense or cover its absence are non-ethical however religious. They tend to the æsthetic side, to religious good form or egoist satisfaction. It is a bad symptom when we find an increased stress on sacraments alongside of a decreased sense of sin. And there are many who seem to observe the conjunction to-day, as the prophets did long ago with bitter denunciation of national judgment thereon. If the prophets are refused, the remedy prescribed for ills that cannot be denied is a speeding up of the old way, multiplying services and sacrifices, tithing the mint and cummin, and making religion punctilious, scrupulist, and expensive. It dare not enter a conventicle, nor let the wafer enter any but an empty stomach. The provision is then only more spiritual vitality to pursue the old path, and not a new type of religion and life, issuing from a crisis in God vaster than anything either in the individual or in the people.

Of course the Stoic intervenes; and he brings a highly ethical note, but without the power to sustain it or to spread it. Be self-redeemed. Stir up all that is within you to put yourself in line with nature, with the moral order. When duty says you must, reply you can. But, except from the untried and self-confident, who have not discovered either the depth of demand or their own poverty, the reply is "I can't." Which plea there is nothing to meet but the fresh asseverations of "Christian Science": "You can. Only believe, and you can." Thus Emerson ends in an Eddy. In such ways reconciliation is cherished without redemption, and peace ingeminated without victory. So transcendental idealism ends where Brahmanism, Judaism, and Hellenism all ended—in the same failure that called for Buddhism and Christianity.

This brings us to the kind of redemption which centres in a historic act; which is easily viewed at first as an eschatological redemption. Faith looks for a moral renovation not of the soul only but of the world, and it looks for it by redemptive catastrophe. Both Judaism and Parseeism rose to this hope, which for its accomplishment required a Messiah or a Soter. And it was this passion which Christ finally converted from æsthetic to ethic, by an act of redemption which was on the scale of the world because it turned on the holy not as the superior and aloof, too pure and proud to fight, but as the intimate act and final moral conflict of the Universe. By His atonement to the holy He converted all worship, all mysticism, and all sacraments from the æsthetical to the ethical; and He set the longings or enjoyments of religious feeling on the eternal foundations of a moral redemption which truly contains spiritual communion for the soul, but on the basis of a salvation for the conscience and the eternal life of a Kingdom. The great gift was a forgiveness rather than a food, a regeneration rather than an ecstasy. The chief criticism of a certain notion of sacrament is that it does not thoroughly establish the morally holy in control of the mystically æsthetic. Æsthetic religion is the religion of human impulse encouraged, idealised, and fed, only not redeemed in the divine and thorough way by a new creation, not regenerated in a moral and personal way. And ethical religion is that of human nature condemned, converted, reborn, regenerated, and revolutionised (though not necessarily with sudden violence). At its height it is redemption mystically moral. For a mere æsthetic religion with its reparatory food, stimulus, or motive, nay, even with its personal communion, is not yet at the level of the Cross with its creative *gift* of eternal life by forgiving redemption. An æsthetic religion saves from sorrow, or in sorrow. It is therefore sedative, quietive, consolatory, refreshing. An ethical religion goes deeper—if morality be the nature of things; it saves from guilt, and it carries with it a new creation and an unearthly inspiration in the name and power neither of the homely, nor the happy, nor the sacred, but of the holy. As the nature of a Church's faith is and its type of religion, so are its sacraments. The æsthetic kind of religion either overrides the moral (or is in a parity with it) or it is entirely controlled by it—as the Cross of Christ controls and interprets all we know and enjoy of His person. The holy sacrament is the sacrament of the holiest act and not simply of a most sacred essence or even presence. From Christ in the Church's midst it is refreshing food, but still more it is personal life creatively new from the one source of the world's new creation in the Cross, which made Jesus the Christ and installed Him as the Son of God with the eternal power of the Spirit of holiness.

§

So, if it is asked whether grace is medicine, food, life, or mercy, we answer thus. There is no Christian who does not set out by saying that for him everything must begin with the gift of God. His God is his Giver. What then is this gift? We may take it perhaps that we are outgrowing the stage in which that question was answered by saying it was truth about Himself. It was nothing else and nothing less than Himself that was the gift. The grace of God was His holy, gracious Self. But that does not come to quite close enough quarters with the real issue. It is enough to meet the Roman view of the sacrament, which interprets the divine self as the divine substance, and sees in a sacrament a greater gift than grace, namely, the communication of God's essence. If the gift of God was not a theology, or truth about Him, was it His person in the sense of His act or in the sense of His essence? Was it something moral—redemption; or was it something material (however fine), something metaphysical, something ontological, something in the nature of a substance, a tincture, a virtue? Was it interpenetration with His will or participation in His being? Was it given to our conscience or to our nature? Was it grace as bestowed mercy or grace as infused vitality? The new life—did it grow outward from the new conscience, or did it suffuse the whole soul and just include the conscience in its sweep? Was it moral regeneration or pneumatic reinforcement? The evangelical view is that the gift was God, holy God, and that it was new and eternal life, but also that it was still more positive and pointed—that it was the holy God's mercy to guilt in His atoning self-oblation at the moral centre where men are made men or marred; it was not the flooding of our enfeebled nature by a spiritual vitality which floated up the conscience among other things of equal moment. The gift was moral mercy, it was not medicine (far less was it magic). The great gift was for the last need. Grace was mercy to guilt, it was not medicine for disease. More than disease ailed us. We are not responsible for disease, except in a secondary way. Somebody may be to blame for my typhoid, but I am not. And who is to blame for cancer? In my sin even, others may have had some share, but I made my own guilt. Grace is the moral, the holy treatment of that, the destruction of that. The great grace is not sacramental grace in any substantial sense, but evangelical grace, moral grace, the grace of holy love dealing with the conscience by a personality, and not of mere generous love repairing our nature by the body even of Christ. That grace is the soul of sacrament, and its right to be.

And, as the gift of grace was the gracious God in person redeeming (and redeeming, not simply recuperating) us, as, therefore, it was more than medicine to our weakness, so it was also more than food for our strength. As it was more than a φᾶρμακὸν ἀθανασίας, so it was more also than a θεῖὸν βρῶμα. All that is too Pelagian, too synergist, too fatal to a real regeneration and a new creation. Christ's own metaphor of the food in His gift, or in His sacrament, had been overdrawn and abused, till it has in many quarters loss its force; so that we feel His beneficiaries but not His property. As a metaphor is a brief parable, that has happened to the one which has happened to the other. The metaphor, like the parable, has been allegorised. Its detail has smothered its idea.

I mean this. The parables have been treated as allegories instead of parables—to their misfortune. They have been treated (and chiefly by the pulpit) as if every detail was by the author deliberately charged with tutorial meaning instead of touched in with pictorial value. Each touch has been treated didactically instead of æsthetically, as if it were there to multiply meanings instead of to complete the picture. That is allegory, which bristles with symbol at every point. The parable, on the contrary, crystallises upon one idea. It is there for the sake of one idea. It is that idea taking lovely flesh. It is an incarnation more than a composition. It is the field in which a pearl of price is hid; it is not salted with seed pearls all along its course. The central idea creates the parable, secretes it as its own integument, so to say; whereas in an allegory all sorts of symbolic garments or figures are hung upon it. So that in the one case we feel the creative power, in the other we admire the reflective ingenuity.

You have only to compare the parable of the prodigal, revolving on the one idea of the absolute and joyous freedom of grace, with Addison's well-known allegory of the Bridge of Life in his *Dream of Mirza*, or the still better-known allegory of the *Pilgrim's Progress*. The parable has more to do with regeneration, the allegory with edification. The one aims at deep impression, the other at detailed interpretation. Well, the like thing has taken place with the short parable in which Christ described Himself as food, and His sacrament as a partaking of it. The metaphor has been treated as an allegory.

Two things have happened by dwelling mainly on this idea. First, religion has come to be viewed as the satisfaction of spiritual desire or aspiration instead of the atonement of moral guilt; the redemption has become more æsthetical than ethical, as it did in Buddhism or mysticism. And second (which is my chief point here), the metaphor of food has been allegorised. Our modern knowledge of physical forces, of the chemistry of nutrition, has been brought forward as deepening and completing the analogy. It has been pressed into the service not of edification only in the way of fancy, but of theology also in the way of truth. The theosophic mind saw in the details of the chemistry of food not only analogies but principles which were imported into the meaning of Christ, though He was conscious of none of them. The forces in the food die, sacrifice themselves, and ascend into the higher life of the human organism, and thereby into thought and action. So the heavenly body of Christ, consumed in the elements, undergoes death and sacrifice in us to rise in our newness of life. And so on, with even more detail in the way of theosophic chemistry, and by way of explaining the inwardness of sacramental action. It is pious ingenuity with a philosophic pose. It is another case of the intrusion of natural law into the spiritual, and above all the moral, world. It is a subtle naturalisation of the higher ethic. No such knowledge of process was in Christ's reach. And yet these details are crowded into His parable, as being within the significance of the entire Christ and the conscious intent of the historic. We might impose upon Christ in the same way any of the speculations which attract us, and get some reputation for mystic insight in doing so. But it takes the moral force out of religion in the end.

Truly, we live on Christ. Truly, we feed on Him. And to men in the natural stages of the spiritual life it gives a solemn sense of union with Him to think that a portion of His body is within them at its divine work upon their supernatural self. But the more we treat that food as substantial the more we lose it in the long-run as moral Witthout moral support, from being supernatural it becomes but preternatural, as the religious life in Catholic lands would seem to show. The more we peer into the qualities and processes of the finest substance and apply them to the action of grace, the more we oust the conscience for the imagination. And at last we lose Christ in the influence that flows from Him. When Christ said that we were to live on Him as He lived on the Father (John vi. 57), was He thinking of the Father as an outgoing essence or influence which He appropriated to be His life? Or was He thinking of that interpenetration of persons (as we now call it) which is the communion of the Holy with the Holy, and which makes the Holy Spirit not an effluence but a person and a power? One is tempted to say that argument from scientific metaphors has done more harm than from poetic, where the touch is lighter and the tendency less dogmatic.

The figure of eating is in the Bible applied to a book as well as a person, as in Ezekiel iii. 1-3. It was a vivid way of saying he thoroughly mastered it, and assimilated it, and lived on it, as many a man has done to Ezekiel's book, or to Plato, or to the New Testament. These works have passed into their very blood. They lived in them till they lived on them. But there is no suggestion of any of the finest particles of the roll entering Ezekiel's system in the breakfast sense of the word. Nor is there any suggestion of the subliminal substance of the higher person passing into action underneath the consciousness of the lower. Deep, latent, and long as the early influences of one person may slumber in the soul of another, they mean nothing in the nature of a dormant ether. A son might say he just lived on his father, or a wife on her husband, in whom her own personality seems lost. "I just live on him." They are in entire and sympathetic communion. But, even if it be the old-fashioned relation of lord and master between the married pair, it is not yet the relation of Redeemer and redeemed. She dwells on and in his character with entire devotion; but she has never been false. She is no Guinevere to his Arthur. Their communion, therefore, is yet not in the region of grace but only of love, the love of peers (as the love of Christ seems for many). It is of sacred love indeed, yet not of holy love. And it has nothing to do with lapse. So much of the moral element it lacks. But is it suggested that if the new communion between them did rest on forgiving grace there would still have to be some passage of an ethereal substance, without which the old confidence could not be restored and made deeper still?[1]

[1] There are certain *risqué* analogies sometimes used here of a kind to which theosophic mysticism is somewhat prone, but which are not unlawful if sacred processes in nature are to be taken as images of holier things. Indeed, it is not unlikely that these analogies may have acted as arguments to such

If we ask where the great gift was secured to us, we have answered that it was on the Cross (unless we are to put even the Cross into a siding). But what was given us in the Cross was reconciliation, it was not amalgamation, not suffusion, not absorption. It was not our absorption into God, nor God's into us. It was not the integration of a divine essence into human nature—not if the Cross, with its moral victory, is the very summit and key of the Incarnation. The boon was not some kind of communion which was the fruit of reconciliation; it was, and is always, the reconciliation itself. It was Christ our reconciliation, and not our new habit. The Cross was not a preliminary to the great gift. It was not a condition of it. It did not free God's hand. It *was* His free gift. It was God in Christ reconciling. And it was, above all things, a moral act. It was the crucial act of the Holy upon guilt, the creative act of the conscience which makes God God upon the conscience which makes man man, but which also unmans him beyond all else. The gift was grace to our guilt more than food to our weakness. It was moral re-creation, not pneumatic reinforcement. We live on the holy person and grace of Christ, about Whose substantial Being or cryptic virtue we know nothing, as there is no sign that He knew anything. Our communion is not with Christ's body except as that image stands for the person; and it is not with His person except as that person in its consummate and eternal Act is our Redeemer. It is not the spell of that person that we own, but its saving grace that we worship. We do not enjoy its kind beauty, nor drink up its sympathy, but live on its act and power.

Grace is a matter of moral and personal relation between holy love and deadly guilt; it is not a matter of substantial continuity, nor of energetic vitality of a pneumatic kind. And our best analogies will come from the region not of occult process but of moral psychology. Christ is more even than our food, He is our life. He is more than what

minds during the formation of the mystico-material doctrine. I will quote from Baader one illustrative passage quite in the vein of his master Behmen:—

> "Der Speisegeber, oder Zeugende, verleiblicht sich unmittelbar als Speise oder Samen, der Speiseesser oder Samenempfänger hebt diesen Samenlieb auf, womit der Speisegeber in einen mit dem Empfänger gemeinsamen Leib sich aufzieht.

refreshes our life, He creates it. But creation has no real meaning to us except in the moral and experient sphere of redemption. It is the action distinctive of the Holy One, *i.e.* of the absolutely moral, Whose very love has "Thou *shalt* love" in it. Christian love is a matter of conscience, of a mystically moral imperative (1 Timothy i. 5). And the Act which gave us our new life gives also the principle of its maintenance. The principle of a sacrament is the principle of the *holy* Gospel. It is moral in its nature, as redemption must be. And we become immortal by a kiss rather than a medicine—righteousness and peace kiss each other. We live not on a sacramental substance, but on a divine person; nor only on a divine person of benignant excellence, but on a holy Redeemer of regenerating love.

Addendum on Theosophy, Theology and Theodicy

THERE are three words which it would be useful to distinguish, both historically and philosophically—theosophy, theology, and theodicy. For they each represent certain strains in the history of the Church, which mean much for the rise and progress of faith in the soul.

Theosophy (which means God-wisdom) is a knowledge of Him on data drawn from intuition, and developed by speculative imagination tending to the mystic and occult. Its knowledge is analogical or cosmological, *i.e.* bearing on God's being, the substantial unity of things, and the relation of it to God. It represents the whole gnostic tendency, whether in the Church or out, in the second century or the twentieth, to seek God in the withdrawn moments of the soul and its thought. In its extreme forms it is represented by Indian philosophy, and by Plotinus at one end of the Christian era and Behmen at the other, descending to Schelling and Swedenborg. But it really covers all the tendency to reduce the Gospel to a speculative system precipitated (as it were) in Christ, and parabled in Christianity, from Origen at the beginning to Hegel at the close. Left to itself it sinks gradually till it debouch into all the negations that, as at this day, disintegrate faith, history, civilisation alike, in one pale burial blent. For it really ends in making man the measure of God. It means ideal man therefore as the authority for God, instead of owning God as the authority for man. The ruling idea of religion here is light or wisdom. And it is often full of beauty and good—if only it had power to the same scale.

Theology, on the other hand, is the content of God's Word or Logos; by which is meant the historic revelation in Christ when He is viewed as the Logos, or moral energy, of God. It was with this idea of the Logos, as God's active reason revealed to man, that the early Church fought the gnostics and their idea of Sophia, or man's wisdom applied to God. The mediæval Church represented a compromise between these two in a magnificent mental fabric, carried by a historic institution magnificent to correspond, and invested with a spiritual spell. When, after the Reformation, the Bible took the place of the Church as authority, and was regarded as the infallible source of pure doctrine, theology was adjusted to this new idea of the Word or Logos as the book. But, since such a Word was not a person, the theology drawn from it became a scholastic system, elaborated from passages of Scripture, which, however, were still read and put together by a logic more or less mediæval, and a system more or less Aristotelian, with a spiritual atmosphere much less impressive. It became an orthodoxy. And the ruling notion of religion was then truth. The ideal of Christianity was pure doctrine. Much use was still made of the old and rational idea of the Logos, though in a harder form. And the collapse of orthodoxy into the flatness, stiffness, and inhumanity that have so often made it a travesty of the severity of holy love, shows how much that Logos idea has come to injure the work and doctrine of the Holy Spirit, and taken the life out of faith.

Christianity as the religion of holy love has for its ruling idea neither light nor truth—in the Western sense of such words at least. It came to meet neither our darkness nor our error, our passion neither for illumination nor for knowledge. It was neither for the imagination nor for the intelligence in chief, rich as it was for both. It came to the heart, and, above all, the conscience. It came in the name of righteousness, and not of culture nor of cultus in the first place. It came to man neither as dull nor as sick, to cure neither spiritual ignorance nor spiritual disease. For those purposes would have been required the gift either of fresh knowledge to dispel the dark, or of some fresh essence to restore vitality enough to cast off our disease. But such was not the trouble, and such was not the boon. The lack was neither vision nor vitality. It was love's holy righteousness. Christ came to redeem us from our last strait; and this deep distress was neither blindness nor sickness of spirit, neither dark nor disease—it was guilt. The difficulty was not our attitude to love alone—it was not coldness needing warmth—it was our treatment of *holy* love, or holy love's treatment of us. The redemption Christ brought was not from our stupidity, nor from our feebleness—it was from our sin. And the question, the cry, He met was, "How shall man be just with God?" or "How shall God seem just with man?"

Christ came as the holy One and the just rather than as the loving Light. The great issue was that of righteousness (Romans i. 17). It had to do with man's righteousness to God or God's to man. That is to say, it was concerned, in the first place, neither with a philosophy of love nor a theology of truth, but with the moral issue of a theodicy; which means God's righteousness, the justification of God. I was writing a book on this subject recently, and everybody told me I must on no account put that word into my title, as nobody knew what it meant. It was another of several such shocks I have had of late. The more you come to close quarters with faith and the Gospel amid blood and fire in heavenly places, the more Christians do not understand you. "Why do ye not understand my speech? Because ye are unable to grasp my Word." To our dreadful education close thinking is but obscurity, and the easy is taken for both the clear and the free. People have been sickened with orthodoxy and its pulpiteers, softened by sentiment and its troubadours in the Press, toughened by vulgar efficiency, and debased by the luxury of peace till the real issues are beyond them. And when the great flood comes in war they are all found eating and drinking of these nice things, and they are carried off their moral feet. They lose, I say, their moral footing—always precarious, for their rock wobbled on the sand. They can only say it is a great mystery, and turn to the ambulance. Wherein God bless them, prosper them, and cure them of thinking that Christianity came into the world only to make doctors, nurses, and comforters, or that the Church is there chiefly as the greatest of the Red Cross Societies. It came as Christ came, as He came to make Christendom do—seeking, before all else, the Kingdom of God and its righteousness, which would increase and multiply all these other good things in tail. Can it be doubted that the pains (in both senses of the word) which the Church has spent during all these centuries upon its theosophies and its theologies would have made a very different world to-day, and one much nearer the Kingdom of God, had they been spent on theodicy, on God's righteousness, as much as upon light, truth, or sentiment? The word would then have been more familiar than even theology, even if no better understood.

It is one of the hopeful features of the time that this matter of a theodicy is coming to be the chief religious interest, whether our egregious education lets the public know the word or not. Find a better word if you can, but at any rate develop the thing. If your soul is not a mere mystic adventurer, with an interest egoist and temperamental, and with the winsome note of flute and viol, seek first righteousness with your religion, whether you rope in people fast or slow. There is no other way to end war or commend the Church. The revival of the passion for righteousness at any price is the mark of the true aristocracy which severs the Kingdom of God from all these egoist democracies that seek, however piously, a whole skin, a full purse, and a good time in a well-warmed world, and then put on moral side in the name of peace. It is the apparent absence of righteousness from the world that makes the chief doubters and deniers to-day; it is that far more than the lack of a system of the universe, or the culture of a hard science that leaves no room for God. Things have much changed since the day of the Agnostics a generation ago. It is the wrongness in things that rouses resentment with either God or man. It is not their tightness that will not let God through, but their crookedness that makes even Him seem to lose His way. It is the moral wrongness in things, and especially in society, that makes the trouble. And it cannot be dealt with by the mysticism in which so many seek refuge from scientific scepticism or philosophic no-where-ism.

The word justification seems in many quarters to be losing the meaning which the word theodicy never won. But it is the word that covers the real, the moral issue, which for society has become the chief. As soon as conscience becomes the leading power in man, and the holiness of His love the supreme thing in God, then the issue between man and God is the issue of justification. It is a question of God's justification of man or man's of God. Now the sense of sin has for the time gone out of commission, or it has changed from the sense of individual sin to social (which feels more tolerable and welcome as responsibility has come to be distributed over a wide area and lies thin and light on each). Therefore the moral interest has passed for the time from the justification of the sinner before God, and it has turned to the justification of God before the sinner. The vindication of God takes the place of the conversion of man. We do not cast our sin on God but our blame. "Why hast Thou made me thus?" "Why hast Thou let things come to this?" The interest has passed from justification by faith to a theodicy. But that must be by faith no less; and by a faith no less moral in its nature, than the evangelical faith was, which engaged the man as conscience with the holy Conscience in forgiveness and regeneration. I cannot go into it here, but God's dealing with the world can only be found to be moral, good, wise, and holy by the evangelical faith,[1] which settles us in His justification of the soul in Christ's Cross. God can only be vindicated by His own Gospel, and not by any expectations or imaginations of ours. The standard for the world is that which is the salvation of the soul. But that the religious interest should become theodical instead of theological, should turn upon righteousness and not orthodoxy, is the best possible thing for theology. It will moralise it, popularise it, and make it the backbone of a religion which intends a new humanity and a new history of humanity on earth. The religion of humanity must have that backbone, else it dies into a mere humanitarianism which is the green mould of democracy, and the blight of its type of Christianity. "A just God and a Saviour." We have lost hold of the Saviour because we have lost hold of the just God. And we have lost Him because we have come to think of the Saviour as the ideal of a young people, the warrant of happy homes and a pot boiling on each hearth, as a divine means of making things pleasant, the future secure, life easy, faith eloquent, work casual, and nothing sacramental—everyone genial, everyone liberal, everything sentimental, nobody heroic, none apostolic, and nothing sacramental. Hence these tears of blood.

[1] See my *Justification of God*, Latimer House Press, 1947.